BEGINNING IN RETROSPECT
Writing and Reading a Teacher's Life

BEGINNING IN RETROSPECT

Writing and Reading a Teacher's Life

Patricia A. Schmidt

Foreword by Sari Knopp Biklen

TEACHERS COLLEGE PRESS

Teachers College, Columbia University
New York and London

Published by Teachers College Press, 1234 Amsterdam Avenue, New York, NY 10027

"My Mother Pieced Quilts," by Teresa Paloma Acosta, is from *Festival de Flor y Canto: An Anthology of Chicano Literature*, University of Southern California Press, 1976. Reprinted with permission.

Library of Congress Cataloging-in-Publication Data
Schmidt, Patricia A. (Patricia Ann)
    Beginning in retrospect : writing and reading a teacher's life /
Patricia A. Schmidt.
      p.   cm.
    Includes bibliographical references and index.
    ISBN 0-8077-3584-1 (cloth).—ISBN 0-8077-3583-3 (paper)
    1. Schmidt, Patricia Johanssen. 2. English teachers—United
States—Biography. 3. Self-knowledge, Theory of. 4. Teachers—
United States—Books and reading. 5. Teaching. 6. Learning.
I. Title.
LA2317.S34A3   1997
371.2'0092—dc20   96-30444

ISBN 0-8077-3583-3 (paper)
ISBN 0-8077-3584-1 (cloth)

Printed on acid-free paper
Manufactured in the United States of America
04 03 02 01 00 99 98 97   8 7 6 5 4 3 2 1

Reflections

We are our
Mothers' daughters
Our
Fathers' daughters . . .

Today I reconstruct
My world,
An unconventional one
A woman of books
A seeker
Beyond the role of
Obedient daughter,
Submissive wife,
Protective mother,
Reluctant housekeeper;

Now I
Live vertically and horizontally
Life is no longer
A dichotomy
an either
or . . .

For Me
Life is a process
A construction, a construing,
Reconstruing—
long distance calls to then from
the sadness of death
the joy of snow flurries on the Square
a taking leave and a return

I am my mother's daughter, my father's daughter,
my husband's wife, my daughter's mother,
I am

Writing and rewriting my life.

—Patricia Schmidt, 1990

Contents

Foreword

This book represents the author's efforts to sort out her life as a person and a teacher, and particularly to examine how these "two lives" intertwine. Patricia Schmidt, as she is represented in this text, is a complex and interesting woman who does not hesitate to share her more difficult, critical, discomfiting, and complicated moments. The text reads a life to examine how this author/teacher—who is trained in certain ways, who thinks of herself as a professional person, who explores many ways of teaching reading, writing, literature, and English, at many university programs over the years—can only be understood if we examine how her personal life, experiences, and history intersect and are taken up in her readings and her choices. The text describes the connections between her personal life and the intellectual approaches she chose, at different periods in her life, to define her teaching. The strength of this book is that the author does not talk about biography's influence on the teacher: She shows it.

We are in the midst of an explosion of work about teaching from the perspective of those who teach. This new corpus is so important in understanding what it means to be a teacher, how teachers think of their work, and what struggles teachers take up as they shift their understandings of their occupations and choices. This book fits in there. As I read through the manuscript, I imagined a teacher friend reading this text, a teacher who has gone through deep struggle to teach in the ways that are important to her, and visualized her taking great pleasure in Schmidt's narrative and story. My friend has both suffered and gained by her choices, and I could see her identifying with the author's willingness to describe her location.

Schmidt works through her teaching in a way that will be especially useful to teachers. Even if they do not agree with all of her choices or teach the same subjects, the themes she raises are ones engaged by many teachers. Two themes seem particularly significant beyond the teaching of reading and writing. First, the author explores how her common-sense and taken-for-granted knowledges about education, curriculum, and learning were constructed. She describes how she came to take these certain knowledges for granted. The discussion of this process—though it does not proceed nor is described in a linear fashion—is important work. Second, the author examines a teacher's authority, both her own in classrooms where she taught, and that of her supervisors and professors. It is a sometimes painful examination, but because Schmidt does not avoid the pain, her discussion is heuristic. When she touches on hearing criticisms, responding to support, and taking on the role of the "good girl," in relation to authority, her descriptions are evocative. It is not that she always concludes where I might, but that she raises issues in a way that permit me, as reader, to conclude someplace else.

It is this kind of openness about her writing that enables readers to see how Schmidt theorizes, to theorize differently themselves, and to gain insight and pleasure from the work. I think this will be especially true for feminists who read this text. The ways that the author makes sense of the intertwining of daily life and work gives space for readers to understand her feminist theorizing. Which feminist theorists she calls on and why, how she identifies herself as a woman and recalls being a girl, and why the kind of feminism she praises resonates for her—these three issues provide a sort of underdetermined arena waiting for the reader's meaning-making processes to engage. Readers interested in how discourses are taken up in the practice of sense-making have a rich territory to explore in this book.

—*Sari Knopp Biklen*

Acknowledgments

Throughout my doctoral work, and especially in the research and writing of my dissertation and then my book, I have sought and found support in the company of other women. So many women have shared their lives with me in powerful ways, encouraging and supporting me while I have been working to complete my research and to write this book.

In my reading life numerous women have offered me insight and understanding about their lives, their roles, and their work, simultaneously helping me to question and to understand my own: Eve and her mother Marie Curie, Louise Rosenblatt, Margaret Mead, Carolyn Heilbrun, Lyn Mikel Brown, Carol Gilligan, and Eva Hoffman.

My friends in research and scholarship, Laura Berns and Barbara Livdahl, paved the way for my autobiographical research by sharing their experiences with me and listening to me when I became paralyzed by fear. New York University friend and mentor Darlene Forrest helped me to feel safe in New York in so many ways, professionally and personally.

A special thanks to Barbara Danish, Director of the Expository Writing Center at New York University, and co-director of two interdisciplinary projects, the Carse Project and the History of Western Civilization Project, with whom I was privileged to work and with whom I learned. Also, I want to thank Jane De Lawter, California Literature Project Regional Director and Professor of Education at Sonoma State University, who works with teachers, sharing authority, encouraging us to make decisions, valuing our selves, our lives, helping us grow.

My committee, John Mayher, and Una Chaudhuri, worked with me in ways that valued who I am becoming, each offering insights, questions, suggestions, and support, always helping me to think more critically. I want to give special acknowledgment to my dissertation chair, Gordon Pradl, who both professionally and personally valued and encouraged autobiography and narrative as research paradigms.

I want to acknowledge my parents, Ray and Helen Roark, who I know love me, and my sister, Pam, who sent me care packages while I was living in New York. I know they had a hard time understanding my decision to move to New York, leaving my own family to study, but they supported me.

I am especially indebted to my husband, Neil, who, despite his personal objections to my graduate work, has always provided technical support and his computer expertise to help me with my work. In the past four years he has spent hours helping me edit and format first my proposal, then my dissertation, and now this book.

To my friends in sobriety, Betty C., Roy L., and Melissa H., I share my gratitude, for they helped me to experience, understand, and begin a spiritual life, which is an important part of my thinking about relationship, not just in living a personal life, but in my reading, teaching, and learning life as well.

A very special thanks to Susan Wellington, who midwived the birth of this book when it was a dissertation.

I am grateful to the staff at Teachers College Press for their compassionate, professional support in the writing of this book.

Last, to my silent partner and companion, who literally kept me and this book company for hours on end, usually stretched out sleeping directly to my left next to the keyboard, on a draft, Charlie, Chuck, my Himalayan cat. May you rest peacefully, my friend.

I dedicate this book to my daughter, Cara Elise Schmidt, and to all teachers who are courageously facing themselves and their students with care and understanding and compassion.

Introduction

I found this story yesterday when a man struggling with his life told it to our group. He sat there in the room with us, but he was somewhere else, in the jungles of Southeast Asia. And as he told us this story, we were there with him in those jungles of memory.

It seems that he served in Vietnam. He flew over 300 combat missions, so he'd known courage and fear. But the fear he described during that hour resonates in my own experience, only my jungles are the blackboard ones, for I am a teacher. This is the story he told us, more or less.

The Python and the Chicken

We used to keep a pet python in a cage in the compound. He had to be fed like any captive would require feeding. We fed him chickens. One day we put a chicken inside the cage into which we had also placed a branch. The python slept peacefully in the bottom. In the meantime, the chicken climbed to the highest part of the cage and clung to the branch, trying desperately to blend in, to appear to become a leaf, perhaps to fool the snake. I looked at the poor creature, paralyzed with fear. I felt and knew the fear we carry deep down inside us. That of death. No words describe the fear, but I can still see the chicken in the top of the cage frozen in time with imminent death sleeping quietly below, waiting.

In many ways, I spent too many years of both my personal and teaching life living like that chicken, living my life in an existential hell based on fear, only I perched on the highest branch in the cage of teaching and marriage and family, watching myself, looking down at the sleeping python, feeling there was no exit, seeing only failure and feeling like I would die. Actually, there were times when I wanted to go to sleep and never wake up. My experiences and perceptions of my teaching life were an existential nightmare, experiences and perceptions of continuous failure. I felt that I had failed to meet both my own expectations of myself and the expectations I perceived that others had of me as a learner and teacher, and as a woman, as a wife, as a mother, as a daughter. My friends, family, students, and colleagues saw me as happy and successful.

All who listened to the chicken and python story that day sat in total silence. The last words of this person's story capture the feeling of paralyzing fear that, from what I can remember and with which I begin this teaching autobiography, began during the second quarter of my first year of teaching high school English.

From writing this book, though, I have learned that this fear I have struggled with has been there much longer. I've had to ask, Was this fear always there in me, latent, waiting only to be awakened by the sleeping python of the teaching life? "No words describe the fear, but I can still see the chicken in the top of the cage, frozen in time, with imminent death sleeping quietly below." That image and those words are powerful, for during many of the 17 years that I taught high school English I was that chicken perched at the top of the cage, frozen in fear, awaiting imminent death, waiting to be swallowed by the sleeping python, my school, my marriage, my family. Why?

What brought about this perception of myself and my life as a high school English teacher?

Initially I researched this book from a need to understand my own life as a teacher and to understand, then, what influenced and influences us as teachers. I discovered that it is the social, the political, and the cultural climate and environment of schools that are also mirrored in our personal lives and relationships with family, and that this relationship is reciprocal and transactional. I discovered, too, that it is the educational life we have lived that influences us: our experience and reading of books and life. I write this book to share with you what I've learned about the teaching life to help us in education find ways to begin to understand, to accept, and to continue to grow in our perceptions of ourselves, our lives, and in turn the lives of those with whom we teach and work, and to return to the joy of reading, teaching, and learning, as I have. It is a book of hope. I hope that you will read on, joining me in the journey of self-understanding and evolution in our lives as teachers.

I begin by asking myself and you, Why do we teachers do what we do in our classrooms? I taught high school English for 17 years. I was surprised by what I found: I met myself, Pat the perfectionist who perceived herself as a failure when only one class was problematic, or a few students voiced their unhappiness, or one or two parents were angry with me. I saw a Pat who said to herself, If only I tried harder I would achieve perfection in my teaching. This was how I have thought about myself as a person and a teacher.

This meant that every year I felt I had failed. Arthur Jersild (1955) tells us that "when teachers face themselves," when we face our anxieties and our fears, our loneliness and hostility, when we accept this in ourselves, "when . . . we feel the impact of one's emotions, one is compassionate towards oneself"

(1955, p. 128). This has been my beginning, writing and reading my life, facing myself, and turning a compassionate heart toward the teacher, the teaching life, the lives we lead as teachers. It has been and continues to be a painful and joyous journey.

At the same time that I was experiencing feelings of anxiety and fear and anger about many external events in my teaching and personal life over which I had little or no control, I was literally mad at myself for not being a good teacher and for failing. During the 25 years since I had entered the educational family, much of the public and administrative criticism of education has reinforced that personal sense of failure that I struggled with and for which I took personal responsibility: floundering SAT scores, poor student performance on standardized tests. Bad teachers and poor teaching were the problems with education. I haven't heard good press on the general state of education since I became an educator in 1969. No wonder we teachers feel defeated and depleted.

As I wrote about my early teaching life, I found myself caught in a web of fear and turmoil regarding my own authority. This became enmeshed with my overwhelming sense of responsibility for the education of my students. I experienced the teaching life as one of tremendous responsibility, but I felt that I had no authority. I did not see myself as a victim, but I experienced authority from the top down rather than from knowing my own authority inside. Authority was in my superintendent, my principal, the department chair, the curriculum, in new critical theories of the reader, in doing what you were told without question, as I'd been taught at home.

Writing and reading my teaching life took me deeper into the heart of my life, to a richer understanding of our lives as teachers. I began to see that the experiences I had as a reader and learner in my own school experience as a child, adolescent, and college student preparing to enter the teaching profession had been haunting my own teaching. Writing our personal teaching and learning stories focusing on our lives as readers, as teachers, as learners (and for me as a female person) is a powerful way to acknowledge and share the past and the role it plays in a teacher's educational process. I have felt that this critical, reflective autobiography has brought me to not only face myself, but to free me to move out of the jungles of memory into a gentle sunlight, a freedom from paralyzing fear.

As I stated earlier, I initially began writing this book to explore what influences the teacher teaching high school English. I did not expect to expose pain, anger, and fear as part of what influences teachers. I did, though. Painful though these stories are, they are about the struggle to make meaning out of my life and to understand the struggle we all have to make some sense of what we're doing here and why.

Be prepared, readers, though, for some of what I write may upset you.

The book is my attempt to look honestly at the teaching life, to make some sense of it, and to help others begin to make some sense of their own lives. I have sometimes written in colloquial or vernacular language and used grammatically incorrect usage (some of which I was unaware until my editor pointed it out to me)—so I caution you English teachers that the text is written in my personal speaking voice and my academic voice, for they are both a part of who I am as a teacher and a person.

I have fictionalized the names so that those who have been a part of my story are not hurt by my own desire for honesty in expressing my experience of events that we share. I cannot tell their stories for them: I am trying to tell my story. I write about pain in this story, and at times I write about my feelings and perceptions of people and events in my life in a critical way. I write about people close to me like my family and relatives, teachers and colleagues, not to disparage them, but to uncover my own experiences and to move on through them. My descriptions of these people and events is my experience of them, of my own lived-in and -through realities.

I have heard that the depth of our pain will also be the height of our joy. This has been my experience. It is my belief and my experience that self-understanding and a willingness to face our fears and do the right thing for ourselves and others is key to the process of change. And I honestly believe in my heart that true change in teaching, something researchers and academics mistakenly term "reform" or "implementation," or in the jargon of the 1990s, "restructuring," begins with the internal life of the teacher: to returning us to the self as a learner, to the self as reader, and to the self as writer so we can honestly face and accept ourselves while being open and willing to change what we can when we can get to the root of our dissonances. Is this not what education in a democracy is about? Becoming the best human beings we can to make thoughtful, informed decisions about what is important in our lives?

We all experience moments in our lives, critical times of change, whether the change be in the form of a personal insight or a professional understanding. A critical time of change for me came in 1986, when I experienced California reading reform and implementation, the California Literature Project at UCLA. One hundred English and language arts teachers from all over California gathered together that summer in Westwood: We connected our life experiences as readers, learners, teachers, and people with the new California English Language Arts curriculum, standards, and framework.

What happened that UCLA summer that set my life on a path of teaching and learning that began to transform me into the educator I am today and who I am becoming? My best description of it is that the UCLA was a magical experience. This is where my journey to a teaching self became a conscious one. Why UCLA? Why 1986 and not 1988 or 1978, when I finished my master's degree in English? These were both educational experiences reading literature. These were crucial moments for me, too. Writing this story and critically reflecting on these two and many other experiences helped me to see the beginnings of educational settings and processes that provide the space, internal and external, for personal and professional transformations. I hope that you begin to ask yourself what some of your teaching and learning experiences are that have shaped your teaching life.

I've come to believe that change happens serendipitously and synchronously: the coming together of experience and learning and our lives. While we may attempt to structure the experience of "reform," of "implementation," of "restructuring" in education by demanding educational objectives and plans, we cannot predict the outcomes in terms of personal knowledge. On the profoundly deepest level, learning and change are dynamic and personal and unpredictable. They occur in transactional settings and are transforming, evolving, ongoing.

In my experiences, evolution, transformation, change—all involve a mythic awakening to the bell, not our usual experience with the school bell telling us when to begin and when to end. When I hear the calling of the school bell, I think, instead, it is calling us to be present in our teaching and learning lives. This awakening and presence that I write of remind me of Maxine Greene's sense of educational vision, a vision that would refocus school to be an experience that attends to the "actualities of lives lived" (1988, p. 7). This seems quite unlikely to happen on an institutional level given the present expectations of schools to be the social conscience, the missing parents, the social workers, the psychiatrists and arbitrators of the "right" American values while teaching reading, writing, and math skills. Control and discipline and standards are the placebos schools are trapped into in their curricula. E. D. Hirsch's series of texts extolling cultural literacy, telling us "what every kindergartner should know," are esteemed to be what real education is: information. This book is about a search to manifest what writing our experiences, our lives as learners, readers, writers, can tell us about teaching and learning that standardized tests and psychometricians miss: the internal life of the learner and the knowledge we gain when we lead reflective teaching and learning lives, something we teachers and our students need to be engaged in in our educational lives.

Most of the current teaching force in the 1990s has been educated in a transmission, information-based Hirschean cultural literacy approach. Most veteran educators are of the generation of the 1960s and 1970s. Until we as teachers can experience and reflect on learning while questioning our past experiences and the value of those experiences in our knowledge reservoirs, we will be perpetually stuck. This process is the process of reflective practice I began to experience at the California Literature Project during that UCLA summer of 1986. It was what I thought to be my most critical moment in education. I have discovered that there were many before and have been many since.

How can we begin to understand and value the personal knowledge we gain in institutional education in the lives of learners? I believe that the way to understand the value and influence of education in a life is to examine our lives. I chose to examine my own life because I realized that I could learn a great deal about myself and put my teaching life into some sort of perspective by doing so.

Literary theorist Louise Rosenblatt states, "But, no one can read a poem for you" (1978, p. 86). I took this notion beyond Rosenblatt's transactional literary theory into my own sense of living life. The "poem" becomes the life actually lived in learning, and no one can know what the knower knows (in the ultimate sense) but the knower.

In 1990, while I was in graduate school at New York University, I was asked to write an autobiography of myself as a writer in the graduate instructors' writing practicum. This was another critical moment in my life as a teacher and learner. I began writing that autobiography with, "I have never considered myself to be a writer. I have always considered myself to be a reader." This, simple as it is, is a powerful statement, revealing much about my perceptions of myself, even as a doctoral student.

However, while I was a graduate student at New York University, my interest in writing and narrative grew. I began to experience and understand narrative, particularly autobiography, as a constructing activity, rather than a product of meaning. Reading and writing and talking about Jerome Bruner's *Acts of Meaning* (1990) and Carolyn Heilbrun's *Writing a Woman's Life* (1988) brought me into connection with my writing self. I began to be aware of how much language and writing my narratives helped me and others to make some sense out of our lives.

Education is always in a state of "reform." The pendulum swings on. The "reform" is always curricular and political in nature: phonics or whole language, English only or bilingual, etc. My own experience with educational reform (like most of us, I've lived through many "pendulum swings" since I began teaching in 1969) tells me that "reform" cannot happen unless reform structures and curricula find ways to work with teachers, with the teaching self, the teaching life. This is where reform begins.

Recently I was talking on the phone with a former colleague. She was describing students as being "inarticulate," and disinterested in school. As I suggested ways of teaching that really worked for me, how I had become more aware of the processes of language and learning as what teaching English is about, I realized that this wasn't helping my friend at all. The more I reflected on our conversation and my work on this book, the more I actually began to understand more deeply what I had undergone in my teaching evolution: continuing processes of self-critical, reflective teaching. She had tried some of the very same strategies and pedagogy that I had, yet we were miles apart.

Most who lead reform (including myself as an advocate of critical, reflective autobiography) have an agenda driven by specific beliefs about what constitutes education. Do we ask ourselves what are we reforming? The kind of reform I write of is a reform that is a dynamic one, one of rethinking, questioning and defining for ourselves as human beings "the actualities of lives lived" in and out of our classrooms so we can actually be present in them and take joy with us each day we teach and learn. The kind I'm talking about is what Gloria Steinem has aptly termed a "revolution from within" (Steinem, 1991).

My hope has been that in sharing my struggles, the pain and joy of teaching, of reading, of writing, of learning through this autobiography, that teachers struggling with their own personal fear and frustration in their beloved profession might begin to tell and understand their own stories in their teaching communities. This book is for those of us who would like to face ourselves and understand, and from this understanding begin to more meaningfully chart our journeys.

My greatest hope is that teachers will know that they are not alone. As teachers we do not need, as Thoreau once said, to "live lives of quiet desperation." It is through self-understanding and learning compassion for ourselves, then others, a compassion found in shared community, that we can know a new intellectual and emotional freedom.

Let's begin by asking these questions: Who am I as a teacher, what do I believe in, why do I believe this? Then we need to look at our pedagogy— what am I doing, why am I doing this, and how does this enact what I believe? We also need to revisit and critically reflect on the lives we bring to our teaching.

On another level, I hope administrators and those in teacher education will read this life and begin to examine their own views of education, of teaching and learning, and of what constitutes curriculum. We can begin to understand ourselves and each other in retrospect.

I have found for myself, working with preservice teachers and with those taking my English classes, that self-understanding, a retrospect of our lives, is a powerful way of knowing the teaching and learning, reading and writing self. Retrospect is not looking backwards only. It is, in my best language, a looking at the past while we're strolling on in our lives. The sense of strolling is key in this notion, for it connotes a leisurely pace, a being fully present in the moment, aware of the past, not living in the future, but fully present in the moment. Writing and reading in retrospect, I notice that my language has begun to change. It is no longer a fear-based language. I have moved from a driven search for meaning to a quieter, more centered notion of strolling, a mindful walk with my life.

My teaching life has changed and is continuing to change. We live in constant change. Each moment we live is gone except in memory. However, we can write and read them and learn from them. I keep journals, teaching journals, reading journals, life journals. They are in one notebook these days, for I tired of trying to juggle the parts and began to view the teaching life and my life as a whole life. So the various parts are together in one journal and I critically reflect on life and teaching regularly. This process is a way of being.

Just last year I wrote this story. I particularly like this story, for it is a story of hope. There are no chickens, no cages with sleeping pythons. I have named it "The Story of the Wise Old Woman and the Girl." It could easily be called "The Story of the Wise Old Teacher and the Young Girl Teacher."

The Story of the Wise Old Woman and the Girl

There was a wise old woman driving a wagon down along a dusty road. She met a little spirit, a playful rebellious little squirt of a girl with speckled freckles and auburn hair—hair kissed by the sun one sunset in ancient times. At least that is the story the sprite told the wise old woman when the wise old woman asked, "How did you get such bright red hair?"

"Kissed by the sunset long, long ago," she replied with mischief in her eyes.

The wise old woman smiled, for she knew the story already. Surrounding this sprite were her friends, creatures of both the earth and the universe, spirits of nature.

The wise old woman looked lovingly at the little one and inquired, "Will you come along with me?"

Unlike most young spirits, this little soul said to her new friend, "No, I'm happy here."

Time passed by and by and the sprite was growing into a bigger spirit.

One hot day with the sun bearing down, she was walking bare-footed. She looked up into the mirage. She could feel the powdered dust between her toes, she saw rising in the heat her old friend, the wise old woman. This time she stared and reached out to the empty air.

The wise old woman, sensing the sprite's sadness, inquired, "Would you like to come with me?" This time the sprite thought seriously about the offer. She remembered that the wise old woman loved her, but something, some doubt, some new sense of fear stopped her from going.

Time passed as it always does. Years passed. The sprite grew and grew and grew up. Now she was a woman. And this young woman married.

One day as she gardened in the sun in her yard, she noticed the sun was going behind the hills and the colors on the horizon became brilliant, and she knew.

A familiar voice called from the distant brilliance, "Will you come along with me?"

To this the wise young woman replied, "Not this evening, but I will come."

Again, some years passed.

One day the wise woman with the auburn hair kissed by the sun was strolling along a dusty road in the warmth of the sun and she heard deep within her heart the familiar voice, "Will you come along with me?"

"Yes," she replied, for she knew herself.

Yes, I used to have red hair as a young girl. Yes, I used to walk along dusty roads. And yes, I am beginning to know myself and to face myself. I began in retrospect, reading in retrospect, writing in retrospect, speaking in retrospect, looking at the past, facing it, accepting it, and changing what I can today when that sleeping python appears and I begin to sit in paralysis.

How do we as teachers come to know the self in the joy and chaos of our teaching lives? We begin in retrospect by reading and writing our lives and reflecting on our lives, not alone, but in the educational community.

CHAPTER 1

Languaging: Developing a Theory of Shared Experience and Authority

When we teach, we do, in a sense, teach ourselves. As teachers, we do not just act as the gateway to knowledge. We ourselves represent, embody, our curriculum. And, in our teaching, we convey not just our explicit knowledge, but also our positions towards it, the personal ramifications and implications which it has for us.

(Salmon, 1988, p. 42)

I began to work with critical, reflective autobiography, seeing it as a research tool complementary to traditional research paradigms, when I wrote a case study with my Expository Writing Center client Rose Budding in 1990, "Languaging with Rose Budding." That case study snowballed into my candidacy paper, then into my dissertation proposal, then into my dissertation, and now begins Chapter One of this book. Something critical happened in the moments I shared with Rose Budding.

Finding out what that something is always begins simply for me—with story. I wanted to tell the story of my experience working with a writer and to research the critical period notion of language acquisition and development. It seems to me that we teachers and educators all need to begin with who we are now to understand ourselves. I invite you to join me in this journey into the teaching self. Read my story. Let yourself respond to it. Be angry. Upset. Happy. Critical. I hope that you, too, will think about who you are now and what you believe about teaching and English now. Write your own teaching story as you read mine. This is what Rose and I did. We were never harsh or judgmental of each other, yet we were extremely critical.

Something special was happening between Rose Budding and me when we met and worked on her writing. As I begin to simply write the story of our shared experiences as writer and teacher, I begin to reexperience and to see the power of telling and reflecting on our stories (our teacher selves) in relationship to the stories of others (our students).

As I reflect in retrospect, I see that I wasn't just researching Rose Budding. I realize that in researching Rose, I was also researching myself. How many of us take the time (or have the time) to write about and reflect on what is going on in both our personal and teaching lives? How many of us look closely at the teaching and learning relationships we have with learners, perhaps focusing on one person and something special that is happening? I have supervised student teachers, and when I ask them if they keep a personal teaching journal, they invariably answer no. They haven't the time or they haven't thought about reflective practice (Schon, 1983). They're just trying to meet their methods class requirements and their master teacher's expectations, and plan and teach their classes (they remind me of myself when I was a young preservice teacher). It doesn't change much even for veteran teachers. Teachers are overwhelmed with the "stuff" of teaching. Another colleague commented to me that when she is teaching, she has no other life except her classroom. Good teachers invariably do this. Do we ever reflect on why teaching and what we do as teachers sucks the very life out of us?

When I began to work with Rose in 1990, I had been reading a great deal of theory. I had been consciously reading, thinking about, and trying various ways to implement the transactional literary theory and pedagogy of Louise Rosenblatt since 1986. Rosenblatt suggests that teachers need to see themselves as readers and that teachers need to know the assumptions (and sometimes set aside their beliefs to be able to listen to students' responses) they have about living, about teaching, and about reading literature that they bring to each classroom experience. In the spirit of Rosenblatt's theory, I wanted to look at the way Rose and I were working together to see if my responses fit my sense of what Louise Rosenblatt suggested as a way of working with readers in *Literature as Exploration* (1938, 1983). You might begin by asking yourself some of the questions I asked myself. What are some of your beliefs and assumptions about teaching? Have you been reading theory? Who? What have you been trying in your teaching? Have you looked closely at your beliefs about teaching and learning in connection to the classroom activities with which you're working?

CRITICAL MOMENTS: BEGINNING THE PROCESSES OF CRITICAL SELF-REFLECTION

We all have critical moments in our teaching lives, in our personal lives. These moments are found in our lives, the books we read, the lessons we teach, including our experiences with and our attitudes toward and perceptions of the world. I began to look at these moments in the early 1980s. In his *At a Journal Workshop* (1975), depth psychologist Ira Progoff terms them "stepping stones," and Gail Sheehy termed these moments "passages" (1976), or predictable crises as we move through the steps of our lives. In a similar spirit, I term these experiences "critical moments," critical in that they somehow make a difference in what and who we are and are becoming. They are critical turning points. They may be monumental, like a nervous breakdown, or they may be metaphoric, like the purchase of a cornflower-blue lamp. Recognizing them and realizing them has been an exciting journey of self-discovery and self-understanding for me. They are not necessarily of the "burning bush" variety. They may, as in my case, come from the simple stuff of everyday living and teaching. I do start with moments that for one reason or another linger in my mind to this day and look to see what about them makes them memorable: for me they are classroom experiences as a learner and a teacher (eventually I came to realize that I cannot separate these in myself as I was taught to), unforgettable books, and people—people who have frightened me, people who have given me pain, people who have brought me great joy, people who have nurtured me, kicked me in the butt when I needed it and were honest in ways that were helpful.

The case study of Rose Budding, of which you will shortly read a bit, was just the beginning. Sometimes the critical moments came as I organized and then wrote about documents I had kept all these years. I had kept many cherished memorabilia, such as a high school book report I wrote in 1963–64 on the one book that touched my heart and soul as a reader; formal papers I'd written when I majored in English in college; tests; course syllabi; lesson plans; personal poetry; and journals. I gathered these together to anchor and to begin to name and story critical moments in my life. These moments then became subjects of critical reflection. The reflective process was similar to peeling off the layers of the onion, opaque yet transparent. This is not necessarily an easy journey for some of us. I was afraid that when I arrived at the core of myself, there would be no one there.

How I wish that I had had the wherewithal to critically reflect on my experiences when I began teaching. My journey might have been less painful. Part of my hope for you who are reading this is that in sharing my experiences with you, you will not feel so alone in the cacaphony and chaos of the teaching life, and that you will begin a critical, reflective pedagogy as a way of life.

Reading and writing reflectively about the book reports, lesson plans, journals, and papers helped me to remember. I had to begin with just trying to describe what I saw in those texts, and from there I began to remember stories. If you have kept papers dear to you in your educational experiences, both in and out of school, you can begin there if you wish to begin in retrospect along with me. If you're just beginning to student teach or are in your first year of teaching, I hope that you will keep your work as a student/ learner/reader/writer and revisit it, reminding yourselves what it was/is like. I was truly amazed at who I saw when I began to reread my writings and tell the stories of those experiences. Beneath those stories lay other stories, stories of childhood experiences. I realized that I learned about life and dealing with the world in my childhood experiences with authority and fear and those greatly influence my life today.

I wrote my story—my stories—and discovered that the core issue, the pattern present in almost all my critical memories, was authority and the relationship to and with authority that we teachers and learners struggle with in education. Writing and reading these teaching and learning stories involves naming our experiences. We begin to recover our lost selves when we can name our experiences.

Many teachers struggle with the educational systems' mixed messages regarding autonomy and authority. Our being as teachers is named by others—be independent, critical thinkers, but do it within the parameters and paradigm of a hierarchical culture and the confines of the discipline. We learned to adhere to the expectations of procedural knowledge.

As I wrote, I became amazed that I was writing and reading my life into self-understanding and acceptance. I wanted to explore how reading theory influenced my teaching, particularly reading Louise Rosenblatt's texts on reading and teaching literature. I discovered that my continuing fascination with Rosenblatt's philosophy and theory of teaching English was influencing my teaching in an unusual way. I was not just examining classroom strategies and activities, I was examining ways of working, ways of believing, ways of being.

In the 1978 text of transactional literary theory *The Reader, the Text, the Poem*, Rosenblatt used "transaction" to describe what happens when a reader reads a text as a literary event. A transaction between a reader and a text is an "ongoing process in which the elements or factors are, one might say, aspects of a total situation, each conditioned and conditioning the other" (1978, p. 17). I thought about this notion for a couple of years. I questioned and explored what the actions, the language, the relationship might be and look like when one teaches "transactionally." Eventually my understanding of Rosenblatt's literary notion of transaction evolved into naming my case study with Rose Budding, transforming my reading of Rosenblatt's literary notion of transactional (which she took from Dewey and Bentley [1949]) into my core issue of authority in teaching, into pedagogical contexts, redefining the teacher and learner relationship.

I wrote the study with Rose believing that what we were doing was transactional in Rosenblatt's sense of the term, but I sensed that we were not just acting on and conditioning each other; what we were experiencing as we worked together was something more. It had to do with language and how we both, two women who did not know each other and who were from different disciplines (I, English Education; Rose, Health Administration) and backgrounds seemed to share, without articulating it in words, a mutual, reciprocal

view of teaching and learning, reading and writing. The way we worked together was in language, with language, and beyond language. This sense of
teaching and English I have just described to you was dramatically different
from my concept of teaching English when I began teaching high school in
1969. For me now, in the 1990s, teaching English is about language and learning. My beliefs about what teaching English was were vastly different in 1969.

So that you can see the person I have evolved into in the 1990s here's a
brief look at one moment in my experience working with Rose. I include my
critical reading and understanding of this moment for you.

LANGUAGING WITH ROSE BUDDING: OUR CASE STUDY

> In order to ensure that I would pursue a doctoral program that would bring
> meaning and relevancy to me, I have been exploring a variety of avenues because
> a doctorate is more than attaining one more degree for me. (Rose Budding, 10/
> 25/90)

The above statement is the opening sentence of Rose's application for
doctoral study at Columbia University (in a recent conversation with Rose,
she told me that she was accepted at Columbia and has nearly finished with
her doctoral work there).

We worked on this statement in her application on November 11, 1990.
Rose came in, sat down in the cubicle in the New York University Expository
Writing Center, and placed two copies of her text on the table, our usual
ritual. During our conversation Rose spoke with the rapidity of a laser-jet
printer.

R: . . . getting scared in the writing. It's funny.
P: Hummmmmm.
R: It's opened up a lot of avenues of why I'm returning.
P: Hummmmm.
R: I think I fell backwards this week because I did not do as much on it as I
   would have liked.

Rose's opening statements expressed fear *in* the writing, not fear *of* the
writing. Her statements and her own realizations during the conversation
reflected how connected her fear of returning to graduate school was to
her ability to write the application. While I said nothing (repeated
"Hummmmmm's"), Rose answered her own thinking. I was listening to un-

derstand and to learn where Rose was in her language and thinking before responding; I had no preplanned response. I listened until I learned what she was thinking so I could think with her.

P: Or you could do, "Because a doctorate is more than attaining one more degree for me and because my concern evolves around the issues and challenges . . . (voice trails off reading the complete text)" . . . anyway, that would mean a whole major revision but what that would do . . .
R: Maybe it would be better.
P: What that would do, then, is connect those ideas.
R: Why don't we do that?
P: We could try and see what happens.
R: Yeah.
P (some confusion, continues to read text): I'm trying to see what you're saying. Are you saying "Because a doctorate is more than attaining one more degree for me" and I'm adding the next one to it . . . "that then your concern" . . . that this degree would address your concern around the issues and the challenges that maintains and improves the health of older people through education . . . Let me read the rest of it . . . "One of the challenges of my doctoral study will be to develop . . ." Okay . . . Yeah, it sounds like there is some connection there that could be . . .
R: It has to be reworked.
P: Reworked. (We said "reworked" together) Why don't you read it again and see what it is you really are trying to say. . . .

This brief episode evidences how we worked together to give language to her writing. I was trying to learn Rose's text by mirroring, exploring, questioning, thinking aloud, and responding as a reader and learner. We trusted each other and shared an unstated common sense of purpose.

In my role of "teacher" consultant I viewed the text as Rose's, but at times when we worked I viewed her text as ours. I was working from my understanding and belief that the process was inseparably connected with her life and the importance of what she was doing with her life. Rose needed to explore and understand her motives for pursuing her doctorate for her to be able to write the application. I was there to help her, by the way we worked, talked, and shared experiences, to do that.

Later Rose read the transcript of this conversation and we talked about the exchange. She felt that my way of working with her was confirming: "You let me think and talk." When I asked her about her use of "we" and her sense of what "we" meant, she replied, "At that moment we are merged or joined, I felt your interest in helping me discover why I'm doing this. You are not too removed. 'We' is support." We were working together in and with language and Rose was acquiring language in a Freirean sense (Freire & Macedo, 1987), naming her experiences with language new to her, naming the world, "reading the word and the world."

When I was working with Rose in 1990, I was also taking a language acquisition and development class. I began to play with the word "languaging" to describe a way of working with people; I defined what Rose and I were doing as "languaging," a form of language acquisition and development. Earlier I described learning as unpredictable and synchronous. This is what I meant.

I became even more drawn to the word when my educational linguistics professor (an "authority") suggested that in the academic community the form I was using (the infinitive, "to language," and my use of the active verbal form, "languaging") was odd, unconventional, not acceptable, and basically undesirable by correct, grammatical standards. A rebellious part of me perversely enjoyed the idea that it is an unconventional form. To use my own word and to have it be unconventional suited me really well at that time of my life. (Just recently I wrote to a friend and found myself being even more unconventional—I wrote without capitalization and only the minimum punctuation. It was quite freeing and felt rather comfortable to me for the first time in my writing in a long time.) Part of the issue was academic ego. In my quest to learn if I had coined a new jargon with "languaging," I asked several education professors if they had encountered the term. I thought, Why couldn't I use a word this way even though it's not the acceptable form or a conventional use? In some small way at the time I was breaking barriers—I was beginning to capture and reclaim my own authority by naming my experience and theory.

What I discovered in the process of working with Rose at the time was that not only was she, at age 50 and past the critical period of language acquisition still acquiring and developing her language, but so was I (at the time age 44).

When I studied our conversations, I found that what we were learning, how we were talking with each other, what we were doing when we read her text was a hell of a lot more than editing and revising text. We were not conditioning and acting upon each other. We were sharing lives, dreams, fears, hopes: languaging.

I continued to turn over and over in my mind the idea of language, of languaging as a shared sense of a naming of the world; I sensed that it was something beyond the ability to use words, to speak words. Rose actually gave language to what was happening between us when she said to me at one point that she realized that she was not writing an application, she was writing her life. Her language also describes what writing this autobiography has been for me, writing and then reading my life and in the processes authoring the self. You see, I've come to know that my authority has to do with authorship, writing the self, reconstructing a sense of who we are and were as teachers.

I hope that you are writing your own story along with me, that you are perhaps telling a story from your teaching life and exploring in it your beliefs and assumptions about teaching, about yourself as a teacher, about learners and what learners do. I suggest that you take a moment to really look closely at the way you are working. What is going on with you? What is going on with the people with whom you are working?

Rose Budding authored her text, and I was part of the languaging process that helped her to know who she was and what she wanted. I also learned a great deal languaging with Rose; I began to learn who I was and what I wanted. This surprised me: I was able to affirm, explore, and question my own experiences as a teacher, a learner, and a woman while helping someone else discover her own life. How many of us do this in education? Too few. This can change if we work to foster critical, reflective autobiography in education. It begins with each of us as teachers.

My ability to help Rose with her writing came from the openness we both had toward finding a common language, not just of words, but of shared experiences, feelings, and emotions in the meaning of the words we used. When we worked together, the shared meaning became greater than the meaning of those individual words we each languaged to the other.

There were times when Rose labored 15 or 20 minutes about one word or its alternative. Together we would talk about the distinctions she was trying to make and whether one word or another captured her intent. I found that we paused over that word and told each other stories. Then she would find the word to represent the experiences she meant. Out of this often came other choices that more closely fit her intent. Laboring over those words together helped me to clarify and reword my own experiences. As I reflect now, in 1996, this was not the hierarchical, teacher-directed teaching and learning I had begun teaching with some 27 years earlier: in 1990, I was now working in a frame of shared authority in action.

THE GOOD WYF OF BATH

Sovereignty. Writing this has taken me one layer deeper into my memory and my journey toward a theory of languaging. In 1980 I was reading and writing about Chaucer's Wyf of Bath. I was struck by the Wyf's tale and by two words: *gentilesse* and *sovereignty*. For me the Wyf's two words epitomized what I see as a right relationship we can live with the world and in our personal lives. *Gentilesse* named the importance of honoring the nobility of each of us, and *sovereignty* captures the importance of recognizing the importance of each person's power. By returning the right to choose to the loathly lady, the knight had honored her gentilesse and her sovereignty. In 1980 I called this action by the knight and the lady "enlightened feminism."

In writing this I'm reminded of the individual power we have when we choose and name our experiences. The Good Wyf's tale is a story of choice and choosing. The teacher's tale, too, can be a story of choice and choosing, sovereignty and gentilesse.

I continue to struggle to give language to my experiences in reading, responding, writing, teaching, and learning: I continue to play with and question my beliefs about ways of working in the classroom. Today it is truly a wonderful journey. It hasn't always been so.

My fascination with the notion of languaging and what it could name continued beyond the Rose Budding case study. It was a critical moment for me. It is only in retrospect that I know this, that I begin to know myself.

Later in that graduate school year, while I was working in a study group in the writing practicum for NYU graduate assistant writing instructors, I began to give language to what "languaging" meant to me in education, and later that spring I concluded my candidacy paper, "A Developing Theory of Languaging: How Transactional Response Transforms Language and Learning" (Schmidt, 1st ed., 1991), with this statement:

> When we work together with each other as co-learners in our classrooms and among ourselves as professionals, not in some hierarchy based on myths of intelligence and as authority which in turn demands a "perfect" text, when we devise a curriculum whose vision we openly share and which is negotiable, then we can hope to begin to learn with each other in the "points of growth in the social and cultural life of a democracy." (Rosenblatt, 1938, p. ix)

This paragraph, though brief, states my evolving philosophy of a way of working. It represents a lifetime of teaching and learning and living. I have continued to re-language it. Each time I revise the statement I have found myself searching for my own language—often the shift of one word or a phrase is the result of months of reading, experiences teaching and learning, conversations, and life's serendipity. Like languaging with Rose, there is the telling of my story, questioning my own honesty, and listening to the stories, the questions, the responses of others.

I have learned to ask myself as a teacher, a reader, a learner, a person: What was/am I doing and why was/am I doing this? How is this affecting others, and what are the ways we can work together in education, in teaching English, to continue to evolve in our own unique, individual ways reading, learning, and growing? This is the Patricia Ann Schmidt whose life you have been reading, the Pat Schmidt who is writing and reading and sharing her critical autobiographical reflections with you, Chaucer's languaging pilgrim, journeying with self-understanding in teaching and learning.

REITERATIONS

So you have a sense of who I am or who I saw myself to be in 1990 as well as my sense of this as a continuing way of living and teaching. It's time to go further back into the past to see who I have been. Who was Pat Schmidt the person, the reader, the learner, the English teacher, before she wrote the Rose Budding case study? What influenced and influences the teacher we see languaging with Rose Budding? In what ways did her experiences reading, learning, and in teacher education influence the way she taught high school English? What did she think and believe "teaching English" was as a profession and a discipline, and what was influencing those beliefs?

So I close this chapter repeating the questions we need to ask ourselves: What influences the teaching of English? What influences the teacher teaching English? I close this chapter reiterating my earlier statement: Most research acknowledges the influence of politics, of culture and society, of the tradition of the discipline of English studies (Elbow, 1990; Britton, Shafer, & Watson, 1990). I learned something more. My daily life and personal experiences as a woman struggling with authority, trying to construct and give meaning to her life, were also daily influences on my teaching. Join me and begin the journey to self-understanding in your teaching lives as you follow my path through the twists and turns of teaching and learning, from sleeping pythons and blackboard jungles to broken shards of glass, Alice's adventures in wonderland, and finally to wise old woman.

CHAPTER 2

A Beginning Teacher

The memories are painful,
like picking up broken
shards of glass with your
bare hands.

—P. A. Schmidt

Somewhere, sometime in our teaching lives all of us have taught the class from hell. My class from hell happened to come the first year I taught English, in 1969. Here I am, I thought as I began to teach that first year: I love teaching English and I have the chance to do what I love. Imagine being paid to do what we love! By the end of the first semester I felt I had been kidnapped into a labrynthine underworld each day when these young people entered the classroom, for nothing I tried seemed to make a difference with this group of 20 honors seniors.

The school year actually had begun quite well. I was 23, newly married, and new to the San Francisco Bay area, having moved there only 3 months before school began. During the summer I had interviewed for teaching positions in several school districts ranging from South San Francisco to schools in my general area. Finally I accepted a part-time temporary job in Martinez, California, teaching three periods of English at Alhambra High School.

Like most beginnning and new teachers, I was assigned two preparations, meaning two different courses of study: two sections of general English called English 2Y and one section of remedial English called English 3Z. When a full-time tenure-track position opened up at the end of the first quarter in the English Department, it was offered to me and I took it. The only catch was that taking the new position meant that I had to give up my three classes and start over with five new classes pieced together from the two veteran teachers who had made changes in their schedules, one to leave the department and the other to become department chair. Still, all seemed well. Appearances can deceive.

First came the change of teaching assignment and students. This change happened without transition for any of us because the new quarter was upon us. I left my three classes on Friday and began teaching five new classes on

Monday. I still had to travel from room to room, but now I had totally new students and taught four preps, none of which I had been teaching the first quarter. This happened so quickly that all I could do over the weekend was get copies of the new curricula, study them, and continue teaching what each of their previous teachers had been teaching. As I look at these moments in my teaching life, I have to ask why the change did not take place more thoughtfully and compassionately for us all. Why weren't we brought together, the teacher leaving and the new teacher, along with the students we were leaving and acquiring to talk about the changes before us? I tried to do this with the students I was leaving, but no such collaboration took place with the teachers I replaced or the new students with whom I began to work.

There they are, the broken shards of glass, the painful memories: the first day, Monday morning, November 1969. I was so pleased and excited with what I considered a promotion, the opportunity to teach full-time in a tenured position. As it turned out, four of my five new classes were just fine. The fifth, the seniors, is another story. Trying to pick up the broken shards with my bare hands, I see them as I pick up the memories with my now bleeding hands: They were the class from hell because they were mad as hell. In their minds they had been given a raw deal in this change of teachers. Their English teacher, whom I'll call Mrs. J., was still at school, but she was now teaching the subject she had dreamed of teaching for many years: social studies. In fact, she taught just around the corner from our classroom and they could and did visit her.

Resentment barely describes how these young people felt at having to change teachers and to have in place of their veteran English teacher a first-year teacher with almost no teaching experience other than her student teaching. Try as hard as I could, I could not understand the anger they directed at me. As a student teacher in Fresno I had taught both juniors and seniors without incident and quite successfully. With this group, however, I had no chance. I began with these young people by being honest about the situation and the little time we'd had to prepare for the change. This is how I began: "Let's continue your study of *Oedipus.* I haven't had time to read it all [I hadn't, for I had had to begin reading *The Scarlet Letter, Oedipus,* and two short stories over the weekend as well as plan for my own substitute while administrators interviewed for my position], but let's discuss what you understand about this play."

Silence. Then one of the young men said, "Mrs. Schmidt, we won't discuss this play with you. You haven't finished it and nothing you have to say about something you haven't read yet means anything to us."

I panicked and replied, "Okay, be ready to discuss *Oedipus* tomorrow. I'll have it finished then." I believed them literally, thinking that was the issue. What I learned over time as the semester continued was that that was not the

issue entirely. It didn't matter whether I had read a text or not, they still refused to work with me. A few came to me some years later to tell me what
was going on that year. They told me that they thought that if they made it
difficult for me, they could make their beloved English teacher return. She
would return because they weren't learning anything from me and I would
give up trying to teach them. Yes, indeed, she was teaching just around the
corner.

Many of them trekked to Mrs. J., complaining about me, about my
teaching. I don't know what she told them; I know what she told me three
weeks later at an English Deparment Christmas party: "Pat, the kids refer to
you as Sergeant Schmidt." She laughed it off. I found this painful to hear, as
I still find it painful to write many years later. I felt devastated. I had been
working so hard to teach these kids, and now I was being told that I was too
tough. Sergeant Schmidt! The shards cut deeply.

I had known that the relationship I had with this class was not good, but
to hear that they called me this awful name made me feel angry, hurt, and as
if I'd been bad. What Mrs. J. told me that day in December is not something
I would tell a beginning teacher who I knew was struggling with a difficult
class, a new life in a new school, and who was inexperienced with community politics.

As I look back on this class, I know that I tried everything I knew of to
try to teach them, to work with them. They were an interesting and powerful
group of bright young people, children of influential members of the community, and they knew this. They were the sons and daughters of judges, the
school superintendent, lawyers, fellow teachers. These young people were the
school leaders and had grown up together in the one high school community.
I was an outsider and not much older than they, and I was guilty of the crime
of inexperience and idealism.

As the year progressed I continued to ask for help in working with this
group. At one point I had the English Department chair visit the classroom
to observe, and then I invited in the senior counselor to observe and advise
me about what to do. The results of these visits were interesting.

In the case of the department chair, I don't remember being told anything except that it was a bright and difficult group. She herself had some of
the same students in her creative writing class and they were fine. The counselor advised me that these young people really didn't like each other very
much, that there were a great many personality conflicts in the group, and
that I could do nothing about that. She empathized with the situation, but
that did not abate the sense of failure and the pain I felt.

Now, having experienced years of therapy, I can name what was going
on then. What was going on was abuse. Pure and simple, I thought that I
alone was the problem and responsible totally for my students' willingness to

learn and their learning. I should have had authority but I didn't. I felt that it was my lack of knowledge and experience that destroyed my authority in the classroom. If so, why wasn't that happening in all my classes or at least a few others, especially the "discipline problems" tracked into Z groups? If I lacked authority, why was it only with one group?

I discovered something as painful as the experience teaching the class a few years later in my informal personnel file in the principal's office. Remember the department chair whom I invited to my class for observations and help? She had slipped a note into my file in the spring of 1970, shortly after her visit to this class: "Pat Schmidt works very well with younger students. However, she doesn't handle seniors well. She can't see the forest for the trees. I recommend that she not be given seniors to teach." When I read this note, I was shocked. As a young teacher, I had trusted her to help me and to be honest with me. A note that I had never been given nor had any conversations about regarding my ability to teach English, and that was critical of the very thing I'd asked for help to deal with, placed in my personnel file was not only unprofessional but certainly without compassion for me or the situation. She was entitled to her opinion, but she also had a professional responsibility to apprise me of an "informal" evaluation and recommendation. Many years later, as a supervisor of student teachers, I try to be open, honest, and straightforward with them whenever humanly possible. I haven't always been successful in this, but at least now I make a conscious effort to work honestly and straightforwardly with people.

There I was, a first-year beginning English teacher, and I felt that I had failed. My sense of who I was as a person and a teacher was shaky after that first year with that class. I had asked for help and worked to the best of my ability to deal with the problems of the class. The lesson I learned from this experience at the time was akin to the thinking of the faithful horse Boxer in *Animal Farm* (Orwell, 1949)—I will work harder. When I read my evaluation years later, I felt like Boxer, that for all my hard work and honest effort to be a good teacher I had been betrayed by the system and sent to the glue factory.

I wanted above all to be a good teacher. So I worked hard to be what I thought was "good": someone knowledgeable about literature, someone who provided a disciplined and controlled educational environment for learning, someone who was respected and liked by students. Book knowledge, discipline, and respect: I thought at the time that this is what gives the teacher authority. Developing and possessing these qualities would make me a good teacher, someone with "authority."

I finished my first year of teaching unsure of myself, shattered, looking at broken shards of my self. My fingers were cut and bleeding trying to pick up the pieces. The transition from student teacher to teacher is difficult and challenging, and yes, sometimes painful.

HOW DID I LOSE IT SO QUICKLY? A GOOD STUDENT TEACHER

How did I change from a good student teacher to the first-year teacher who finished her first year of teaching shattered? As I recall my early English teaching experiences, I remember that student teaching in Fresno in 1968–69 was a joy, especially the class of seniors I taught at Roosevelt High in the winter/spring semester. The preparation and practice to teach English, student-teaching one class each semester, did not begin to prepare me for the reality I faced with five English classes a day, four preparations, and changing classrooms.

The senior class I student-taught at Roosevelt High consisted of 19 students: 14 males and 5 females. My master teacher told me he had given this class to me, a 23-year-old female, to see if I "could handle the boys." Though now I would view this as sexist, I didn't question his thinking. After all, he was the master teacher (very male in this double nominal). These young people accepted me as their teacher, though initially they told me, "We're tired of being the training class for young English teachers." Many told me that they didn't expect much from the class because I was a student teacher.

I was told by a professional authority (whom I understood held my career in his hands with his professional recommendation) that my ability to teach an English class would be assessed on how I handled the boys. So I thought about how to control the class while teaching English. Good English teachers tightly control student behavior. After I met the class I soon forgot about controlling behavior. It wasn't necessary. Giving me this male-dominated class was probably more a reflection of his problem with 14 adolescent male egos clashing with his own than his concern for my ability to teach young men. Was it sexist? Would the same question about control be asked of a male teacher being given 14 adolescent females? Should control be the issue? Isn't meaningful curriculum and working with learners to connect with their lives a different type of "control" that is more connected with learning?

I came to teaching thinking that the teacher automatically received respect because I was a good student and I respected my teachers. This has always been one very problematic assumption of which I continue to be reminded: I believe that people will automatically respect you if you respect them. I assumed that the people I worked with shared my desire to work together on a common goal of education, learning. I had also stated in one of my psychology papers at the time I was student teaching that I felt that if I respected my students, they would respect me. As a beginning teacher I did not have a sense of myself in relationship to others or how to define that self in relationship. I wanted to be good. My assumption regarding shared respect is a good theoretical principle from which I work, but not everyone else does, and I need to consider that in teaching as well as in personal relationships.

So my master teacher dictated the text I would teach, what was important for my evaluation—discipline, and the general curriculum (a term paper). Since my master teacher had set up this issue of behavior control, I went into that classroom worried and quite stiff. As it turned out, my experience with them was quite different from what my master teacher had suggested it would or could be. I developed a comfortable, easygoing rapport with the students once I let down the walls I took into the room at the beginning of the semester. They were not the problem my master teacher had set them up to be. I began to learn not to let other teachers' perceptions of students or a class influence my teaching.

I loved my student teaching.

Along with my student teaching, I had immersed myself in the schools while I was an English major at Fresno State by working 10 to 15 hours a week as a teacher's aide in high school English classes. It was a powerful preservice experience. I read papers, corrected tests, typed and ran tests, and created and put up bulletin boards for three English teachers. Planning and teaching one English class was my dream come true. I realize now what a romantic idealist I was as I entered the profession (I'm not sure at all that I have yet transformed these notions). I gave a tremendous amount of time and energy to the one class I student-taught. The kids respected me. I respected them and encouraged them to read and discuss literature and to have their own opinions even though I was teaching in a traditional paradigm: teacher in front, desks in rows, some lecture and discussion from a list of literary analysis questions I'd prepared. I always tried to get my students to think in the same critical ways that I was being asked to think in my own college English classes. I really don't remember ever having "control" problems with that class, and I didn't have to manufacture authority in external ways. The kids challenged me in innocuous ways (playful even), but they seemed to want me to succeed. I really liked them and they liked me (we often chatted outside the classroom while we waited for our class to begin), and I wanted to give them the best English experience I could. I listened to them and shared some of my own experiences. We were going through similar experiences. They and I were graduating that spring and we were looking forward to beginning new stages in our lives. As I was writing and rewriting this experience, I realized that the seeds for the notion of shared authority and its challenges, which I wrote about in a 1990 piece about the Wyf of Bath, were planted early, it seems (much earlier than I had imagined).

Whenever my master teacher and my college supervisor were observing, those kids bent themselves over backwards to be cooperative with me during the lessons, and they always inquired the next day about how they'd done for me. I don't remember the class being unruly or difficult when I was teaching them unobserved. If there were any "behavior" problems, they surfaced in the form of kidding and practical joking with me and with each other. Teaching them may have been easier since we were so close in age (several of them were 18 and 19 and I was 23). I felt very comfortable with these young people.

I found it strange that they were concerned for me when I was being observed. My guess now is that they knew the power they had to influence my evaluation. They knew that my evaluation would be based on their behavior while I was teaching them, and they were genuinely concerned. It was spring and I was their second student teacher that year. Over the course of time they told me that the previous student teacher had had a difficult time working with them and they knew that that young teacher had not received a good recommendation.

I was deeply touched and overwhelmed with emotion when, at the end of the year, they threw me a surprise party with a cake and card. Their comments about my teaching and their experiences in my class were written in a "Best Wishes" card. The comments generally ran along the lines of "You were tough," "I didn't expect to learn much from a student teacher but I did," "Thanks for the decent grade for a bs term paper," "I enjoyed your class," and, "Good luck in your marriage." (I had shared that I was getting married soon after my/our graduation.)

I ended my student teaching feeling that I was successful and that I was a good English teacher. The experience I had the very next year, the first year of my professional teaching career, shattered and nearly destroyed me. I prided myself in choosing to become an English teacher, but I had just started my career and I felt that I had failed at being the kind of English teacher I'd worked hard to become. Today, having written these stories, I am beginning to understand in retrospect.

CHAPTER 3

The Good English Teacher

I am an English teacher.

Even when I haven't felt good about myself, I have always said this with great pride: "I am an English teacher." There is something wonderful about being an English teacher, saying that I teach English. Everyone knows (so I assumed) what an English teacher is, and almost everyone remembers his or her English teacher. I thought I knew what an English teacher was: someone who loves books, someone who is well read, someone who has a disciplined mind, someone who is a good communicator, someone who is organized, someone who is enlightened about life. I'd have to say that now that I am writing about what an English teacher is, I realize that I probably fashioned myself after my high school English teachers, Mrs. Linson and Miss Hompson. I admired both tremendously as teachers and as women. They were both, generally speaking, "commonsense teachers" (Mayher, 1990).

Miss Hompson, my senior English teacher, was an especially powerful force in my life. She was the quintessential English teacher: She exacted high standards, taught the great books, was intellectual, led rigorously academic discussions about literature, and carried herself with great dignity. She dressed elegantly, a 60-plus-year-old, and she wore her naturally curly reddish hair in a soft bun at the nape of her neck. I was not a top student in our very elite university prep group: I struggled with B's and felt lucky since we were graded using a bell curve, which allowed only two A's in the class (when I became an English teacher I refused from the beginning to grade on the curve, feeling that if there were more than two people who did outstanding work, they could earn an A). Much about Miss Hompson reminds me of the essences of the fictional British schoolteacher Miss Jean Brodie in Muriel Spark's *The Prime of Miss Jean Brodie* (1961) except that Miss Hompson was no fascist. It wasn't her political stance that appealed to me; I'd say it was her primness, her intellect, and the sense she gave us that we were special. She led an independent, intellectual life in farm country in the California Central Valley.

IMPERTINENT QUESTIONS AND MORE UNEXAMINED ASSUMPTIONS

More critical moments. Yes. Many more. In 1992 a New York University colleague queried me about the nature of my work on this memoir: are you writing about yourself as an English teacher or a literature teacher? Initially I was angry with him for asking me a question that I had failed to think about. That old feeling from that first critical year I taught English and felt that I had failed was raising its ugly head, the wounds opened again, and I retreated into fear momentarily. Where did this feeling of failure come from?

When this same colleague pursued his query, asking me, "Are you going to talk about teaching grammar, punctuation, writing, etc.?" I was annoyed with his question and I bristled secretly (and, I might add, defensively), primarily because I thought I had not considered teaching English as either teaching skills or teaching literature, which I thought his question was suggesting (I now see that I was feeling judged). I perceived him (through his questions) to be separating the content of teaching English from teaching literature: That English teachers teach literature separately from teaching grammar, spelling, punctuation, and writing, and that that was what I should be doing now in my teaching. My research was, after all, about what influences the teaching of English, not about what English is! I didn't want to fuss around with what English is. I wanted to write and read about the influences on the teaching of English. A bit foolish of me, now that I can look at this experience from a greater distance.

Before I could do much more at the time of his query, I had to look at my response. When I reflected a few days later on my response to his inquiry, I realized that his questions were actually not condemning me for my inadequacies as a researcher, but were actually meant to help me continue to learn about myself and to see how I had changed. This is the power of reflection I have come to know in my teaching and learning life.

My transformed view of teaching English from common-sense traditionalist to transactional languager was not at question here. But I had bristled at him and his questions because for me they reflected that traditional, common-sense stance I now abhorred (Mayher, 1990), one that views the teaching of English as a discrete, teacher-centered content and skill-based curriculum in which teaching literature does not include "teaching skills" (teaching skills can be generally described as teaching grammar, spelling, usage, vocabulary, punctuation, and even reading). I had evolved, and I was now viewing teaching as a "languaging experience" inseparable from experiences of reading, writing, and sharing and living lives. Languaging even went beyond literature. Worse, I did not want to return to what I had been as a teacher, anticipating pain and disgust with myself and my failures. I realize that I only wanted to write about the positive moments that influenced my teaching life, moments like the California Literature Project summer.

A haughty person I was indeed! When I began teaching English in 1969 I did think of teaching English as teaching literature and teaching grammar and writing as separable and separate skills. I did the very best that I could at the time, given my education and experience. My ideas about teaching English were fostered by my desire to be a good English teacher, a desire that came out of a long tradition associated with English and teaching and one that I had experienced as a student.

If you reflect on my responses with me, you might come to see, as I have today through many years of critical reflective practice, that I lacked compassion for who I was as an English teacher and for what I had been as a teacher. I am the teacher that I am today because of the experiences I've had in my teaching life, good and bad, painful and joyous.

Today I am grateful, for the questions my colleague asked me really jogged my thinking and resonated long after he posed them. I would ask you to honestly ask yourself the same questions whether you are a beginning teacher or a veteran teacher: What is it to teach English, and who am I as an English teacher? I find that Peter Elbow's book *What Is English?* (1990) is a useful guide to exploring this question.

ANOTHER UNEXAMINED ASSUMPTION

This is the unexamined assumption that I discovered in my thinking: English teachers who majored in English teach literature and the love of reading— we study literature, then we teach literature. I hold two degrees as an English major (I earned my English B.A. in 1968 and my English M.A. in 1979), and throughout my academic experience we read, analyzed, and interpreted literature: new Critical theory—close analytical reading of text. Literature was an object of intellectual and aesthetic beauty. To read and analyze literature critically was the highest calling for an English major and English teacher.

Literature has always been my first love, and I chose to become an English teacher because I loved reading literature so much. You who are reading this book, like so many teachers I talk with, probably chose to teach English or your own special field for the same reasons.

In 1992, when my erstwhile colleague queried me and angered me, I did begin to consciously and critically reflect on these questions and I invite you, my readers, to reflect on these questions as well. Do you teach English the ways I did? Are you angry that I'm implying that that is not good teaching? Anger is good. It's what we do with it that matters. We can't stay with it, even if it's justified. When I began teaching I did not allow myself to be angry or to express it. Now I write about it, look at it, and then work on what I can change, which is always only my reaction to what is angering me.

Start with the questions with which I started: What is English and who is the English teacher? That is where the stories that you are reading begin.

I have come to think of myself as an evolving English teacher. If we cannot change the structures in which we teach and live, what can we change? Ourselves through growth, academically and personally. As Arthur Jersild (1955) ever reminds me, teachers must face themselves. When we work with these constructing and reconstructing processes, we are evolving.

I use "evolving" to describe this process because evolving captures the sense I have of the movements of change, growing from one way of thinking and doing into another. Evolving is the process of becoming. We are always becoming and yet we are always who we are. Interesting paradox.

As I began teaching high school English in Martinez, California, in 1969, I declared my vision of myself as an English teacher: I wanted to share my love of literature with my students while somehow instilling a pleasure and love of literature in them. I wanted to be a young Miss Hompson. Thinking again of recent conversations and conversations over the years with teachers, I know that many English teachers I talk with share this way of thinking about teaching English. At the core of what many of us teachers bring to teaching English is a love of literature and a desire to share that love with young and adolescent learners, instilling it as a legacy to be continued beyond the classroom.

What I was unaware of was my own assumption and blind acceptance that I and perhaps you, we people who love literature, also teach English in ways (the ways I had been taught) that do not foster that same love in students and, in fact, drive students away from literature and from becoming lifelong readers.

ON BEING GOOD

For most of my life, beginning in childhood, I'd say, I've wanted to be good. Being good for me means being perfect, never making mistakes, and being accepted and liked by others. This desire to be good and to please left me without a self, for when I am good in this way I usually abandon myself, betray myself to outside authority. Since teachers contend with outside authority throughout their careers, ranging from school boards to state legislation, administration, and parents, we find ourselves in constant tension, being pulled between our sense of self and our sense of what we must do to be good in relationship to those outside authorities.

THE "GOOD" ENGLISH TEACHER

I wanted to be the Good English Teacher, like Miss Hompson or Mrs. Linson, so I began teaching by religiously following the traditional curriculum I was given by the English Department; it was basically the same curriculum and we used the same texts I had myself experienced as a student only five years earlier. As a new teacher I was unconsciously doing what Phillida Salmon in *Psychology for Teachers* (1988) describes teachers as doing: "When we teach, we do in a sense teach ourselves" (p. 42).

So I found myself to be a first-year teacher trying to emulate my belief in the Good English Teacher, but I was not accorded, nor did I take responsibility for, my own authority to question and explore with my colleagues any assumptions embedded in the school curriculum or in my pedagogy. I did not know what reflective teaching was, so I did not practice it.

Fear of failure worked heavily on my heart and soul as a teacher. I felt that if I failed to teach the curriculum as I was expected to do, I would not only not have my students' respect, I would not garner my colleagues' respect, nor would I receive tenure. The possibility of rejection and failure in the academic and educational cultures and communities within which I chose to define myself as a human being frightened me.

I felt alone.

I now know that I was not alone. A great many teachers silently live in this cacophony of authority: We live, teach, and read in contradictory language (McNeil, 1988; Sizer, 1985). Take an authority, be an authority, be responsible for your students' learning, but do nothing to question or change the tradition, the form, or the structure of education.

How did I teach English when I began teaching in 1969? I began teaching high school English just as my inquiring colleague had suggested with all my classes except one, the honors university prep English class that I wrote about in Chapter 2. In the other classes I taught as I had been taught, teaching skills separately, discretely, then testing the students' knowledge of the skills. I taught literature as I had been taught, as an academic skill, devoid of the pleasure of reading and with only feeble attempts at connecting to our lives.

For the most part I was teaching students how to prepare to read literature in academic ways. I followed the time-honored New Critical and Structuralist theory and pedagogy I had experienced in my own education: Teaching literature involved doing a close reading of text, giving an authoritative lecture on the text to my students, discussing interpretations of the text, and then having students write prescriptively and formulaically about them, using Warriner's composition exercises on standard essay forms (Warriner & Griffith, 1963).

I determined my classroom reading assignments by referring to the re-

quired anthologies and my own academic reading: that is, for American literature my junior English class read almost exactly what I had read in my two
academic English major American Literature survey classes in college. I did
not question my choices. The authority for these choices came from the traditional curriculum and my experiences in school as a learner. I had been taught
and learned early on in my life that authority was outside me, with the system
and with all adults, and I, though now the teacher, did not recognize that I
now could claim my own authority.

Why couldn't I recognize my own authority? Why can't we know our
own authority? I'd suggest that all our early experiences learning within education systems and family systems influence a teacher's choices in how and
what to teach. The concept of authority I had at that time came from my
childhood experiences with authority, both at home and at school.

I had been taught by my family to unquestioningly accept authority, all
authority. People (everyone but Pat the kid) had authority, which meant they
had physical power and used it to bring my unacceptable behaviors into line.
As a child, being spanked with a switch and then being told not to cry because
you felt pain made an indelible mark on my way of thinking about authority.
I wanted to be good, but I was bad and when you are bad you are punished.
At home, when I tried to speak, to question, to negotiate my own experiences
with adult authority, I failed, and I was punished for being rude, disrespectful,
a "bad girl." I just grew quiet and read. I became silent about my self.

School expected the same good behaviors from me, but at school I found
I learned and teachers did not berate me or hit me for being a kid. I toed the
line at school because I was afraid of what my parents would do if I got into
trouble in public and disgraced them. I disgraced them early on: kindergarten.
I only remember the experience vaguely. Somehow, in a fit of anger, I grabbed
a classmate's dress and tore it. I was sent to the principal's office for this. I had
been bad. I lost control of my feelings and acted out in anger. My parents
were angry at me and I felt ashamed that I had acted so badly.

Another incident still colors my feelings about myself as being a bad girl
when I was young. When I was four or five my cousins and I were playing in
the well house at my grandmother's house in the country in rural California.
One of my younger cousins had been teasing me and making faces at me
through the window. He wouldn't stop it and I felt angry with him. I had had
it. No one interceded, so I took care of the problem. I was so angry that I
punched him—through the glass window. I have a one-inch scar on my right
wrist from the cut. I must have bled profusely. He escaped unscathed, thank
God. Of course, I was punished. I had a bad temper and I didn't control it and
I was bad. I learned that when I am angry, lose my temper, and strike out at
others, I hurt myself, and I am bad. Even as I write this in 1996, at age 49, I
fear my anger and my temper. For years I have hated myself, thinking that I

was a bad person if I lost my temper. Many friends and acquaintances see me as quiet, laid back, and pretty easygoing, if not intense about teaching and school and relationships. Beneath this exterior is a pretty frightened person at times, a chicken hovering at the top of a cage with a sleeping python below. How I wish that as a young preservice teacher I had had the opportunity to explore my experiences and understand how they inform my actions and thinking. It has taken years of psychoanalysis and self-help and recovery to begin to understand that I am a human being with human emotions that don't condemn me to an eternal hell for expressing them.

I'd have to say that the teaching profession and schools themselves reinforced this good/bad behavior paradigm. Good students don't misbehave and good teachers don't get angry. So what do we do with these feelings we're not supposed to have? I'm still working on how to deal with normal anger and that normal people get angry. I, however, went into teaching with no understanding of myself regarding feelings and teaching.

So, many levels of personal experience, inside and outside of educational settings, influenced my thinking and my teaching. As a young adult beginning to teach English, I found that I accepted with good faith that the academy, the experts in American literature, the literature anthologists, the English Department, and the curriculum held unquestioned authority.

From my perspective as a beginning teacher, these people, like my family, had much more skill and knowledge and power than I, and they had determined that these texts were important and valued them. So, I thought, based on curricular authority, high school juniors should read them. I had read and written papers about Ben Franklin, de Crevecoeur, William Cullen Bryant, Thoreau, Whitman, Anne Bradstreet, Jonathan Edwards, Poe, and Hawthorne, all in the standard college text for American literature, *The American Tradition in Literature* (Vol. 1, Bradley, Beatty, & Long, 1962). So would my students.

Even though I hadn't enjoyed my academic training as a personally satisfying reading experience, I had learned to value and enjoy the intellectual exercises reading literature afforded me. I was happily seduced by tradition. Like many of my present-day students, I loved searching for the "hidden meaning" in texts.

I derived my sense of self from external authority. I proceeded to teach the texts that I had been taught to read, and I taught them (my students and the texts) in the same way I had been taught. I filled the containers, as Lakoff and Johnson aptly describe the metaphor for schools and teaching in *Metaphors We Live By* (1980). Because I had read these texts and authors and had received the authoritative word about interpretations (I still had my papers and almost verbatim lecture notes), I felt knowledgeable enough to talk, to take authority for knowledge about these authors and their texts to (and, ironically, away from) my students. I lectured to my students about authors and texts, but I never felt comfortable teaching this way. I thought that if I lost my notes I would have nothing to say. I was doing all the work, and I had lost myself as a reader to academic reading. I now see how this way of teaching robs learners of their own authority.

I allowed the content of English, then, to be defined by what I had read, by what I had experienced in my own English academic training. The way I taught was hierarchically determined. I accepted it, and in so doing, I perpetuated the discipline and its traditions.

OF FORESTS AND TREES

That painful first year that I described earlier is full of contradictions and paradoxes in my memories of it. I have the remembered experience, something Zinsser (1987) calls "inventing a truth" which the mind creates from the stored memory. Then there are actual "data" that reveal another truth of the experience. This is why it is important for us to keep the papers we write and reflect on them in the years to come, for they tell us much about who we are becoming.

I kept a set of lesson plans I taught to three of my five classes that first year that I taught English in 1969: 7 weeks of daily lesson plans for my junior college prep English classes (December to January 1969–70). I taught these classes very differently from the senior honors English class I struggled to teach that I wrote about in Chapter 2. Earlier I stated that I entered teaching with a love of literature and that I wanted to instill this love into my students. These plans still horrify me when I look at them. I see no love of literature. I see little or no literature. I planned my weekly lessons using the form I had used in my student teaching in Fresno. I did not teach much literature, as I thought I did when I shared this in the initial memories that I wrote about earlier.

As a teacher writing and reading this account in retrospect, I continue to realize that the imprint of experiences and the memories may be dramatically different from what I actually did. The actual lessons show me a different picture of my early teaching than I remember. I remember the struggle, the pain, the feeling of failure. I had to write that story to get to the story I just described to you. The imprint of the experience of struggle, pain, and failure has been deep inside. The story is in Chapter 2.

What I see in my early planning indicates to me that I was trying to do it all. Sadly, those kids learned the traditional curriculum with my emphasis on the thinking processes of learning literary and language skills. Knowledge was information and interpretation. There was little joy of reading, of entering people's lives, of knowing our own lives, of connecting with the world beyond us. It is ironic that these classes did not rebel against nor dislike my teaching, to the best of my memory. They were good kids. As Eliot Wiggington (1986) tells us in his book on the teaching life, there were sometimes shining moments, but there were few for me.

Let's take a close look at my actual lesson plans which were the same exact plans I had used as a student teacher (see Figure 1). These lesson plans for three sections of Junior X English (we tracked in incredibly inhuman terms: X meant college preparatory, Y meant general English, and Z meant remedial English) show that I had assigned exercises in reading the classic texts from the anthology *Adventures in American Literature* (Secondary English Editorial Staff, 1965), and grammar exercises from Warriner and Griffith (1963). In addition, I assigned and then tested my students with meaningless vocabulary and spelling worksheets. Do you know these books? I had them when I was in high school and I see them still in high school classrooms today, some 30 years later.

(Several years later, for some unknown reason, probably intuition, I began to question the amount of time I allotted in my classes for studying vocabulary and spelling alone. I calculated that I spent around 40 percent of the whole class time on these isolated skills. Lesson plans reveal two days a week.)

Quite noticeably, I assigned very little writing. I discovered I had given only two writing assignments that I authored; that is, assignments I did not merely assign from the textbook or the anthology. Again, I am horrified by one of the writing assignments I authored: "Write a descriptive paragraph describing a classmate—due tomorrow—use adjectives." I thought I was personalizing the writing experience by assigning a personal topic while students were practicing using descriptive adjectives. Teaching was organizing and giving assignments. Assignments were exercises. Writing this takes me even deeper into the memory of my own experiences as a learner, first in reading, now in writing.

THE ACADEMIC WRITER COMPLEX

I am not a writer!

I have never considered myself a good writer, so I do not consider myself a writer (interesting notion to consider as I write and you read this book). What is a good writer? Is this the same problem as the good English teacher?

I began teaching with no consciously stated notion of what it means to write, nor of the complexity of constructing meaningful writing assignments. Since I did not view myself as a successful writer, I did not see myself as a writer at all. I believe that the paucity of writing assignments I gave came

Figure 1. *Weekly lesson plan, 1969–70.*

TEACHER *Roark*   COURSE *English*   WEEK OF *Jan. 13–17*

PERIOD(S) *2*   ROOM *A14*   GRADE *11*

TEXT _____

MONDAY
Go over Ex. 1 · 11–20
in Warriner's
Go over Ex. 2, even

HOMEWORK ASSIGNMENTS
Ex. 2, Warriner's—odd
Ex. 3, even

TUESDAY
Go over Ex. 2+3
Homework, Warriner's
Ex. 23c—Explain
Warriner's
Collect final rewrite

Ex. 4 (1,2,3,6,8)
Warriner's
Ex. 3, even

WEDNESDAY Review Sentence
Variety,
Ex. 3, Warriner's
Language and Systems
Poetic Systems, Ex. 5+7
Chapter 10, Ex. 5+7

Bring
Adventures in
American Lit.
Review
Exercise—1+3

THURSDAY Review for
finals

Language
and Systems

FRIDAY
Review

History of Engl.
Colonial Period
Huck Finn
Vocabulary

from not experiencing meaningful writing much in my personal or educational life. I did not consider myself an author of texts or ideas. It may also be partly attributed to the fact that I had no idea how to teach writing. I think it also had to do with time: I found it difficult to read, give grades on, and meaningfully comment on a minimum of 130 pieces of writing a week.

The way I taught writing in my English class had a great deal to do with having few experiences owning my own authority as a writer. There is that word again: authority. As a writer I found myself in relationship with a demanding reader who expected technically correct writing and clear prose using an introduction, developing support in the body, and then a conclusion. As an English student, an English major, an English teacher, to write in any flawed, incoherent, incorrect way was to fail. Typically, my papers were returned with a letter grade, bleeding red marginalia comments such as "frag," "run on," and "unclear." All deficiencies, all failures to write correctly, precisely. Most of the students I've worked with don't intentionally write from their deficiencies, and being told we are deficient, empty, and flawed doesn't help us as writers to "correct" the errors of our ways. The margin comments served to condemn my writing, not encourage me to write, to be a writer.

I always wrote for an authority, to please an authority, to get approval on the terms others demanded or expected, whether it be the personal idiosyncrasies of teachers or, as Stanley Fish stated in *Reader-Response Criticism*, "Interpreting the 'Variorum'" (1980b) would say, the "interpretive community" to which I wanted full admission. I wanted to be a good English student and then a good English teacher.

So the passion that I had declared in my first year of teaching, to instill the joy of reading literature into my students, was being driven by my stronger desire to be a "good" English teacher, which was influenced by the traditional education experiences I'd learned in English classrooms. I was primarily teaching English using the same traditional New Critical pedagogy I had experienced: assigning book-centered exercises, using a skill-driven content (punctuation, grammar, vocabulary, and spelling). It was teacher-centered and dominated by the textbook companies that produced the structures. It was also dominated by the metaphor that time is money, characterized in Lakoff and Johnson's *Metaphors We Live By* (1980). I thought that my classes and I must complete the curriculum. In those first years of teaching I just taught lessons day by day and week by week so that I could complete teaching the course of study by the end of the year.

I've also heard many other teachers talk about the frustrations of trying to teach the course of study by the end of the year and the accompanying sense of failure if they only make it to the Romantic poets or did not have time to teach a key play.

I remember the feeling at the end of each day in those early days of my teaching career of total physical and mental exhaustion. It is no wonder! Time and external structures drove me and ultimately their learning. When my students and I did read a short story, "The Mystery of Thor Bridge," in our standard English text *Adventures in American Literature* (Secondary English Editorial Staff, 1965), for example, we read it one day, answered the comprehension questions at the end of the story, and discussed it the next day. Then we were done and moved on to another story or assignment. Assignments in my classroom were connected by virtue of their sequence in the book, certainly not by any understanding or knowledge of why or how my students might be learning or might need to learn. Like my own experiences as a student, I, now the teacher, was expected to be the authority, and they as the students were not.

ENCOUNTERS WITH REALITY, 1970–1985

In those early years teaching English I never really thought about what it meant to teach English, neither about the way I was teaching nor the components of my curriculum in theoretical, pedagogical, or philosophical terms. Like most young, inexperienced teachers, I was just trying to survive the 5 periods a day, 130 to 150 students a day, and 3 or 4 curricula preparations.

I did look around me, and I did remember what I had enjoyed about my own learning experiences. I tried to infuse these experiences and lessons in the curriculum I was teaching.

Though the curriculum remained the same, I changed the order of my curriculum each year. I prided myself in never teaching any level or even the same-level classes the same way from year to year or from period to period. I'm not sure why I did this. At the time I might have been thinking that it would ensure fresh experiences in the classroom, for I noticed that other English teachers taught exactly the same lessons and units year to year and that the students had copies of tests, assignments, and so forth, which meant that they could predict what they were expected to learn. I took pride in this unpredictability because at the time I thought students could not cheat if lessons, assignments, and tests were changed. Naively, I thought this would make students concentrate on learning.

Soon after I started teaching at this school I noticed that students said that they loved Mrs. Such-and-Such or Mr. So-and-So because these teachers had established reputations as being tough, and usually they taught exactly the same lessons from year to year. The kids practically passed the tests and assignments on to each other. Mrs. Such-and-Such was so busy grading papers at her desk at the front of the class she didn't notice them cheating on her 10-page test, they reported.

I changed lessons from year to year to prevent cheating. I also changed lessons from year to year because I did not want to become bored repeating the same ideas, the same lessons, over and over. Repeating the same assignment in the same way three times in one day (if I were teaching three sections of English IIX—the sophomore academics) just never worked. Each class was different and required different lessons. Discussions often took on the nature of the class, and each class was different. No class ever ended in the same place naturally. So I planned change each year, both for them and for me.

In "The Swinging Pendulum: Teaching English in the USA, 1945–1987," Simmons, Shafer, and Shadiow (1990) aptly characterize the influences not only on the teaching of English generally, but very specifically address the political, social, economic, environmental, and professional contexts that characterize the major external influences on the way I taught English.

I wanted to be thought of as a good English teacher, a person willing to listen and to compromise. As a beginning teacher, a good girl, I did not openly state my opinions or disagree with English Department colleagues, for I felt that it was not politically or socially safe for a first-year untenured teacher to do so. I felt that any failure to be accepted or to break from traditional English teaching could mean losing my job.

I did not know about the National Council of Teachers of English (NCTE) or the California Association of Teachers of English (CATE), so my involvement in the profession of English teaching did not extend beyond the department level. The English Department at my school subscribed to the NCTE professional journal for secondary English teachers, *The English Journal*. For many years I relied on the department copy of the journal for my professional reading. Eventually, I joined both NCTE and CATE, subscribed to their professional journals, and attended regional and statewide conferences. The only other source of professional reading I used was the English Department's professional library. I did not read much in this area. I barely had enough time to prepare for my daily lessons, read students' papers, attend meetings, and enjoy the life of a newlywed. There was no other life than teaching, no rest until the school year ended.

There was another life going on internally, a psychological one. I was living a life dependent on others' acceptance and approval. Stanford educator Nel Noddings in *Women and Evil* (1989) describes the problem of goodness for women in our lives and goodness in education settings. The good girl, the good wife, the good mother: all come from a legacy Noddings calls "the angel in the house," a societal expectation of women to be morally and innately good, living under the law of kindness. "Women were (are) taught to think of themselves as good when they lived lives of obedience and service" (1989, p. 3). Does this sound familiar for teachers, not just women? Further, Noddings tells us that if women are anything else, they are perceived as evil; that is, to be rebellious of male domination is to be "the devil's gateway." Look at Hillary Rodham Clinton and Marcia Clark in the 1990s.

I've always thought that I was just bad and crazy. In *Women and Evil* Noddings (1989) further tells us that:

> As early as kindergarten and first grade, for example, teachers associate all sorts of good traits with good readers, and many studies have documented that teachers often treat good and poor readers differently; they talk to them differently and offer them different opportunities. At every level of schooling teachers refer to bright students as their "good kids." "With my good kids," they say, "I do . . ." and they go on to explain how lessons progress in classes populated by academically bright students. (p. 197)

Noddings further suggests that we educators need to be aware of the moral stances we take and help our students to understand these stances.

I thought that I had to be approved of and accepted by those I worked with in the system. It never occurred to me that what I wanted was a reciprocal relationship, not a dependent, conditional one. That the reason I was so fearful was that I was rebelling against the norms of goodness. I couldn't give language to myself. As a person, as a teacher, as a reader, as a learner, I didn't know how to approve of myself first, to know my own power and authority first before I tried to work with others in relationship.

I would describe my thinking at that time in this way: I wanted to become a member of the English teacher culture and community, so I felt I had to accept the rules of the culture. If I was uncomfortable with them, I had to change to be accepted on their terms.

In a recent article in *College English* ("Resisting the Faith: Conversion, Resistance, and the Training of Teachers," April 1993), Nancy Welch tells a similar story, only she was caught in the cacophony of authority as a doctoral student in education. She thought that "they" (professors, curriculum) had the answer and that her job as a learner was to learn the right language and give the right answers (theirs), but that they really had her best interests at heart. When she finally realized that they didn't have her best interests at heart, she was able to make changes for herself and recapture her own authority. "Many women, perhaps most, have internalized the expectations described in these ideals [of womanhood] and have come to depend on the rewards associated with meeting them" (Noddings, 1989, p. 60).

That senior English class my first year of teaching was a critical moment in my teaching life. That experience negatively influenced my sense of myself as an English teacher for many years. I realize now that I was trying to teach in a way I valued but that my students couldn't and/or didn't want to deal with: I assumed that because I was their English teacher they would respect me and accord me the authority of being their teacher, but I didn't have the wherewithal to know how to deal with the daily sense of failure in working with them when they or my colleagues or the system didn't reciprocate. I respected them, so I assumed that they would respect me. They didn't. They were used to authoritative, hierarchical leadership and learning. So, too, was I. I gave them and myself mixed messages.

Like Nancy Welch, I was trusting, trusting that everyone else shared my values and sense of trust. Thus, I defined myself as a teacher by others' perceptions and opinions of me. It's as if the view of the feminine has constructed the view of American education. Educators have been predominantly female. Teaching is often viewed as a feminine job, and many of the expectations of teachers and other helping professions demand self-sacrifice, nurturing, and innate goodness. The American culture and our educational system perpetuate the confusing notion of Other as Authority (the system) but hold teachers individually and collectively responsible for all students' learning. Perhaps this is why education is so devalued in terms of funding and respect. It is a feminine profession.

Following that first painful year I became very unsure of myself, though by traditional academic standards I was both formally and informally well trained to be a good English teacher. I had been educated by my family, my schooling, and my academic training to be an authority but not have any real authority. I lived emotionally in a chaos of paradoxical authority.

On the curricular and structural levels, my teaching of English was content-driven and controlled through a high degree of organization. On the psychological level I lived in conflict, and the struggle almost destroyed me.

None of the stories in this narrative surprise me when I remember how as a child I "taught" my cat Smokey and my doll collection. I'd line them up, read to them, mark their imaginary work, and keep records of their scores. We learn what teaching is from our own childhood experiences in school. That kind of teaching I have been describing is what I had experienced in my elementary school years and in many of my high school years: basals, anthologies, worksheets, spelling tests, vocabulary sheets. The same structures were transformed into common-sense New Criticism in my college years.

So what I've discovered as I tell my stories of who I was/am as an English teacher is that what influenced my first years teaching English were my childhood experiences with authority at home and at school (Brown and Gilligan, 1992) and my sense of what constituted a good English teacher and the "subject" of English (Grossman, 1990; Elbow, 1990). Much of what I remember about those early years centers on my fear of my failure to meet the expectations of my parents, of the profession, and of the educational community— my fear of failing to be good.

Indeed, my NYU English Education colleague asked me a most important question when he asked, "What do you mean when you say 'teaching English'?" And I hope that as you've read about my experiences and reflections on teaching English, you've been writing your own stories and talking to colleagues about what teaching English means to you and who you see yourself to be as an English teacher. I hope that you've moved into the labyrinth of the soul of the teacher, the psychological and emotional life you've lived. I suggest that if you're keeping a reflective journal as you read this that you stop and think back to your own schooling, your own childhood. What memories do you have? Teachers, events, experiences. Pick one or two and tell the story. Know yourself. Then begin to reflect.

I would like to say that when I taught English, I was genuinely concerned with how my students were learning or even that I was thinking about the issue of learning. But I can't. Fear crept into my life, and my sense of who I was as an English teacher was shaky. I retreated into control. My classroom epitomized the greatest sense of hierarchy I could implement (teacher-directed learning and students sitting in rows), though I was not comfortable with it. I was concerned about students' behaviors in my classroom. I felt I was expected to be the authority in control and that I was responsible alone for their progress. I had no clue how to include them in the process of learning.

To my colleague's apt question, What do you teach when you say you teach English?, what I've been discovering as I write and read this teaching life is that I taught more "commonsensically," more traditionally (Mayher, 1991), than I'd ever imagined. The way I thought about the "subject" English was driven by my love of literature, but that love of literature was certainly not evident in my teaching pedagogy. I was teaching the way I had been taught both in and out of classrooms, and my beliefs (unexamined) were held even as early as the theory of teaching I enacted in my back yard classroom lining up my cat Smokey and my dolls.

My experiences with the profession and discipline of English informed the way I chose to teach high school English, and so did my experiences as a reader, as a learner, as a child who was female.

Another critical place for critical moments in English teachers' lives is their reading and writing lives. I had to examine my experiences here as well to better understand my teaching life. We need to ask ourselves many questions to begin this exploration. What were my reading experiences in school? In elementary school? In high school? What were my reading experiences in college? In my personal life as a reader? In what ways might those reading and learning experiences have influenced my teaching?

CHAPTER 4

Living in Books

But no one can read a poem for us.

—Louise Rosenblatt (1978, p. 86)

We all bring a reading life into our teaching. As English teachers we bring a personal, an academic, and a professional life into our classrooms. Who we are and how we see ourselves as readers informs how we read with our students, how we teach literature.

My father read to me, and he taught me to read before I went to school. I loved my dad and I wanted to please, so I learned how to read and read as perfectly as I could for him: I had a quick memory and remember memorizing the texts he read to me. I turned the pages and recited memorized stories.

But in the rest of my life living at home, I could not and did not want to make one mistake because I feared my father, who was smart and intolerant of mistakes. I learned to be as hard on myself as he was on us. The motto I constructed in my mind, which I learned from him and took with me into my life was "once taught, always learned." There were two ways of thinking about mistakes: (1) you were stupid and/or (2) you didn't listen.

I aspired to perfection and his approval in all my chores: washing the car, mowing the lawn, hoeing and weeding the cotton on our farm. I washed our family car and followed his precise instructions: first hose down the car, then wash the roof first, always hosing the vehicle to keep everything wet and prevent spotting. After a great deal of effort following these instructions and carefully drying the car with the chamois, I presented my work to my dad. To my chagrin, he spotted water spots on the chrome bumpers. I had failed to be perfect. Whatever work I did, I never heard the approval I longed for. There was always the looming imperfection to point to rather than the accomplishment of the work. Just doing the work was expected and was nothing to be commended for.

So I went to school a reader wanting approval and afraid of making mistakes. And I wanted to be perfect, get the answers right. The lesson and worksheet blitz of school did not faze my love of reading because I was successful at completing them correctly. They reinforced my desire to get things right.

After my kindergarten bad-girl episode, I tried to be a good girl and a good student by performing as perfectly as I could. I was rewarded with good grades and my family's approval for such performances.

As I search my memories, I don't find memories of reading any good books in school, yet I did very well on the standardized tests and worked to be tops in reading, dutifully completing the worksheets. I really enjoyed getting these lessons right and doing well. Had school been my only place to read, it could have hindered my reading. My reading life was not limited to school, but the experiences as a reader at school certainly influenced my sense of teaching and reading. You might begin your search for the reading self you take into your teaching by searching your memories for texts that were meaningful to you as you reflect on your own reading lives.

Powerful personal reading experiences (those that I remember having an emotional and personal response to) happened out of regular school for me. Throughout a childhood and adolescence of voracious reading I remember reading two books that touched my soul. A third comes to mind now, and that was an experience I had in summer recreation during storytime. Our teacher told us the story of Silas Marner. I cried. We forget the power of story and storytelling. To this day I love to read to my students, whether high school or college. There is something wonderful about hearing a story.

Whenever I have asked readers to recall and write about the book that most powerfully touched their lives, the book they recall is almost without exception one that was not read in school. Though I do acknowledge that school reading was an equally powerful reading experience, I must characterize that reading experience for the most part as a soulless one.

The first book that touched me deeply and still does to this day is Frances Hodgson Burnett's *The Secret Garden* (1987). I just loved that book. As I think about it now, I believe the reason I loved it was that I identified so much with the rude, neglected child Mary (her mother was beautiful and self-absorbed), and the children's discovery of joy and hope in the secret garden with animals.

When I was about five we moved to Arizona, from California and my mother's family, and I lived a pretty happy life as a child growing up and going to school in the Southwest. As a child, I felt the silent pain that children feel trying to sort out who they are and learning to deal with their feelings. My mother, like Mary's mother, was beautiful. My little sister was beautiful with her long, carrot-red curls. I was not beautiful, not even pretty. I had red hair, bony knees, a fiery temper, a deep raspy adult voice, and freckles. I rejected much that was feminine, choosing to be like a boy: athletic and strong.

In 1991, as I was writing a story in my journal during my life in New York, that secret garden surfaced from my unconscious. It seemed to come out of nowhere, but at the time I was listening to, responding to, and writing with my students at NYU in World Mythology—a writing-across-the-curriculum project called The Copse Project. This response and this way of working were yet another unexplored aspect of the notion of languaging I wrote about earlier.

February   1991

The Garden was a safe place for her just like for Colin. But one day a robin fluttered in. He had been wounded. The wounded robin broke her heart. She looked at its frightened eyes and its shaking body and cried inside. She cried so deeply inside that somewhere in there she lost her smiles. She couldn't smile anymore: somewhere lost inside was a smile, lurking, waiting to pounce on her and play with her. Some days she saw the sun dancing in the garden. She'd run over and dance, too, but the smile stayed lost inside with the memory of the wounded robin.

One day a wise old woman suddenly appeared in her garden magically through the high stone wall. This wise old woman took her onto her lap and spoke kindly to her (as wise old women do) saying, "You're a kind and gentle child. I see you playing in the sun, dancing, but you seem troubled."

As children do, she spilled out her sadness. "There is a robin who comes here and he's hurt. I'm so worried. He looks so scared. I'm scared, too."

"I know," the wise old woman comforted her saying, "it's okay to be scared. Let yourself be scared, for you are a child. It's brave to be scared and to love the robin."

The wise old woman put her gently down from her lap, turned and disappeared through the wall. The little girl still felt scared and the wounded robin in the garden still made her sad. But, the smile moved closer to her heart.

As I said earlier, my mother, like Mary's mother in *The Secret Garden*, was beautiful, and I remember that she worked long days, first as a waitress, then in my father's gas station as bookkeeper and cashier. In an era (in the 1950s) when the majority of women did not work away from the home, my mother worked full-time, leaving my younger sister, Pam, and me at the neighborhood child care home. One of my aunts came to take care of us for a while, and when I was old enough I baby-sat my younger sister. Our parents worked hard to achieve their American dream: They provided well for us. They made sure we were kept busy with activities—church, clarinet lessons, swimming lessons, ballet lessons, Job's Daughters—but I just didn't feel loved. In typical sibling rivalry I felt that my sister was the favored one. She commanded my mother's love and attention with her sickliness, sort of like young Colin. As a child I always felt responsible for my own pain. Once I made a makeshift teepee in the backyard using a flat hoe, a three-pronged hoe/rake, and a regular rake. In my wild Indian play mode I stepped on the three-pronged hoe/rake and ran it through my foot, slicing a gash between my big toe and the next toe and pushing the other tine almost completely into my foot. When I ran into the house crying and bleeding, the words that I heard from my mother and still hear as I write this were, "It's your fault. You should have known better than to use that hoe!" So I thought, "This wouldn't have happened if you had been good, Pat." I thought that I was bad for accidentally hurting myself.

School and reading, church, playing the clarinet, swimming, baseball, and other sports were my life. I was trying to be a good girl, a good kid, so I accepted school and the authority of the adults in my life and of school unquestioningly.

During those hot Arizona summers when I was in junior high school, I remember reading the encyclopedia in my spare time. I began with and worked on a volume at a time. I wanted to know about everything. I don't remember ever finishing, just the joy of reading and learning about everything.

The second book I remember as a soul-touching, powerful reading experience is *Madame Curie* (Curie, 1937), a book I read in my teens. I read this text while I was going to high school in the California Central Valley farmlands. After spending 10 years of my childhood in Arizona, my parents moved our family back to California when I was a sophomore. As I read Marie Curie's life story, I romanticized the idea that a woman could make a difference in the world, and the world of science at that. It fueled my adolescent romantic dreams of going to college to study math when I graduated in 1964. At the same time, I was reading women's lives in the movies and on television. Lucy, Gidget, Tammy, Annette. My virtual role models were conniving and manipulating women like Lucy Ricardo, who got herself into trouble and couldn't be honest lest she find more trouble, which she always did. Women just couldn't win in Lucy and Ethel's case so they learned to manipulate and lie to meet their needs. Gidget and Tammy and Annette. All virgins, good girls. Virtue would win the knight in shining armor after he'd been seduced by the "wild" girl. These were the social and cultural models I experienced.

I would characterize my life on the farm during my high school years as a silent, intellectual one. I lived my own romanticized fantasy by riding my horse, the wind blowing in my hair, feeling free. In *Meeting at the Crossroads* (1992) Lyn Mikel Brown and Carol Gilligan studied adolescent girls in school, ages 11 through 15, and found that when girls aren't encouraged by their social and cultural environment to speak their truths about themselves and their feelings, they become silent and often go underground. After years of critical reflection on this, my sense now is that these dissonances are not limited to the issue of gender, they are issues of heart and soul. As Nel Noddings indicates, at issue is our way of being in the world, our reading and writing our lives in relationship to a world where women and men fall prey to sexist expectations derived from traditional roles ingrained and encultured in us.

Aside from school, family, and living in books, I had no contact with people with whom I could discuss ideas, my love of books, and math (I was initially going to be a math major). My mother's family of six brothers and three sisters and their spouses and children had little respect for education and generally disdained people who used more than one or two syllables or nonracist, nonabusive language. The more I protested and argued, the more abusive the men in particular became. I remember that they told me to get down off my high horse and speak English. I struggled to be myself while living in this isolated and silencing community with a different set of values serving as their lens to view the world than I was aspiring toward. Reading gave me an escape to another world. I lived a vicarious life through books. Recent studies done by Orenstein in *School Girls* (1994) and Lyn Mikel Brown and Carol Gilligan in *Meeting at the Crossroads* (1992) address these critical shifts into the silent underground that adolescent girls make. Going underground may not necessarily mean that we are rebelling, but that we are protecting our relationship with ourselves. To break with images of perfection publicly is not safe for women, so we split. In retrospect I learned a great deal about my fears as a woman who is a teacher from Brown and Gilligan's study which resonates with my experiences, helping me to name them:

> One of the most difficult questions for the women teachers was whether it was legitimate for them to show girls their sadness and their anger and also whether they could reveal such feelings without losing control of themselves and of the girls. It seemed easier for the women to try and model perfection for girls— perfect women, perfect relationships—and yet women's images of perfection were at odds with what girls know about women and experience in relationships. . . . For women to bring themselves into their teaching and be in genuine relationship with girls, however, is far more disruptive and radical than for men. It means changing their practice as teachers and their changing education. (1992, pp. 230–231)

I'd say, too, that it means we need a revolution from within, a critical, compassionate look at our beliefs and assumptions about ourselves and life.

During my doctoral work at NYU I began to explore the feelings I bottled up inside me in childhood and adolescence, feelings about being a smart girl in a male-dominated world. Those feelings surfaced when we read Deborah

Tannen's *You Just Don't Understand* (1990) in a doctoral seminar. I responded quite emotionally to Tannen's notion that the major problem between men and women is that men and women speak different languages and all we have to do is understand and recognize the differences: If women know men's language and men learn women's language and we accept that they are different, then relationships can work. I argued with Tannen. Her view was a limited view in light of my own personal, social, and cultural experiences. Her theory was limited to middle-class, educated men and women who, if they were willing to read such a book, at least were interested in the differences and might be seeking understanding to begin with. It wouldn't work with the likes of my grandfather or my uncles. I couldn't imagine my uncles, male cousins, or grandfather reading Tannen's book. If someone told them her ideas, they would simply laugh: relationships are easy—man is the boss, woman is the servant. They would probably smile through their rotting teeth, pull out the cigarette, and again smile while they asked, "Why is the bitch bothering with this understanding each other's language bullshit?"

Reading Tannen took me back to the jungles of my memory: back to the teasing, to the beating with a belt that one of my uncles administered to me when I was about 5 because I was so stubborn and he wanted me to cry. I wouldn't. I thought about the verbal and emotional abuse I experienced living around my mother's six brothers, men who teased me and my female cousins about our femininity (commenting openly about our tits), our naive sexuality, and in my case, my "highfalutin" intelligence. No one deserves such verbal and psychological abuse, but I had no recourse. My words simply were no defense against theirs. Writing this book is my best defense against such abuses, for perhaps other people will become more conscious of the experiences we bring into our teaching lives, which touch so many children's lives.

Only in the past few years have I understood how my parents, too, experienced abuse from these men. My father had always struggled with the verbal and emotional abuse heaped on people by my mother's brothers. He had been physically abused by his own alcoholic father.

A couple of years ago I was visiting my parents as they prepared to move to Washington. My uncle was angry, angry that my parents were leaving, so he began to abuse them with his anger. My father refused to speak up for himself and my mother when my uncle became abusive. My father seemed to know what I knew about self-defense with words against the detonated bombs my uncle set off. He had taught me this form of self-defense. My father feared his own anger, should he reply to my uncle. So he raged about my uncle's actions to mom and me. My mother became equally upset, but she remained silent to my uncle and tried to appease him, to make him happy by giving him what he was demanding. When I witnessed this scene, I realized I had learned about authority, mine and others, from my home environment. I was so angry at my uncle I was ready to march over to his home just yards away and shout into his face, "My parents are good people who have done their best. Leave them the fuck alone." This was the same uncle who had beaten me mercilessly with a razor strap when I wouldn't cry.

Though my parents did not know what I had in mind to say to my uncle, my parents dissuaded me from confronting him. They thought they would leave the next day and his abuse would be over. They just wanted to get the hell out of there and not have my uncle say anything bad about them to the rest of the family. I knew that saying nothing only allowed it to continue, but I accepted my parents' fear. I also knew he would say exactly what they had feared he would anyway.

Before I left, my mother and I sat in their empty home and I asked her if she remembered the beating that my uncle had given to me. She did. I was quiet. She said that she was sorry she hadn't stopped him. He had gone too far. Those were healing words for me. She was there, she had seen the beating, and yes, she should have protected her daughter. She didn't tell me that it was my fault. It wasn't! No child, no human being should be hit just for the sake of hitting and causing pain. I know that I took this belief into my teaching. Do not hurt other human beings, for you know what it is like to be hurt, to be punished for just being.

READING A WOMAN'S LIFE

Reading *Madame Curie* (Curie, 1937) when I was an adolescent living in a male-dominated and sometimes abusive environment offered me a reprieve from the real world and a wonderful journey into a romantic world of love and hardship, and the story of a woman's pursuit of knowledge. I kept my book review of *Madame Curie*, which I wrote in a high school English class sometime between 1962 and 1964, either for Mrs. Linsom or Miss Hompson. The book report I wrote tells me a great deal about what I valued as a young woman. I have included the text in its entirety below. The report constructs a picture of me both as an adolescent reader and a writer.

Madame Curie by Eve Curie

Marya Sklodovska was a marvelous person. At the age of four she was a child prodigy. She was a studious person, living and yearning for perfection. When in her teens, because of necessity, she became a governess to help support her sister.

Manya (an affectionate nickname) was born in an intellectual family during the time Poland was occupied by Russia. Her father was a professor, while her mother was a musician, professor and accomplished wife. Manya was the youngest of five children: Zosia, Bronya,

Hela, Jozio, and Manya. All of the children excelled in knowledge. The family was a closely knit one.

In her childhood Manya developed a love for the country. She had relatives all over and her family visited them. One time for a period of about a year Manya lived in the country. At that time this shy young girl forgot—or rather laid aside her intellectual search.

Manya, many times in her early life, lived on practically nothing. When she attended college at Paris she starved herself, froze herself, and many times drove herself to sickness. Even her love life was nothing until she met Pierre Curie. Although [*sic*] once she fell in love with the son of one of her mistresses. That was shattered by his parents. Marie never thought much of love after that.

All these contributed much to Manya's person, and yet none did. When Marie finally found love and her life's work, she gained a searching mind. She grew to love science.

When Marie married Pierre this book turned into a biography of two people combined to make one. Marie Curie and Pierre were companions. One couldn't live without the other. They didn't have material things, for they weren't rich in that way. They had a common love—science. They were two of a kind.

Marie Curie with Pierre discovered radium, polonium, and many other radioactive elements, but when Pierre was killed in a tragic accident, Marie was distressed, weakened, and torn apart. In fact she would have welcomed death. She courageously overcame it and worked on her experiments.

To show what these two people had when they got the Nobel Prize for the radium, they loaned their money to anyone needing it.

There is a lot more to Marie Curie's life in her old age. She did many outstanding things: she made a trip to America, got a gram of radium from the American people, she had her leisure hours, and she had her students who loved her. Marie Curie was a most outstanding person to the day she died. I believe this is one of the best books I have ever read. The description of Madame Curie is one given by a loving daughter who knew what a great human being her mother really was. Madame Curie is not a story of one person discovering a substance vitally important in the world today, but of the person of a Polish girl—shy and brilliant—who came into fame through the family, husband, and world.

What is revealing about what Pat Schmidt, English teacher to be, read and wrote about in this book review, is what I choose to say about the book and the language I used to say what I thought and felt in response to the reading. I focused on the human aspect of Marie Curie and mentioned her brilliance, her shyness, her love of science and her husband Pierre, and her humanitarian side. Most of the text is in the form of report, but in the last paragraph I included my response to the text, saying that it was "one of the best books I have ever read." My English teacher, either Mrs. Linson or Miss Hompson, could not have known that I really meant it. The instructor's comments were simple and affirming: "Review A, Theme A, Excellent." No other remarks! There were only a few corrections in spelling and sentence structure. All of this may seem good.

What a missed opportunity for my English teacher! She read my report as an assignment well done, making standard, affirming yet empty comments that respond to what I have come to call the "good writer, perfect text" syndrome. That is, the focus of the response is on the mechanics of the writing and a value judgment on the structure and organization of my written text. She missed an opportunity to connect and share with me as a reader on a human level, to even communicate what she understood about what I was writing about. The language I'd experienced from my English teachers was the language I used to work with my own students. My comments were usually short, structural and functional, and generally useless except that I had passed judgment and been given a grade with an ideal, perfect text as the paradigm.

I've given a great deal of thought these past nine years to what constitutes meaningful, useful response to student texts. I've learned to consult students. I strive to respond as a co-reader and co-learner, mirroring what I read, exploring and clarifying what a writer is saying with the text he or she is writing. I try to work with students, learning from and with them. I try more to notice what readers are doing and to acknowledge that in order to to help them and me become more aware of what we do as readers. I make suggestions and I try to listen deeply. It is mutual, reciprocal. This is languaging. I don't language perfectly, thank goodness, but I do aspire to improve and I am conscious of what I am doing more often than I used to be.

I was surprised when I actually found the book review of *Madame Curie* (how many people keep a book report they wrote in high school?) I had written over 30 years ago. Even though I was reporting, I believe I was making choices to share what I found important in the life of Marie Curie, and I was revealing my own values and concerns about life, about being a woman, in doing so. For the most part, the text of my book report was written very objectively; that is, I summarize the plot of Curie's life. While I wrote a retelling the story of Curie's life, my personal pleasure and excitement about the book seeped into the book review format.

From looking at the structure of the report, I can say that I wrote about *Madame Curie* in typical book report fashion. I had been asked to name the main characters and to summarize both the plot and the theme. The book had touched me so personally that my personal response was not silenced in the report. I see that my own personal theory of living in mutual relationship in the world, the seed of my languaging theory is there: "Madame Curie is not a story of one person discovering a substance vitally important in the world today, but of the person of a Polish girl—shy and brilliant—who came into fame through the family, husband, and world." Until I looked more closely at what I had written about *Madame Curie*, I hadn't realized that even at age 17 I was working out a theory of relationship and authority and had unconsciously stated my own ideal of a successful woman.

I am happy to discover that I had written a report of profound admiration for a female scientist who suffered much, found and loved her husband, her soulmate, and valued family. I was a young woman contemplating a career in mathematics and I identified with Marie Curie's life: the struggles, the losses, the roadblocks, and the loving relationships.

In the early 1960s my parents were struggling to make a living farming, so I went to the local junior college. I planned to major in math because I had done much better gradewise in math in high school than I had in English. However, that changed quickly. I earned a D in my first semester of calculus (though my male adviser told me I had one of the highest math entrance placement scores of any student, male or female). I had a B in that calculus class at midterm (based on completing pages of problems and the midterm exam), but when I took the final I earned a D. I have no idea what happened to me between midterm and finals. I do remember that while driving to my finals I was hit by an uninsured driver who literally backed through a stop sign and into my parents' car. Though I was not injured, I was shaken up by the collision and the prospect of facing my parents. My fear of their wrath was a reality. I was guilty of being unable to control the other driver.

The final grade, which was based solely on the final, really threw me. I couldn't understand why the whole semester's work rested on the final exam. I knew a young man in my class who had failed the midterm, did not complete a good deal of the homework, and somehow had earned a C on the final. He received a C in the class. I silently resented what seemed to me at the time to be discrimination based on gender. (I hadn't heard of Gloria Steinem or feminism.)

I rationalized to myself (after talking to the guy who received the C) that he needed the grade, for he was going to become an engineer and needed at least a C to continue in the engineering classes. I was a young woman and had little future (my aunts and uncles teased me about being an old maid because I was not engaged or married at age 18). I was considering teaching and not engineering. I had no idea what a woman could do with mathematics except teach. It never occurred to me to challenge the grade or to question the instructor about what seemed to me to be a male bias. I was one of only two females in the course, and my calculus instructor was also my counselor. He encouraged me to stay in the major because "we needed a pretty face in the class" (my instructor/counselor's exact words). Amazing how some things remain etched in memory so clearly! Without much feeling, I decided to not major in math. I loved reading and had just met Shakespeare big-time (a whole semester of his works), so I turned to literature courses. I'd never received a D in any class, so this experience really stunned me.

I'd stayed out of trouble since my kindergarten skirmish, but during my senior year of high school, the dean of women called me into her office. I went there full of fear that I was in trouble (the only reason people were called into the dean's office), though by my teens I had learned to control my anger in outward ways and I would never have considered doing anything remotely close to breaking any rules at school or anywhere for that matter. What I learned was that I had received a $100 scholarship based on my English teacher's (Miss Hompson's) recommendation. She had described me as a "thinker." I would never have known what she thought of me as a student had the dean not told me. To this day that one word means more to me than any letter grade I have received. It was a form of recognition of who I was as a learner. What a loss that she never shared that with me personally.

THE ENGLISH MAJOR READER

A novel or poem or play remains merely inkspots on paper until a reader transforms them into a set of meaningful symbols.
—Rosenblatt, 1983, p. 24

As I think back on my junior college academic, literary reading experiences, I would characterize them as frustrating. Well-meaning professors usurped our authority to read and to learn how to take intellectual pleasure reading when they gave critical readings and lectures, filling us (the filling-the-empty-vessel approach) with information about literature, with their authoritative readings and the authority of other critics, without honoring us as readers, readers who bring lives and responses to texts. Being a good student, I did not question my experience.

I thought that the problems I might be having with meaning were with me, since I was failing to read and write well. I just needed to read and write more and work on form and correctness. Meaning was located in the text. I couldn't see that the source of my frustration was the giver of knowledge, the appointed authority. I loved to read, but I didn't care for most of the selections in my American Literature class. The selections and the class were dry, formal, and with the exception of author Anne Bradstreet, totally male.

I did enjoy my first Shakespeare class, though I was frustrated that we read so many plays—one a week. Until I reached graduate status and we read in small seminars, focusing on one or two authors, I found myself always frustrated with the academic fly-by-night survey course approach to reading literature. We usually read a novel or a play each week. This allowed time for no more than a superficial reading experience. I wanted to read more fully and have some time to discuss the text and remember it.

The general pattern I experienced in all my English classes was that we read the assigned text and then we went to class, where the instructor lectured to us, telling us what he (I had only one female professor during my whole English studies as an undergraduate) knew and deemed important. I copied pages and pages of his ideas about the text. Certainly these lectures offered new ways of thinking about the text; however, there was no transaction fostered between the readers' reading and the professor's reading and research.

My undergraduate years as an English major brought to bear a critical influence on me as a preservice English teacher. I want to tell you the story of my reading and writing experiences in two courses. These two courses are standard for English majors, a survey of American literature and a required course in literary theory. These courses seem representative of most undergraduate English courses (sadly, not just in 1964 and 1968, but also in the 1990s).

The first course I want to write about is the survey course in American literature, English 30, and the reader and writer I was being trained to be. We read major American writers from *The American Tradition in Literature, Vol. 1* (1962) by Norton. The second course, English 193 T, "Problems in Modern Criticism," provides a critical glimpse at who I was as a reader, because it gives a sense of how, after four years of English courses in the academic discipline of English, I was reading and writing about literary theory, and also gives a sense of the level of understanding I had of the role of literary theory in the life of the reader and what I took from these experiences into my own classroom teaching.

UNDERGRADUATE READER

The content of English 30 began with readings from William Bradford and continued chronologically, concluding with texts by Abraham Lincoln. We were required to write weekly essays in response to the reading assignments. The class met twice a week for lectures and teacher-led discussion questions. When I returned to research this part of my college reading life to research,

I found papers I'd written in response to the reading and writing assignments for English 30: "Queequeg," "Ideas Pointing to Ben Franklin's Individuality," "St. Jean de Crevecoeur's Interpretation of an 'American,'" "Freneau-Bryant," "Hawthorne," "Starbuck's Role," and "Billy Budd." I numbered the paragraphs of the Queequeg paper for referencing in the reading of the paper, which follows:

Queequeg

Note: These are my ramblings on Queequeg and what the character evokes from me.

1. Melville uses the character of Queequeg as a symbol of the bridge between Puritan prejudice and Christian, in the essence of the word, brotherhood. He introduces Queequeg in a humorous manner but if read into one can see the irony in Ishmael's reflections of the words "cannibal" and "pagan." When Ishmael asks "that aint the harpooneer, is it?" and the landlord answers "Oh, no, the harpooneer is a dark complexioned chap. He never eats dumplings, he don't—he eats nothing but steaks, and likes em rare," little did Ishmael or the reader know this was a hint that the man was a so-called "paganistic cannibal" and that rare meant raw.

2. Melville then leads the reader and Ishmael on, being careful not to bring Queequeg on the scene directly, but building up to a climactic entrance. To make the characterization more mysteriously revealing, Melville uses this dialogue, "But tonight he went out peddling, you see and I don't see what on airth keeps him so late, unless, maybe, he can't sell his head." This statement adds to the dismay and wariness of Ishmael, but still the landlord persists in not revealing the actual character of Queequeg and not until the later in the novel is the real character revealed.

3. What strikes me as being ironic is that Queequeg the "pagan" has all the qualities that his contemporaries were trying to find. He doesn't possess the prejudices of an educated man, but the qualities of an informed man. The reader and Ishmael find this out as the friendship of Queequeg grows on both.

4. Melville keeps the reader in suspense of the coming meeting between Ishmael and Queequeg by building up slowly to the surprising entrance which comes like a slap in the face when Queequeg finally appears.

5. Melville uses Ishmael as his voice to present his own feelings about his world—the Puritan world. Queequeg seems to represent man in his changing state—a non conformist [*sic*] in a non-mobile or fixed

society. This society was a materialistic one, while Queequeg didn't place his values on his materialistic needs to be happy, but on what was natural and free.

    6. To end the introduction of Queequeg, Melville leaves us with these lines—"Better sleep with a sober cannibal than a drunken Christian."

My instructor, Professor B., wrote to me, "A good beginning, I am sure you can do even better in the future." This, the first paper, was not graded, a good idea (now I teach entire courses without letter grades, using critical reflective self assessment, and find it a powerful step forward toward freeing us to be readers and writers).

    This paper is probably a first draft, for I had marked a paragraph sign on the second paragraph to indicate a new paragraph rather than recopy and revise the text (usually I tried to rewrite and turn in technically "perfect" texts). I made a note to the instructor at the top of the paper indicating that I was sharing my ramblings and that this paper was "evoked from me" by the character (this phrasing surprises and amuses me, for Louise Rosenblatt uses evocation prominently in her transactional literary theory). Other phrasings I find in the language in my text point to the reading and understanding that I found from trying to state the author's intentions: "Melville uses Q . . .," "Melville then leads the reader and Ishmael . . .," "Melville uses this dialogue . . .," "Melville keeps the reader in suspense . . .," "Melville uses Ishmael as his voice . . .," and finally, "To end the introduction of Queequeg, Melville leaves us with these lines . . . ." All but one paragraph begins with language that states the author's intentions or my sense of the author as directing the text, directing the character Ishmael, and directing the reader. The one exception is paragraph six, which begins, "What strikes me as being ironic is that Queequeg . . . ."

    In that paragraph I share my response to Queequeg. I, the reader, saw myself in the same position as the character Ishmael, finding out about what constitutes a pagan. Much of my paper deals with characterization and the way in which I saw Melville crafting the character.

    Curiously, I used the passive phrase "but if read into . . . ." Readers "read into" text to discover, to see, the irony buried by the author. My reading stance reflected what I now refer to as an archaeological dig approach predominate in New Criticism and its offshoot, Structuralism; that is, the author buries his intentions in the text and my job as a reader is to dig out meaning, meaning that is buried or hidden, but nonetheless there.

    All the papers I wrote for this course seemed to follow this characteristic stance and voice. For the most part I received marks of B or B−, save one test on which I received a C−. Mr. B.'s remarks, usually one or two lines, were prescriptive evaluations, words that I found virtually useless in terms of improving my reading of texts, my writing about them, or my thinking about literary scholarship:

> I want more of your ideas, your interpretations, your insights please be more specific!

> This answer is too general. You must be more specific, and you must use care to hit the essential points.

> Again, you must come to the point, your answers are too superficial.

I certainly wasn't aiming to write papers that were too general, lacked insight, or did not hit the essential points, nor was I aiming for superficiality.

These comments were negative descriptions citing the deficiencies in my writing, my reading, and my thinking. These remarks and this way of teaching were not helpful to me as a learner, but then this course wasn't about learning, it was about American literature. The papers were one-shot deals: We wrote them, he graded them, and we went on to the next author, the next assignment. There was no chance to rewrite or to work with the instructor to discuss the writing, the texts, or the way I was reading. No chance to move into the text deficiency of generality, let's say, and work on specificity. Communication was one-way. Guess what? This way of working, responding to student texts as deficient and focusing on what needs to be corrected, is precisely the way I responded to my own high school English students' writing.

Around halfway through this American Lit course, I wrote in one of my short papers, "Irving and Cooper are the first writers which have been enjoyable." Mr. B. took exception to my statement and corrected the relative pronoun from *which* to *who*, commenting, "This is not a fair statement." He didn't elaborate on why my personal response, which I had thought he had earlier encouraged me to share in my papers, was "not fair." The problem was one-way communication and structures that reified top-down, external authority. I took his comments to heart, but we never shared what either of us meant in order for understanding to take place. I thought that he was right. If he said that I was being unfair and he knew more than I knew, then he was right and I was being unfair.

At the time I read his comment about fairness to mean that as a reader I shouldn't and didn't have the right to make such evaluative statements, finding pleasure in one text and honestly stating that I did not enjoy others. It could have been that he was trying to encourage me to enjoy the other texts.

I received an A for one paper I wrote in that American Literature survey course. It was my Hawthorne paper. When I look at it, as you shall in the following paragraphs, I see it as a text written in a literary, academic tone and, as in my earlier Queequeg paper, I'm still writing about the author's intentions.

Nathaniel Hawthorne

1. Hawthorne seemed to be searching for "truth." In *Young Goodman Brown* [*sic*] Faith represents a hope or "truth" which is eventually lost by Young Goodman Brown through the evil he saw in mankind; an inconsistency in mores. The pink ribbons are the only gay part of the whole story and represented man's "faith" and in the end, with the fall of these ribbons—it is a loss of faith.

2. To Hawthorne the hardening of the heart was the greatest of all sins. In *Young Goodman Brown* the loss of Faith was a hardening of the heart. Mr. Hopper in *The Minister's Black Veil* [*sic*] shut himself off from the world by a simple black veil. In doing so "Thus, from beneath the black veil, there rolled a cloud into the sunshine . . . which enveloped the poor minister so that love or sympathy could never reach him." Wakefield too had a hardening (coldness) of the heart in his eccentric plan. In the action Wakefield cuts himself off from the world without the use of a black veil, but achieves the same end as Mr. Hopper. In Mr. Hawthorne's words he was "the outcast of the Universe."

3. In the two stories, *The Birthmark* [*sic*] and *Rappaccini's Daughter* [*sic*], Hawthorne shows man trying to do the impossible—perfecting nature. The triumph of intellect over the heart. There must be some symbolism in Hawthorne's use of women as merely innocent bystanders drawn into these evil plots by man's depravity. Giovanni's sin was that it was true love that he experienced with Beatrice—if so how could he hurt her so much?

4. In *Young Goodman Brown* the dark loomings of the forest represent the mind of man—the wandering through the forest, the indecisiveness of Young Goodman Brown, and the final extinction of man's individuality and resignation to his fate.

5. Each of his characters is cut away from the world through their own misgivings; Young Goodman Brown through his loss of faith, Mr. Hooper with his black veil, Georgianna with the birthmark, Beatrice with the deadly perfume, Wakefield's undecided length of self-banishment, and finally, Ethan Brand searching for the "Unpardonable Sin."

6. Just as a last point there seems to be a similarity in *The Birthmark* and Edgar Allan Poe's *The Tell-Tale Heart*. How both of these men became so obsessed with the idea to remove from this earth something

they really had no right to do—again tempering with God's or Nature's creation.

    7. Original depravity and criticism of Puritan concepts is a reoccurring theme of Nathaniel Hawthorne's.

What made this paper an A−, more valued than the others? There were no comments about what I was thinking about Young Goodman Brown in my paper, only general marginalia:

A good quotation.

This is not clear. (Para. 3, in reference to the section on Giovanni)

She is not cut off is she? Her husband interprets the mark, she doesn't.

A good point! (Para. 6, in reference to the Poe connection)

I had no idea about what to do to improve my writing from reading these comments. As a writer I learned that I had been specific rather than general, that I made clear points (save the one). Had I been a more involved reader? When I revisit this text I remember that I loved reading Hawthorne, a love that continued for many years. My paper included many points about Hawthorne that Mr. B. had lectured to us. I also loved both Poe and Hawthorne. In my first 10 years or so of teaching English I always assigned my classes to read these two authors with great pleasure. I was intrigued by the power of Hawthorne's moral sense and literary aesthetic. I enjoyed Poe's macabre and was fascinated with his "Philosophy of Composition."

    When I was first teaching American literature in my high school English class, I typed and dittoed Poe's theory of composition as stated in the philosophy and assigned my classes to study it. Then I'd test their ability to understand and apply Poe's philosophy against his own writing. Was he practicing his own philosophy? At the time I enjoyed the assignment, but now I think, God, how could I have assigned this to those kids? This assignment was an esoteric and futile academic exercise for 16-year-olds. But, it was what I knew how to do, what I was interested in, and it was valued by English academia. It's ironic that I didn't think to check my own philosophy of teaching English with what I was actually doing in my English classrooms when I taught. I missed my own lesson. I did not put myself into the shoes of a 16-year-old reading this stuff for the first time. Not having experienced a sense of myself as a reader other than academic, I carried this way of reading and writing into my classroom.

    For this American Literature survey course I also wrote a major paper on the novella *Billy Budd*, reprinted in *The Tradition in American Literature*, *Vol. 1* (1965, pp. 895–962). I have the original draft of this paper (long before the age of word processing). As a writer I spent a great deal of my paper writing about Melville's characterization of good men and his use of symbols, irony, and personification. What I also did in this paper was include my own response to the character and the ideas, something quite different from the short papers I'd written. As I wrote about this I realized that, as in my life, the issues that I write about are "being good." I made such comments as, "As a character Billy Budd is unbelievable. I just can't picture any person with his physical make-up and his moral make-up. He just couldn't exist. Maybe this is why Melville gave Billy these characteristics—to make us more aware of good. To make us think a little about doing good deeds, having a good attitude, being likable."

Billy Budd drew me in as a reader. It presented a moral dilemma that interested me, the nature of evil and good. I read the text carefully, giving the text and Melville full authority: It would be a completion of itself, for I had been taught that authors wrote texts that were always structurally "perfect." I thought that Melville was in control.

I closed this paper by making a personal connection with a film I had just seen, an association with my own experiences with the world, and by raising moral questions regarding taking a life in the name of good, of justice:

> This book reminds me of a movie I saw last weekend—"The Hill." In "The Hill" the conflict was in trying to prove an officer guilty of murdering a soldier. The final scene consisted of a final breakthrough and the men are almost to the point of winning—in fact they have won, but they reverted to the same means they were judging the officer on. They killed the officer and in the background one of them was shouting, "We won, We won" while in reality they lost. Ask Captain Vere if the ends justify the means or vice-versa? Wonder what he would say? He wouldn't have to justify the ends or the means because he was within the law. What about conscience?

The paper I wrote on *Billy Budd* paper shows me as a reader who viewed the author of his or her text as the authority for meaning. What Hawthorne wrote reflected his moral, thematic plan, and he was in control. As an "academic" reader I learned to search for this plan. In the case of *Billy Budd* I also became involved personally as a reader, raising moral questions for myself, for us all as readers. I raised these questions as if these characters were real people. I recognize my own voice in much of this paper.

I have no memory of what mark I received for the *Billy Budd* paper. As I studied what I wrote, I found myself surprised that I had so much to say about the novella and that I was, in academese, "clear and specific." I think that happened because I was engrossed with the book, I lived in it, and I wanted to communicate what I thought. I wasn't writing for a grade but because I was deeply interested in thinking about what constitutes good behavior. It didn't matter to me that the book was about men and focused on men. My real life living on the farm mirrored the male culture. All the literature I was reading throughout my undergraduate academic reading life was written by dead white males (sometimes living males), but at least these male authors raised moral questions. At the time, the moral questions *Billy Budd* raised for me as a reader came alive. Since most of my experience in the world as a young female had been in male dominated hierarchies, I was eager to read what academia required because I wanted to succeed, to be "good."

I authored the *Billy Budd* paper on December 9, 1965. I earned a B in that course, a grade that told me you're an above average something. I say "something" because I'm not sure what the grade meant, other than that my ability to write an academic literary analysis was above average. If I wanted to become an English teacher, then I felt that I had to meet the academic standards of the discipline. Those requirements and standards were high, subjective, and not negotiable. With a B I felt deficient—I should be getting As.

THE GOOD GIRL: ENGLISH MAJOR AND LITERARY THEORIES

When I entered Fresno State College (FSC) in the fall of 1966 and through 1969, I took upper division English courses in "Romantic Poets," "Shakespeare," "Twentieth Century Literature," "Problems in Modern Criticism," "Survey Literature Early Period (American)," "Senior Reading," "World Literature Ancient to Medieval," "World Literature Renaissance Through Modern," "Wordsworth to Shaw," and "American Literature to Whitman."

The curriculum for English majors and minors was organized by culture and that culture's historical periods, by genre, by author (e.g., 19th-century Russian novel), or by literary movements such as the Romantic poets. The literature we read was still almost exclusively male-authored, with a female writer—such as Christina Rossetti or George Eliot—here and there.

I was taught to read, to learn, and eventually to teach by that academic curriculum, one that had nothing to do with its readers' meaning-making processes and everything to do with the subject and content of literature: historical contexts, author's intentions, biographical interpretations, and close New Critical analysis.

The English department at FSC, though traditional, was innovative. During my undergraduate years the "fourth hour" of class was a major department curricular reform. The "fourth hour" meant that English classes were four-credit courses and that we attended three hours of class, with the fourth being met by attending any of the fourth-hour sessions, varied and open to all. Department professors lectured or read poetry; visiting poets read; we watched films. It was an exciting part of the curriculum. Experiencing the literary life meant literary performance. While this was enjoyable and brought literature to life, readers were still left hearing other's ideas, watching other's interpretations of or being told about literature.

When I began to teach high school English, the curriculum I found in literature anthologies was designed for teachers to teach using the same New Critical paradigm—organized either in cultural historical periods (i.e., American Literature), or by genre such as the short story, drama, or the novel. It was all familiar to me. Reading selections I used in the American lit anthology were followed by discussion questions such as those we find in much later American literature anthologies still in use in most English classrooms. This is what we find for Washington Irving's "The Devil and Daniel Webster" : "1. (a) What is the meaning of the Woodman's scoring of trees? (b) What do the trees symbolize?" (Miller, de Dwyer, Hayden, Hogan, & Wood, *United States in Literature*, 1979, p. 163). There was a meaning in this text, a right interpretation, and we were to find it. The answer keys in the back of the teacher's edition assured us of the answers.

The courses of study the English Department gave to me to teach in my high school English classes were watered-down reflections of my college literature courses. Good, trusting, accepting woman that I was, I continued the tradition of submitting to outside authority that I had experienced throughout my life both inside and outside classrooms.

DEATH AND UNEXPECTED LESSONS

He comes to the book from life. He turns for a moment from his direct concern with the various problems and satisfactions of his own life. He will resume his concern with them when the book is closed.

—Rosenblatt, 1983, p. 35

During the fall of that first year at Fresno State College, 1966, my grandmother died unexpectedly just before Thanksgiving. I spent that Thanksgiving going to her funeral and mourning, and though it was midterm time, I did not tell any of my professors what had happened. I felt that a death in my family made no difference regarding my responsibility to complete midterms and mid-term papers. It did make a difference, however, for my term paper for Mr. S.'s course in Contemporary Literature was a disaster.

I couldn't concentrate, and I ended up turning in a paper because there was a deadline. I received a D on the paper (the paper was a mess), and I vowed to myself that the next one would be different. I would just go about researching and writing more methodically so personal matters couldn't interfere with my work. For the next paper, I read and wrote a comparative paper on Truman Capote's *In Cold Blood* (1965) and Ralph Ellison's *Invisible Man* (1952). I was pleased with my reading of these texts and the paper. Mr. S. gave the paper a B (still above average) and commented on my work, "This is a dramatic improvement over the first term paper, account for the change." I thought that he was questioning whether I really authored this paper after the disastrous midterm paper. I was indignant. If he'd known me at all, he wouldn't have asked such a question, implying that I was dishonest. The truth of the matter is that he did not know me at all as a reader, as a person. He knew me as a student who sat in his lecture class.

It was hard for me, but I decided to go to talk with Mr. S. to clear my impugned integrity. Gathering up all my courage, a pile of papers on which I had noted my research (and my drafts), and a measure of youthful indignation, I made an appointment and took all my work in. He saw the piles of notes and drafts and seemed impressed. He asked me, "Why is there such a difference in the writing?" I told him about my grandmother's death and that I thought that would not be a legitimate reason to ask for more time to write the paper, so I'd done the best I could. He told me not to be so hard on myself. "Professors are people, too," I remember him saying. At the time I felt happy and relieved because I had proven that I was a good, trustworthy student. It had never occurred to me to question the system or to negotiate with the system. I feel sure that my accepting response is related to how I saw authority, whether that authority was exercised or not. I clearly saw myself as having none, and in my experiences with the education system I had not developed much of a sense of my own authority. Everyone had the face of one of my parents or teachers, who exercised ultimate authority while I lived with them. I would ask us all to consider the issue of developing authority in teacher education.

The means instructors and professors used for evaluating knowledge in literature courses rarely varied: a midterm, a final, short pop quizzes, and two research papers, one at midterm and one at the end of the semester. I don't remember reading books I selected for my own pleasure reading (I had no time), as I had done in elementary and junior high school. I only remember reading assigned texts, and I think that most of the time the papers and tests rarely revealed my understanding and knowledge of a text in anything more than a superficial way. I would spend a great deal of time thinking, trying to write something original, ending up with little time to write responses.

There is one exception. I read Jacqueline Susann's *Valley of the Dolls* (1966) during the summer of 1968. That was the summer my best childhood girlfriend, Chris Simpson, got married. I returned to my childhood town in Arizona with my parents, and I took along some trash reading. *Valley of the Dolls* was that trash. I stayed up all night to finish it. I immersed myself in the book, the characters, their lives. When I returned to Fresno State in the fall of 1968, that book became important in my thinking about reading and teaching literature. I wrote a paper on pornography and salacious reading material in secondary classrooms in which I raised several questions about the "merits" of *Valley of the Dolls* and what constitutes "great literature."

In all of my undergraduate studies, I can remember only one female professor in either my education or English classes. Her manner was tough, and she scared us all with her keen, demanding, intelligence. She appeared more male (brusque, rigid, authoritative) than the male professors I had, yet I was glad to see her at the podium. She was intelligent and professional, another good "woman" English teacher. I admired her.

While I soaked up reading literary texts like a sponge, many texts were incomprehensible. They were not incomprehensible because of the language, but because I simply had not lived life enough to be able to read it. One text assigned for Contemporary Literature particularly escaped me. I was too young and inexperienced, and I had little knowledge of human sexuality to read Durrell's *Justine* (1957). I remember shyly asking one of my male friends, rather naively, what's a Spanish fly? He relished filling me in on the answer.

MONKEY SEE, MONKEY DO

But all the student's knowledge about literary history, about authors and periods and literary types, will be so much useless baggage if he has not been led primarily to seek in literature a vital personal experience.

—Rosenblatt, 1983, p. 59

When I became a high school English teacher in 1969, I continued teaching literature in the ways I had been taught to read and to write about literature: The teacher was the expert reader and director and students were the receivers of knowledge. I loved reading, and I wanted my students to know in their own experience that same love of literature. I thought that I was working with my students to help them know literature as an aesthetic experience connected to their lives. I didn't know how to do this in a conscious way. I was not aware of the New Critical theory that was embedded in my pedagogy, a largely unexamined pedagogy.

From the beginning I experienced teaching the high school English curriculum as a yoke, a labor. I took all the responsibility for knowledge of a text and left my students with very little responsibility or room for personal evocations of the text. It's no wonder that they and I were frustrated. The lessons I planned and the assessments I used consisted of traditional five-paragraph essays, book reports, research papers, multiple-choice tests, true–false tests, and short-answer essay quizzes to check reading—most of these dictated by the text or the textbook. Readers had to identify literary devices, give plot summaries, write book reports, take spelling and vocabulary tests, and identify characters and themes.

In the midst of these rigid practices I began to develop "creative" reading experiences for my classes once we'd read and studied the texts in the academic way. We enacted scenes, wrote monologues from the point of view of a symbol or a character, sent letters to the author, or put a main character on trial. But these were always extended activities separate from the academic study and reading of the text.

I had been trained to read academically in a literary community of interpretation (Culler, 1975), and I was teaching high school English the same way. I can say in retrospect that I led two lives as a reader (at least): one trained for the discipline of English or the subject of English; and the other, like Burnett's Mary, of the personal secret garden variety. Rarely did the two lives merge. Reading and teaching serious classic literature was what good English teachers did. Reading for personal pleasure, for the human, vicarious experiences in which I, like the image of Wallace Stevens's reader, became one with the book ("The House Was Quiet and the World Was Calm," 1965/1985), simply did not happen in the academic world.

You might want to pause here and revisit your own reading life, both academic and personal. What are some of your favorite texts? In what settings did you read them? As an English major or English teacher, what is reading literature? What is teaching literature? What are your own experiences reading in the academic world? What was your experience with authority?

HUMPTY DUMPTY SITTING ON A WALL

The professional preparation of the English teacher, moreover, often has little relation to actual conditions in the classroom.
　　　　　　　　　　　　　　　　　　　　　　　　　　　—Rosenblatt, 1983, p. 65

Another influence on the way English teachers teach English is our preservice teacher education. As teachers, beginning or in retrospect, we need to ask ourselves more questions: What was (or is) my preservice education and preparation to teach high school English like? How do (did) my experiences reading and writing about teaching English in my methods course(s) influence how I teach or will begin teaching English?

What is interesting is that the English methods course I had as a preservice teacher was included in the Fresno State College secondary education strand and was taught by an English professor, Dr. K. What this meant is that English professors taught English majors how to teach English. Believe it or not, the same structure of teacher education and preparation that separated the English Department from the Education Department still exists in the state college system here in California in the 1990s.

I took courses in curriculum and instruction, school and society, and the psychological foundations of education, all of which were in the Secondary Education Department. None of the other teacher preparation courses were taught by a member of the English Department. My roommate, who was also majoring in English but planning to teach in elementary school, took her teacher preparation courses in the separate Elementary Education Department. The primary coursework in our teacher education programs was and still is tracked, split into primary and secondary and now further grouped into bilingual. The challenge of untracking students in our schools may lie in untracking teachers in their teacher preparation and education courses.

What I find disturbing is that there was and is so much to be learned from teachers working together in heterogeneously grouped education courses. I have learned a great deal about teaching and learning from my experiences with K–12 teachers in the California Literature Project (CLP) and my doctoral work at NYU. Many of the primary and middle school teachers I met and worked with talked about language, learning, literacy, and learners when they shared their teaching experiences.

As a high school English teacher, I had tended to view teaching English solely from the narrow perspective of the discipline of English. For most of my teaching career I had almost no contact with what was happening in English language arts districtwide in my own school district.

In the preservice course I took in 1968–69, "Secondary Education, English Materials and Methods," we read one text as the authority on secondary English methods for the course, *English in the Secondary School* (1961) by Edwin H. Sauer. Sauer wrote the text using and proposing a structural linguistics view of language for teaching English. The basic philosophy was that English teachers should be students of language, combining New Criticism, Structuralism, and linguistics in an approach that focuses on the "delight" of language rather than meaning. While approximately half of the book, "Part I: The Science of Language," addressed language as a function of history, grammar, and writing, Professor K.'s course emphasized literature and literary concerns as the central subject of English in secondary schools, found in "Part II: The Art of Language." We read the first half of the text, Part I, in the first five weeks of the course. Each week we studied and wrote about such salient topics (listed in the order from the course syllabus) as:

Week 1   Philosophies of English teaching
Week 2   Philosophies of language and teaching the "new" grammars
Week 3   Words and dictionaries
Week 4   Integrity in language and logic
Week 5   Rhetoric and composition, the development of Modern Prose
Week 6   The literature program in general
Week 7   Teaching fiction. Censorship or Guidance
Week 8   Pornography and the teacher's approach to it
Week 9   Keeping poetry palatable
Week 10   Teaching the play, Shakespeare and/or the Contemporary Play
Week 11   Essay and biography. Modern Prose Styles
Week 12   CREATIVITY and creativity and creative writing
Week 13   The English profession, academic freedom and trespass. What you teach when you teach English.
Week 14   Final Examination Date. All work must be turned in by 4:30.

Each week we were required to write on the subject of the week in short, informal reports related to the weekly topics. These reports were designed "to compel you to think critically about some of the foregoing class subjects. They will be graded for effectiveness of presentation as well as subject matter" (Course description, Dr. K., S.Ed. 161 syllabus).

Dr. K. taught this course through lecture. We as students received his thoughts and information, which he lectured to us, and then we wrote papers for him. We did not think about nor did we talk to each other about language and learning issues. Actually, we listened to Dr. K.'s lectures most of the time. For me, the language of the course was the language of philosophy, theory and abstraction, and logic. English (primarily literature) was the subject, and teaching literature was the content. We wrote about subjects but did not examine our views, our pedagogy, or our philosophy other than from an abstract position. For the most part, Dr. K. knew me as a student from reading my writing for his literature courses. He knew about the errors I made writing and he corrected these writing errors, editing the structural elements of text in red pencil, writing such comments as "make ideas parallel," "distinctions not clear," or "okay," while inserting commas, circling spelling, and using checks in the margins. Guess what? Again, this is how I responded to my students' writing when I started student teaching and then teaching English.

These were surface structural issues that did not help me reflect on teaching English, nor did the comments help me become a better writer, be-

cause he followed the format of response typical to him and many teachers
before him: to point out the deficiencies of my writing. Dr. K. always lectured
and spoke about things with such authority and certainty, with such well-
defined logic (he lectured from pages and pages of prepared notes), that I
never felt it possible to have a conversation with him about teaching English.
Even in his written comments there was no dialogue with the writer (me)
regarding my thinking, my ideas. There was no real questioning, nor were
there suggestions regarding particular ideas. None of this helped me think
about teaching English, but it certainly influenced the way I taught English.
His response was to the externals of presentation and the correctness and organization of my writing.

I wrote a paper for Dr. K. proposing *Valley of the Dolls* as a reasonable
yet problematic text for a high school teacher to encourage students to read.
Interestingly enough, for this paper I received the lowest grade on any paper
I wrote in this course (it was a futile attempt on my part to write ironically).
I titled the paper "Teacher's Attitude to Suggestive or Salacious Literature."

In this paper I wrote that I was afraid of and concerned that the teacher's
position was precarious, like sitting on a fence, being the guardian of moral
correctness regarding sex and religion in English classrooms. I wrote ironically about how I viewed the teacher's position in relationship to social and
cultural standards. I used the words "good" and middle-class "gentility" to
describe what we as English teachers are "bound" by in terms of social and
moral codes.

The irony seemed to escape Dr. K., but I find myself laughing as I look
at the list of books, which reflects my tongue-in-cheek humor, that I included
as posing moral problems that were as problematic as *Valley of the Dolls* for the
English teacher: a list of texts such as Orwell's *1984*, Wright's *Native Son*, and
Ellison's *Invisible Man*. I chose to place *Valley of the Dolls*, a popular "trash"
novel, among texts I had been assigned in my Contemporary Literature
course at Fresno State. It is the only contemporary text I remember reading
written by a woman about women while I was majoring in English. Of course,
we had read Jane Austen and George Eliot. I was suggesting that *Valley of the
Dolls* wasn't any more "suggestive" or "salacious" than the accepted contemporary literary canon, specifically *1984*. I argued the teacher's dilemma. What
do we tell a student who wants to read *Valley of the Dolls* to fulfill a reading
assignment? No, if we are to meet middle-class, academic "good" (moral) literature standards. That same summer my mother had forbidden my younger
sister to read a book called *The Bastard*. She felt that any book with that title
couldn't be any good. I took my mother's position into my own dilemma as
an English teacher. I didn't understand, however, how *The Bastard* or *Valley of
the Dolls* was any different from Balzac's potboiler *Eugénie Grandet*. I wrote
this paper in a serious yet facetious tone, but not well enough for anyone save

myself (or someone familiar with me as a person and my sense of humor) to recognize and understand the irony in it. I cited *1984* as an example of salacious literature because it had ideas concerning human reproduction and children playing at sex in the first few chapters. Heaven forbid teenagers read such stuff!

Though I wasn't arguing in the rhetorical tradition, I was turning phrases in on themselves and mixing up the academic language with my own dry, sarcastic thinking. My closing paragraph, which was not meant to be ironic, indicates my position, my thinking as an English teacher. I was Humpty Dumpty sitting on a wall, and I perched precariously with no place to go: "The teacher is forced to walk a fence. He must be careful to go one way— down the middle. If he should lose his balance and step haphazardly to one side or another he may fall off. Either way, in choosing to teach literature of any type the teacher is in a precarious position."

How ironic! I was writing about a teacher, myself, in such detached language that I used the pronoun "he" to refer to my female self.

Dr. K. left me sitting there on my fence, ignoring a young female teacher's fear-based dilemma (he did point out a problem in parallel structure, but he missed the female author/pronoun agreement problem). His sole comment, which accurately described my text, "You do a good job of raising the questions, but then you leave me balancing precariously," said nothing to me as a person who was really fearfully stuck regarding the teacher's moral and ethical responsibilities. He had accurately described my dilemma, but he did not help me make some sense of what the choices might be besides sitting pecariously on the fence in fear. He said I left him balancing precariously. I did and it was intentional, because that is how I felt. It was not necessarily a failure of my text, but a real dilemma I hadn't resolved.

That sense I had of a good English teacher's dilemma proved to be sadly prophetic during my first year of teaching. Another young English teacher hired that same year at my high school fell victim to the moral dilemma I had posed in the teaching suggestive or salacious literature paper. She innocently taught an e. e. cummings poem to her sophomore English class. She naively selected it thinking it was about a 16-year-old interest: driving cars. The kids read the double entendres in sexual terms, and my young colleague was confronted by irate parents who visited her classroom and demanded that she not be rehired. More than the poem, she had openly considered bringing a Black Panther into her classroom to speak. As an untenured teacher, she wasn't rehired the next year, though she was considered a bright light in our department who had just come into teaching from the University of California at Berkeley. The administration denied that the poem and the parents' protests played any role in her losing her job at our school. We all knew that wasn't true.

READING LITERARY CRITICISM AND THEORIES OF THE WORLD

In 1968–69, while I was still a preservice English teacher/undergrad English major, I took a course in literary criticism, "Problems in Modern Literary Criticism." I was student-teaching and working as a resident adviser in the dorms at Fresno State to pay for my room and board during my graduate year. In this course we read Hollander's *Modern Poetry: Essays in Criticism* (1968) and Kenneth Burke's *The Philosophy of Literary Form* (1957). One of the papers that I wrote for the course was a paper on Wimsatt and Beardsley's (1954) article "The Intentional Fallacy." I really thought literary theory was heady stuff and that literary criticism offered the answers to interpretation. Authority! And every theorist was male!

The professor was, again, Dr. K. In all, I took four courses with Dr. K. I found him to be very calm, methodical, very controlled. I found this manner comforting. His approach to teaching literature (hence, English) was a type of moral didacticism, and his rational, philosophical approach served as a paradigm that I used to model my own approach to reading, to writing, to teaching. Again, as with the paper I wrote on salacious literature, I fell short of his high and admirable standards in the research paper I wrote for this course: I (my reading, my writing, and my thinking) had some "serious confusions." And, I agree, I did. I was wrestling with some tricky stuff. But is all confusion necessarily bad, meriting a mere above-average evaluation, a B? One cannot receive an A for confusion. Or is confusion possibly a challenge of the idiosyncrasies, of the logic of the text, necessitating a greater effort by the instructor to work with the reader to understand her ways of thinking and reading the text?

From an academic perspective, I enjoyed writing this paper, and again I chose to write a bit felicitiously (I was still trying to write ironically). Reading theory and thinking about it gave me personal intellectual satisfaction: I really loved thinking about the nature of things, playing with ideas and the relationships of those ways of thinking about literature. I liked to read and to think.

In the paper I wrote for Dr. K. in 1968, I argue with Wimsatt and Beardsley's dismissal of the usefulness of knowing the author's intentions as a standard of literary criticism; I felt that knowing the author's intentions could help readers enhance, understand, and appreciate as well as evaluate a piece of literature. The author's intentions should not drive our reading of a text, but help us to understand the text. I argued that to assert that "the poem should not mean but be" (Wimsatt & Beardsley, 1954) was to ignore the historical and biographical contexts of a text. I closed this paper by stating very clearly, "The work sets its own standards, but the artist's intentions help to understand and read the poem or work of literary art."

My theory of literature did not embrace one strict philosophy. Both theories seemed possible, and I did not think they needed to be mutually exclusive. I was addressing and working out the issue of authority in relationship in terms of readers, authors, and texts. I sometimes described myself in those days as a "relativist." Things depended on circumstances, on the individual, on the text. Nothing was true of everything except that how we read was situational.

Unlike all the papers I had previously written for Dr. K., this paper received a major response from him. Marginalia notes to me in barely decipherable handwriting heavily peppered almost every page. He summed up his feelings about my reading of these theorists by giving the grade first then writing his remarks: "B—A thoughtful, provocative paper which suffers from what I believe to be some serious confusions. See the marginalia." Guess what? I was again confused. The marginalia notes he wrote to me corrected my thinking, my reading of the text, with comments such as "No—if one plumbs his unconscious it is to come up with archetypes (common for centuries) and if we look to his biography, it is better to understand his signature." It never occurred to me to talk with Dr. K. about his response to this "provocative" text. Could the problem be philosophical difference? Though I took four courses with him, I don't remember ever having any conversations with him about my reading, my thinking, or my writing.

As I have previously discussed in this book, in "Teacher's Attitude to Suggestive or Salacious Literature," I wrote in a lightly sarcastic tone. In the "Intentionalism" text, I was romping about with these theories in my own satiric voice (I had opened with "'Only Connect!' is the cry of the fearless intentionalist . . ."), and Dr. K. again didn't seem to read my text's ironic tone. Is not the phrase "the cry of the fearless intentionalist" not a bit exaggerated or a bit on the tongue-in-cheek side? As I revisit Wimsatt & Beardsley (1954), I see their tone as sarcastic, almost playful—my paper was my attempt to write in the same vein.

I concluded the "Intentionalism" paper with a clear statement of my position and theory of reading literature. I stated that "The intentions should not be used as a standard to judge, but are helpful in appreciation and then evaluation. As Isabel Hungerland clearly stated 'the poems, the paintings, the symphonies are there. The standard you seek is to be found in the work itself.' The work sets its own standards, but the artist's intentions help to understand and read the poem or work of literary art" (Roark, 1968).

Yes, I might well have read these theorists differently than the expert reader my professor was, but as a learner, I could have really benefited more from a discussion with him, a give-and-take conversation. He did not suggest it, nor did I request it. Neither one of us dared disturb the status quo. Good common-sense teaching and learning.

As a reader, you might want to take some time now to think about the theories you've studied and how you view them. What are the theories of literature, of reading, of writing even, that you've studied? In what ways do they influence your thinking about yourself as a reader, a writer, a teacher, a learner?

A BEGINNING TEACHER'S PHILOSOPHY OF EDUCATION

Along with cultural, social, and political influences on teaching, I found that my attitude, beliefs, and philosophy of life, of living, and of education were influential on my teaching. As I begin to explore this with you, I ask you to also consider the questions I have considered as I began to write about these experiences. What beliefs about life, about education, did/do I as a preservice teacher take into my teaching life? I found a brief statement of my beliefs that I wrote while in my Advanced Ed 174 class—ironically, during the final exam for the course in my postgraduate year.

When I began writing this book, I thought that I had evolved, changing and replacing my ideas as I continued to experience, read, write, and grow. What I continue to learn is that much of what I now state that I believe in my theory of languaging, which I wrote about early in this book, was there all the time, cluttered and covered with unexamined good intentions. The process has been one of self-discovery in that the way I work and believe have been there in some form all along, and it is the experience in and out of language that powerfully influences my teaching. Norman Holland in his psychoanalytic reading theory calls this foundational self our identity loops (*The Brain of Robert Frost*, 1988). So, what has been evolving, changing, if my basic identity has been in place? My sense of it is very simple: experience. Not so simple when we really look at the nature of our experiences and what is changing, evolving. I had to reexperience being a learner, a reader, a teacher, a writer in a collaborative community. My sense of who I am and knowing and understanding myself through reflective, critical autobiography is one aspect of my evolving theory of languaging.

To complete a teaching credential, all California secondary teachers have to earn a subject matter B. A. or B. S., then take the required two semesters of student teaching in the fifth year. In my fifth year I elected to take Advanced Ed 174, a school counselor course. In the final test for that course I wrote a response to the question, "What philosophy will I take into counseling?" As I look at that statement, I see that those beliefs speak for my way of being, for the stance toward the world and teaching that I took in 1968. A key concept in my philosophy statement included my belief that "man [notice the universal male pronoun] is a rational being with the ability to and capability of handling his [not her?] own problems. He is, in my feeling, basically good and his character is governed by his environment." I further stated that man has free will and that our environment and experiences shape our lives. I would work with the individual to help him [now it is painful to see that I excluded the *she* and the *her*] make informed choices until "he proves himself otherwise [untrustworthy, undependable]. A student would have my trust and confidence until through his actions he proves himself [*sic*] otherwise." I said my approach would be non directive: "I would present the possibilities to the counselee then let them make the ultimate choice."

I see so many similarities to my theory of languaging in this statement. The statement itself is masculine in tone and style, and grammatically correct with my universal male pronoun encompassing all students, both male and female! I was using the same language that was valued in academic discourse, Dr. K.'s rational academic language, abstract and theoretical. I can still hear his voice when I read my text.

The then–Pat Roark was buried beneath all this language that she thought admitted her to academia. Not knowing how to use my own language actually blocked me from who I was for many years. I still struggle with this issue, especially when I lose myself while trying to be falsely academic, that is, not true to myself. The style and voice of this book are a struggle to both speak in my voice and to write in the "standard, correct English" one expects from an English teacher. They don't always go together. Working out my languaging theory some 25 years later, making a statement of my philosophy and beliefs in my own language, has been a critical moment in my growth as a teacher. I didn't write about my beliefs or values as an English teacher again until 1986, when I became a fellow [*sic*] in the California Literature Project and then it was like watching a baby learn to walk (notice that women are still living in male names).

Though I held this basic ideal belief in "man's" nature and the nature of the universe (we are basically good, we have choices, we can make informed choices about our lives and behaviors), I didn't include myself in my ontology, especially in my teaching. There are several reasons why: (1) I was afraid to not be "in control" of my students; (2) I assumed authority as I had experienced it in my own student days, which in turn negated choice; and (3) I hadn't worked on my own sense of myself in relationship with the world. It took several years (and, eventually, psychotherapy for personal depression beginning in 1980, following a near divorce) before I began the critical ongoing process of personal self-reflection, before I began to look at what I believed and made connections with what I was doing and why that might be so. The experiences I eventually had in the California Literature Project in 1986 introduced me to the processes of collaborative, professional self-reflection.

All of my classroom preparation, my reading of theory, my experiences in education, my subject matter preparation did not prepare me for the emotional, personal struggles of that first year in the classroom, for the politics and culture of the classroom, for the politics and sociology of teaching. Are my experiences a single aberration, or do we all struggle with these issues in our teaching lives?

I suggest that we stop and reflect on our beliefs about teaching and what we hope for ourselves and our students. Write about this and let it sit awhile. Then return after a few days and read it again, reflecting on what you see in your statements. If you have a group of friends, share this and listen to each other's statements. My belief is that we all struggle on one level or another, and usually alone. We can begin to change this.

RETROSPECT: READING AND WRITING A BEGINNING TEACHER'S LIFE

All of these stories and critical reflections construct a picture of an idealistic beginning teacher. These are the critical aspects of her experience that she brought into her teaching: her reading, her learning, her writing, her academic experiences in education and English, and her experiences and perceptions of herself and the world through a girl's, then a woman's eyes.

Who was I as a 23-year-old woman from the middle class beginning to teach high school English?

I was a young woman, a young wife who wanted to be good: a perfectly good daughter, a good English major, and most of all, an idealistic good teacher. I was my father's daughter, who accepted all adults as authority (even after I had chronologically become one). I was my elementary teachers, my high school English teachers, my college English teachers (primarily Dr. K.), I was a structural/New Critical English teacher who taught almost exactly as Sauer had outlined in *English in the Secondary Schools* (1961): the history of the English language, a historical functional grammar, Latin and Greek roots, prefixes and suffixes as the foundation of all vocabulary learning, teaching language as something that must be appropriate to the situation, and teaching literature from the perspective of form, function, and the "delight" of language.

In the years since that first painful year, I have learned that there will always be dissonance between what I believe and what I do in my classroom (that is, it should never come together at one point permanently because for me that would mean that growth stops) and what I experience as a learner. I am learning to recognize and accept differences in beliefs about ways of working and being. When I first began to teach, and for many years thereafter, I didn't have a clue as to how to deal with the dissonance I experienced. At least now, through telling my stories, I am aware of the problem.

During that first year I knew that things weren't working right (the dissonances were tremendous) in the senior English class. In the rest of my classes
I was just surviving day to day (typical of most first-year teachers), but I wasn't
uncomfortable enough to change much more than externals to somehow
match my teaching with the paradigm of the subject and the teaching of English I had constructed. I thought everyone else in teaching had the answers
and that I was the only one floundering, the only one with whom something
was wrong.

I felt alone. Arthur Jersild in *When Teachers Face Themselves* (1955) tells
us that

> Ultimately loneliness is not simply a condition that exists in a person's relations
> with other people; it is a condition that exists in his [her] relation to himself
> [herself]. . . . Who, then, is the loneliest one? It is the person who is not at home
> with his own thoughts, the one who is alien to his own feelings, the one who is
> a stranger to himself—he is the loneliest person of all. (1955, p. 75)

I didn't consider the possibility that teaching and learning in English
classrooms was a shared responsibility, and that I, the teacher (and learner),
carried limited responsibilities. I couldn't learn for my students, they had to
take responsibility for their own learning; I had lost myself because I didn't
know that I couldn't take responsibility for their behaviors, that they had to
learn responsibility for their behaviors. I thought as I had experienced with
my colleagues, my professors, and my childhood teachers, that teaching English meant that I controlled behavior in a supportive classroom environment
focusing on the contents of English. And I tried so hard to be good. I was a
romantic idealist lost to teaching in a New Critical, Structuralist, traditional,
common-sense paradigm.

That first year I was exhausted and overwhelmed by it all. I sought help
to solve and change problems in my teaching, but was not prepared for the
realities of my classrooms. I wanted to achieve the impossible—perfect
teaching.

My thinking and the thoughts of my friends in my immediate teaching
community were very much described by Linda McNeil in *Contradictions of
Control* (1986):

> So long as the school ran smoothly, no administrative attention was forthcoming
> . . . . Feeling little support for their professional authority and even less provision
> for efficiencies of time and effort, the teachers set about to create their own au-
> thority, their own efficiencies. To do so, they needed to control the students. . . .
> Their solution was to control knowledge, the course content, in order to control
> students. (p. xx)

I was an untenured teacher, afraid of making mistakes in a field I perceived as intellectually unforgiving. According to McNeil, I was practicing defensive teaching. In defensive teaching teachers select teaching strategies to control knowledge and student behavior (1986, p. 159). The problem that needs to be addressed for both teachers and students, according to McNeil, is the legitimation of processes or ways of knowing: to be able to question, to explore, to offer new ways of thinking, to learn to work independently. We need to look not so much at how much is learned, but at the nature of what is learned (1986, p. 207).

I close this chapter with a favorite passage of mine from Arthur Jersild's *When Teachers Face Themselves* (1955):

> Meaninglessness is a common condition in college and graduate training. Much of what goes on in the name of learning is simply an academic enterprise . . . .
>
> If we educators are to face the problem of meaninglessness, we must make an effort to conduct education in depth—to move toward something that is personally significant beyond the facade of facts, subject matter, logic, and reason behind which human motives and a person's real struggles and strivings are often concealed. This does not mean the rejection of subject matter—far from it—but it does mean helping the learner to relate to himself to what he is learning and to fit what he learns into the fabric of his life in a meaningful way. (p. 80)

CHAPTER 5

The First 15 Years,
Alice in Wonderland

When a person seeks to realize the meaning of his own emotions, he cannot help but be humble. He is baffled by the play of love and hate in his life. He cannot penetrate the clouds of anxiety that move across the horizons of his inner world. He is perplexed by the conditions that sometimes move him toward depths of longing. He is bewildered by the complexity of his feelings, which lead him at times to accept what he should reject and to reject what by rights he should accept.

—Jersild, 1955, p. 97

Much happened in the first 15 years. A baby. Many changes in principals, much happiness, and growing depression and pain. In both my personal and professional life, those first 15 years can be described with the word "searching." I was trying to find, searching helter-skelter for ways to take control of my teaching and my life. I was searching to be the best teacher I could be, the best wife I could be, and after much struggle with my husband to begin a family, the best mother I could be to our daughter, Cara. Creating my own family was a critical part of my personal life. My husband was less enthusiastic about creating a family, and there was much friction between us about what shape our lives would take. Since I wanted family more than he did, I made a vow to be supermom and superwife while already driving to be the good (actually perfect) teacher. We could have it all! I also assumed total responsibility, as I did for my students in my teaching, for raising our daughter.

The late 1960s and 1970s were the times of female consciousness-raising and women's liberation. I loved and embraced feminism. Women's liberation—finally, some role models I could identify with and who encouraged me to pursue my profession and accept my intelligence. I'm not sure now to what we truly liberated ourselves, but we had to begin to change the lives of women, and this period marks the beginning for my generation of consciously striving to make those changes. During these years we Schmidts bought a new four bedroom home in suburbia, traveled to Europe, bought a 1971 Mercedes, had our daughter Cara in 1973, and acquired a rascally Manx cat, Pebbles, a brown-eyed Irish setter we called Lollipop, numerous, now-deceased fish, and a gray cheeked parakeet we called Tootsie. Our marriage was intact, though wobbly.

I poured my energies into my professional life and my family. At various times during those first 15 years or so of teaching English I was our school librarian, taught virtually every course and course level in the English Department, and advised cheerleaders, flag girls, the school newspaper, and several classes and clubs. Nothing out of the ordinary for a teacher. Most of us do this. For a really good book that captures the general experience of English teaching read Sizer's *Horace's Compromise* (1985) or Sylvia Ashton-Warner's *Teacher* (1963). However . . .

Not much was left for me. I could not and did not walk through these years, I ran and ran and ran. I was in Wonderland. I was Alice pursuing the white rabbit.

In 1976–77 I was elected president of my teachers' association for the school district. My work for approximately 180 teachers during that year was exciting. I truly enjoyed working for improving the lives of those involved in education, both teachers and students. It was not an easy time personally. I neglected my daughter and my husband for teaching and professional political work. The experiences in community leadership and working with colleagues who valued me enabled me to look at the problems of our marriage, and what I saw I didn't like.

In the middle of my presidency, in the spring of 1978, my husband and I separated for three months. He moved out. At the time I believed that the marriage was over. I thought that the problem was the marriage and our relationship. I had not searched in myself for answers. We both began counseling to address the problems of our relationship. We reconciled after three sessions and I took responsibility for his pain and mine both, in the same way I had taken responsibility with that painful first-year senior English class. The academic year ended with a new collective bargaining contract and a 2.7 percent salary increase for our teachers. My family, like Humpty Dumpty, had been broken into fragile pieces, and I was Alice who had disappeared into a crazy world inside the rabbit's hole. My heart and soul were cheerless, dark, and empty. I thought that the problem was that I was trying to do it all, so my solution was to do less. I was exhausted and I vowed that next year I would concentrate on my classroom and my family and *nothing* else. That vow was short-lived.

Two of my colleagues and friends, both women, were just finishing up their master's degrees. I looked around my school, around my life, and felt that something was missing. I was still searching for a center. I decided to return to school to get a master's degree in English. I did not feel good about the work I'd done as an undergraduate English major, and I felt that this return to school would enable me to become more knowledgeable in my field:

an authority. I'd been taking professional growth units like health fanatics take vitamins (about 30 units since I'd begun teaching), but they went nowhere. I reasoned, why not take a year off and pursue a master's degree in English? I'd worked hard at teaching, I'd worked hard at change in education for my educational community, and I deserved it. I thought it would give me time to be a real mother to our five-year-old daughter and "rest" psychically from all the personal and professional stress. It also served to buffer the sense of loss I anticipated in no longer living in the drama of being president. So, after nine years teaching at the same high school, I gave myself the gift of a year studying, reading literature, and not teaching.

I loved being a student again.

During those first nine years I took little time for personal reading. I can remember reading only two texts that profoundly touched me and influenced my life: Wallace Stegner's *Angle of Repose* (1971) and John Fowles's *The Magus* (rev. ed., 1977). Over the years I have read and reread them both. Why? Stegner's novel focuses on the crumbling marriage of the narrator, who discovers that the relationship between his grandparents parallels his own circumstances. His grandfather, a taciturn civil engineer, marries a writer, moves her wherever his work takes him, and eventually chooses to close his heart to her because of the tragic death of one of their children (for which he holds her accountable). Theirs was a lonely relationship that reached an "angle of repose," a resting point in mining terms. I was struck by the narrator's sense that he didn't have to choose to turn a stone heart on his wife as his grandfather had done to his grandmother. I searched for understanding of my own marital problems in this text written by a man.

The other book I loved, actually, the other author I loved and read everything I could get my hands on was John Fowles, another male author. I loved *The Magus*. It is a male rites-of-passage novel, but I identified with the female protagonist, Alison, and felt Fowles treated her well. Fowles seemed to understand the male view of women as sexual objects and possessions, and he wrote sensitively about women, teaching us through his protagonist Nicholas that men should not objectify women, nor should they seek authority outside themselves—in a God who is not present. I saw him as a male feminist. His protagonist, Nicholas Urfe, had to experience his own imprisoned thinking to be free of it, and in the closing scene he and Alison are reunited at the Tate Gallery in London, educated with the possibility of freeing themselves existentially. I read everything I could get of Fowles's at the time: *The Collector, The French Lieutenant's Woman, The Ebony Tower,* and *The Aristos.* I was fascinated with *The Aristos,* which is a book of philosophy dealing with existential concepts: *aristos* derives from the Greek and it means roughly "the best for a given situation" (Fowles, 1970). I was especially intrigued with the section "Adam and Eve," for in it Fowles gives a feminist retelling of the creation. Fowles states that generally males are responsible for the sickness that prevails: he sets up dichotomies for male/female relating, Adam as stasis and Eve as kinesis, Adam as hatred of change and Eve as the assumption of human responsibility. I could identify with these descriptions. Eve is intelligence and the assumption of human responsibility, progress; and Adam is hatred of change, conservatism, forced to change by Eve. This retelling of the story offering a feminist perspective by a male really caught me: a male author advocating women's intelligence. With my fundamentalist Christian upbringing in the Assembly of God and then Baptist churches, this was revolutionary thinking.

I read *The Magus* many times, checking Fowles's stated feminist beliefs in *The Aristos* with his treatment of men and women in *The Magus*. These issues just interested me. Wimsatt and Beardsley would cringe. Was he consistent? He seemed to be. This interest in Fowles and in feminist issues resurfaced in my master's degree work in the form of my master's thesis, *Romance Parody in John Fowles' The Magus* (1980).

Ironically, again, I was checking another person's beliefs and philosophy against what he was doing, against his writing. I still wasn't doing this with my own beliefs.

ALICE MEETS THE QUEEN OF HEARTS

I chose Holy Names College nearby because I'd been rejected by the University of California at Berkeley English M.A. program (my undergraduate grades in English courses averaged merely a B and my GRE scores weren't high enough) and Holy Names was my alternate choice. UC Berkeley did me a favor. At the time I was ashamed to tell people that I had been rejected by Berkeley, since many of my friends in the English Department had graduated from the Berkeley English program. It was an ego and status issue for me.

As usual, life worked out the way it would be best for me in spite of my own desire to attend the prestigious UC Berkeley. The program I took at Holy Names College was incredible in that the classes were so small, between six and fifteen persons, and most were seminars. And, most critically, the professors were almost all women, a true godsend. Yet, for the most part these classes were lectures and traditional academic literary analysis, save one class. That one class was Sister C. M.'s T. S. Eliot seminar.

I had emerged from Wonderland and entered a beautiful garden where I met a wise old woman teacher. I remember Sister C. M.'s graduate seminar in T. S. Eliot well. We sat in a circle. Sister C. M. was no doubt an Eliot expert, but she did not lecture. We read, explored, questioned, selected passages, puzzled, and gave our personal responses to Eliot's poetry. Our written work was not assigned, except that we were told to write a response and it could be personal. Freedom to read, think, and respond. Many times we gathered around the table and simply read aloud to hear the rhythm and sounds. There was such freedom to read and make meaning. That experience was the first one I can consciously name, through writing this narrative and reflection, in which my personal and intellectual experiences merged, and I knew at the time that that was happening even if I did not in a conscious way change my own teaching.

At Holy Names College, during my postgraduate study as an English academic, my academic reading experience with literature and what constitutes literary scholarship, "close reading and interpretation," though traditional in many ways, was somewhat different from my undergraduate experience. I would describe the difference in terms of relationship and intimacy. I worked more closely with my female professors, and they responded to my writing thoroughly, beyond marking deficiencies, to my ideas. My professors knew me personally, and though all but one taught through lecture and discussion, they encouraged us to talk to each other and with them about our readings of the assigned texts. Most critically for me as a reader, I had a memorable academic experience reading T. S. Eliot in which my authority as a reader and writer were valued, honored, and expected.

Since I viewed my English M.A. as "academic" study, I did not reflect on my teaching of English nor on my role as a teacher when I returned to my high school classroom. All of my work had been as an English academic, and I continued to teach, though with fewer grammar and punctuation lessons, in a New Critical paradigm. As students in an English M.A. program, most of us already teachers of English or postgraduate English majors student teaching, we did not reflect on our literary study in relationship to our pedagogies of teaching English or education.

I returned to teaching in the fall of 1979 vowing to focus solely on one thing—my English classes. I wanted to be the best English teacher I could be, and I now possessed the Academic Knowledge and Authority I thought I needed to be an expert English teacher, still thinking to erase the painful, haunting memory of my first year. The changes I made in my teaching and my life that year still focused on the externals: I changed my schedule and tried to keep life simple and simply teach. No more committees, no more curriculum revisions, only the minimum required extracurricular activities (like chaperoning the Senior Ball). Just teach and be with my family. I still did not look at Pat herself. I continued to cycle through my "successful" classroom pedagogy, but I now felt that I was more expert in my academic discipline. I now had a master's (notice the maleness of this nominal) degree, the measure of the good English teacher.

The approach I used and my decision to isolate myself was so "successful" that when I returned to my classroom in 1979, I found myself taking a leave of absence around Thanksgiving, ostensibly to finish my master's thesis, which I did complete. It was the teaching year that I did not complete.

In my zeal to just teach, my teaching life that year was one of almost total isolation. As I sequestered myself in my second-story chemistry room converted into an English classroom, with fixed lab desks, I found myself returning to Alice in a land more foreign than I could have imagined. I was isolated in my own mental rabbit hole, and the white rabbit was setting off firecrackers in my psyche. The real kids were setting off real firecrackers in the real lockers outside my classroom and I went over the edge.

What I returned to that fall was what many English teachers juggle successfully, even if stressfully. Things hadn't changed at my school and after spending the year in the academic, intellectual ivory tower at Holy Names, the gap between my personal intellectual life and my personal needs only widened. The high school where I taught was in turmoil. Teachers were griping, they were unhappy with and critical of the whoever-was-the-current-administration (our school had swallowed 6 principals in 10 years), and the atmosphere was generally one of unrest, dissatisfaction, and negativity. I told myself that I could escape this negativity by staying in my classroom at lunchtime and getting the hell out of there when our negotiated contract allowed, 30 minutes after the last class bell had rung. I did not consider would happen to me in such total isolation.

That's what I did, but it didn't block out the environment or my response. As John Donne wrote, "No man is an island" (I'd like to think that in a different cultural milieu he would have included women). In my case, no high school English teacher is an island. But I felt the isolation I had experimented with and sought change in my job for the solution. I thought that I needed to leave teaching and try something else. I thought that this was what my husband wanted because over the years he had resented teaching. Teaching took all my time and energy. And when I came home from teaching, motherhood took the rest of my energy. Combined with my superwoman approach to life, perfect English teacher, perfect mother, and my failures at perfect wife, I decided that something had to give before I did.

> The ghosts of old hurts, the souls of agonies of an earlier day, live on in many of our children at school and in the colleagues with whom we work, and in ourselves. And it is to the extent that each of us has the courage to look into the haunted house within himself where these ghosts reside that he can gain some insight into the way the lives of other are ravaged by anxiety. (Jersild, 1955, p. 55)

So that temporary leave of absence became a permanent resignation from my profession in January 1980. I was so depressed and upset that I could barely find the words to respond when the superintendent called me at home to thank me for my years of service to the school district. Alice had met the Queen of Hearts and there was no way out of Wonderland except to quit the game.

I explored other worlds for the next 43 months, first the world of corporate work in the form of technical writing jobs for the banking and petroleum industries. These solved one problem but created another: I experienced an emptiness, a hole in my life, without the classroom. The personal struggle I experienced is reflected in the poetry I wrote during that time (1984–1985) and in my reading life. Now I find this poetry and my state of mind to be pretty scary stuff!

July 1984
DEATH BY DRAGON

She fights to see light
In the darkness of the night
Ominous portent
Impending
Death by Dragon
She lay on the divan
Struggling to overcome the darkness
To see light, to feel light, to live.
But the Dragon
Approached her prone figure
Ominous portent
Impending
Death by Dragon
She reached up for the light none too late.
He skulked away from her lifeless body
In the darkness of the night.
Leaving her family to grieve her
death by dragon.

March 24, 1985
NIGHT VISIONS

He left me in a house
Of strangers, by mistake
Driving away—
I tried to call him back
Leaving an unanswered message;

Then the winds of death came
Blustering winds
Like a hurricane,
Pushing the house over,
Sweeping away my father,
Then my mother;
I clung to the pole
in the house,
And, to my daughter
Screaming as she slipped
Further and further
Away:
The raging winds pulling us apart.

Both "Death by Dragon" and "Night Visions" were written during six months of psychotherapy for depression, something I had been fighting and almost succumbed to since leaving teaching.

Two texts I recall reading during those final commuting months into San Francisco are Gail Sheehy's *Passages: Predictable Crises of Adult Life* (1976) and Dostoyevsky's *The Possessed* (1980).

The Possessed moved me deeply. I remember reading it each day on the 35-minute commute to my corporate job. Spiritual quests and personal quests. Reading literature offered me safe avenues to explore and understand what I wasn't willing to risk exploring and understanding in my own personal life and my teaching life. Reading opened the windows of my mind to new experiences.

In the last year of those 43 months away from teaching I left the technical writer consulting business I'd successfully built and tried to "become a writer." During that year I was again in therapy for depression, and I wrote a great deal. The desire to "write" came about in part from a weekend course I had taken in Ira Progoff's "Intensive Dialogue Journal," conducted at Vallambrosa Center near Stanford University by Progoff. I had begun to feel free as a writer and sought to write a variety of texts, among them an article analyzing the three French epigraphs from de Sade's *Justine* (1965). These epigraphs introduce the three sections to John Fowles's *The Magus*. I also wrote several poems, a children's book, *Kelly's Dream*, and a children's story still in draft form, "The Great Goose Rescue." I completed and "field-tested" a short story about our Irish setter and one of her adventures boarding a local transit bus, "Lollipop, Ker Plop," with my daughter Cara's fifth-grade class. They responded positively to Pop's story.

Lollipop's story was really my psychic story. Lolly had actually found her way out of our back yard and jumped on a local transit bus. She was brought home to us by a kindly bus driver. The story resonates with my healing psyche, having been cared for by very kind women in my life during this time.

I worked with these fifth graders to help them write their own stories and found I enjoyed teaching them. Though I enjoyed being a "writer," that time I spent with my daughter's class gave me much pleasure, but I was not earning a living, something I equated with being a successful writer. So my perceptions of success and failure continued to guide my life and my decisions.

In 1984 I found myself considering returning to the classroom. Forty-three months away had been good, but I was lonely still. I missed teaching. This time I wanted to make a difference in education, and I knew I needed to make changes, both personal and professional, if I were going to return, stay, and enjoy teaching. The year I was president of our teachers' association made me think I might explore educational administration. I began working on a credential in educational administration at California State University, Hayward (while I was working as a tech writer I had begun an M.B.A. and had taken two semesters of business classes), and I began to ease back into teaching. Whenever I felt I needed to make changes, I found myself always turning to graduate school to seek new knowledge and, probably, new authority. I continued to turn to education as a solution to my problems.

I eased back into teaching: I taught the programmed, self-paced courses at the Adult School, and I also taught summer school at my former high school. Resonate with my preservice teaching experience, I taught the kids, 90 percent boys, who had failed English and the required proficiency tests, as well as people needing English credits to graduate.

Then in the fall of 1984 I accepted a one-period position at my former high school, teaching students who had failed English and needed to repeat English to graduate. I'd always enjoyed teaching the "remedial" kids, although I hated the tracking. I didn't view these kids as failures (again, almost all of them were male) and by semester's end they had all passed the class. I viewed these kids as intelligent, just lacking in skills. There was no curriculum for the class, and I had the freedom to choose what we would do. I deviated from the regular curriculum, spending a great deal of time talking with them and holding a reader's workshop with students reading individually selected books at their own pace. All that control and organization I had begun teaching with were disappearing. A couple of these "failing" students went on to college and graduated, one with a degree in marine biology.

During these early years of my return to teaching I also taught a creative writing class after school at the junior high school in our school district and a poetry workshop at another elementary school. Students selected their own subjects and forms of writing based on personal interest, and I helped them, giving mini-lessons connected to what they were doing in their writing. My own experiences as a writer during those past 43 months away from teaching influenced my sense of what writing is and what teaching writing could be: Writers write best when what they write is meaningful to them and when they have a desire and a reason to write. Coupled with my experiences in assisted self-examination and reflection in psychotherapy and the Progoff intensive journal workshop, being a writer and working toward self-understanding enabled me to begin to make small but powerful changes in my teaching.

CANCER, FEAR, CHANGE

In the summer of 1985, after a three-week trip to the Middle East and while I was taking another course toward the administrative credential I had just started (still searching for authority), I discovered a suspicious lump in my right breast. Four days later I had surgery to remove the suspicious lump. I went in confident that everything was okay, and by the time my surgeon had finished stitching up my breast, I learned that I had breast cancer.

What an emotional time that was. Two weeks later I sat at the district office interviewing for a part-time English job at my former high school. After having checked with my surgeon, I learned that I had to tell the interviewing committee at the time of my interview that I had breast cancer. These words are among the hardest I've ever had to say to other human beings. It was hard enough going through the interview, but I had to also say, "I've just had surgery for breast cancer. I'm going to be okay. My doctors expect a full recovery, but I have to tell you that I have this existing condition." That was a critical moment for me. My voice cracked with emotion, and I was close to crying as I spoke. As I write this down I find myself staring at the memory and my thinking, Who would hire a woman who has had breast cancer to teach?

They hired me anyway (in circumstances strikingly similar to my first go-round being hired into this school district), and I began teaching English part-time again that fall while I underwent daily radiation treatments during the first two and an half months of school. I also resumed psychotherapy to deal with the emotional rollercoaster of dealing with a life-threatening illness. I taught in the morning and went for radiation treatments in the afternoon. Teaching English in the morning kept me focused on others and not myself, though I was scared to death of dying. I was grateful for the chance to teach high school English again. To ease the pain of this, I began a daily numbing-out ritual, sipping lovely glasses of wine to wind down from all the stress.

Earlier psychotherapy I had begun in 1980 when I crashed and burned and left teaching had initiated the process of reflection and self-exploration that I now sought again and hoped would help me to make changes in my life. This third go-round with therapy was different. I began to tell, to explore, and

in the process understand and make some sense of my life experiences. This process helped me to grow, and to become aware of and to begin the process of personal change. Change meant that I needed to face my fears, name them, and begin to take risks in spite of them. There are two really good books that deal with the psychology of teaching and the teacher's life. I've been sharing some of their text with you as I write about the teaching life. I highly recommend them to those of you reading this who wish to continue to explore your personal and teaching lives: *Psychology for Teachers* (1988) by Phillida Salmon and Arthur Jersild's *When Teachers Face Themselves* (1955).

Through therapy I had explored and begun to understand the physical, emotional, and verbal abuse I experienced in my early childhood, then later in my adolescence. When I talk with my parents about this they feel that the kind of physical and emotional abuse I experienced growing up were discipline and teaching respect for authority. They contend that if one doesn't have bruises or something broken, physical and verbal punishment is not abuse. I do understand this stance to a degree. I understand that my father truly suffered physical abuse when his drunken father beat him with barbed wire, causing blood to dry his shirt to his back. However, I disagree with the notion that abuse is only physical violence, not inflicting foul language on others. Abuse is when people we love, trust, and respect exert control over our lives with intimidation and threats of physical and emotional punishment. Inflicting that punishment, either physical or verbal, destroys the person's, especially the child's, soul. I've seen this abuse in education, and it is not restricted to teacher–student relationships or parent–child relationships. It can be administration–teacher or teacher–teacher. It is often well-intentioned. It walks around in pedagogy dressed in words like *discipline, control, back to basics, standardized tests,* and *grades.* The unexamined practices in the name of learning can destroy our very hearts and souls. That is the tragedy.

In the spring of 1986 I found myself wanting to learn to be a better English teacher, wanting to try new experiences and to somehow change what I did in my classroom. One day that spring my principal slipped a brochure from the California Literature Project into my box. The deadline was the next day.

The descriptions of the California Literature Project in the state's brochure really appealed to me: I wanted to know what the new English Language Arts Framework was, teachers would work together to read texts and learn new ways of working in their classrooms, and everything for the entire seven weeks would be paid for by the state. I was thrilled to finally see that the profession was being valued (most of us pay for everything to better our professional lives). I had only been teaching for five months that year and I was already frustrated with my department. Even with the passage of time, extensive psychotherapy, and an attempt at a new attitude, the structures had

still remained the same, and my response was not much better. There were three demigods in our English Department, one at each grade level. This reminded me so much of that first year and Mrs. J. The expectation of what constitutes a good English teacher hadn't changed much in the past 15 years. Each of these English teachers was "the" English teacher for his or her grade level: they were each good, traditional, common-sense teachers. I was really odd woman out.

By this time I'd dropped teaching isolated grammar, having realized several years earlier that it didn't make my students better writers. My years away from teaching and my practical experiences writing helped me to change my pedagogy. The anxiety and fear of dying changed my life. They went together. I didn't lecture on or about the texts we were reading: I opted for class discussions, though still teacher-directed. I dropped the five-paragraph essay and tried to create a junior term paper project that somehow addressed the process of research (this came from my M.A. thesis experience), and I included student speeches on "how to" do something in which students collaborated on designing the class evaluation sheets and evaluated each other, along with my teacher evaluation. I knew that my teaching was better, and so was my classroom environment.

My principal was new to the school that year and he supported change in our department, too, so he was delighted when I approached him to recommend me to the California Literature Project. Though we had our differences, I am indebted to my principal for his initial support of my involvement in the Literature Project.

So, that spring of 1986, with the support of my principal and the school district, I applied for and was accepted into the statewide teacher education/staff development program for implementation of the California English Language Arts Framework, the California Literature Project (which I will refer to hereafter as the CLP). That year was the beginning of major transformations in my teaching and in my thinking about teaching literature, and of a redefinition of what teaching English is for me. It was also a year of major life transformations. As you read this, I ask you to consider what professional experiences have made indelible marks in your memory and in your teaching life. Spend some time and write these down. Once you have them down, then choose one and really write about it. Write it all. What happened? How did you feel? What changes did you make in your classroom after the experience? What worked? What didn't?

My school district fully supported me in making the application, which meant a commitment by them to two years of follow-up training, the district providing substitutes for a total of 20 days of release time. My active involvement in the CLP lasted four years, culminating with my work as a teacher-leader at the CLP Sonoma State Summer Institute from 1988 to 1990. I

worked alongside other CLP teacher-leaders and institute participants, and then led my own California Literature Project follow-up group.

You now know me better than many of my close friends and colleagues ever did. This was the Pat Schmidt who drove the family silver Toyota mini-van to Westwood, California, and UCLA in July 1986, wanting to know more about teaching English and open to new experiences. I had figured that my life might be short, and I wanted to experience and enjoy it. I didn't realize that that summer experience would change the course of my life in ways beyond my limited vision of curriculum reform.

Carpe diem. Seize the day!

CHAPTER 6

Experiencing Literature and Theory, 1986–1990

Why do you tell us these stories?

—imaginary frustrated reader

Because they were the source of my authority.

—Rouse, 1978

Pat, don't bullshit! Don't capitulate your story to "research." Stay true. Stay honest.
—Pat Schmidt, 1993

But I was lucky. I managed to get redefined.

—Mike Rose, 1990

Unlike Mike Rose, who made this statement in his important book *Lives on the Boundary* (1990), I did not get redefined. I was lucky. I feel that I was beginning to redefine myself. 1986 through 1990 are the years when I began to consciously redefine myself professionally and personally. I began to seek adventure in life. My idea of adventure was to spend a summer away from my family, living and studying in Los Angeles.

Just what are the circumstances, the contexts, the personal issues that contribute to adventuring professionally? As I write and reflect on this question, I hear deep inside the words *experience, community, broad, open structures* and *an open heart and mind.*

I drove our silver minivan to southern California with few preconceived ideas concerning the California Literature Project or what I would learn. I was looking forward to enjoying the experience, to meeting others who shared the same willingness to think about teaching and literature, and to learning. It wasn't easy to set off on this adventure. My husband was angry at me for leaving him for the summer, and our 13-year-old daughter, Cara, was happily off to Texas on her own adventure to study ballet with Robert Joffrey and the Joffrey Ballet.

I was first attracted to the California Literature Project because it focused on literature. I loved literature and reading. I was taking a false sense of authority with me. Because I had my M.A. in English, I felt that I was a "certified academic." I certainly did not question what that meant, but I thought that that M.A. finally gave me authority to be an English teacher.

Though Berkeley was only a 15-minute drive from my house, I had not studied in the Bay Area Writing Project in Berkeley, something many Bay Area teachers automatically attended. In the early 1970s I had read James Moffett's *A Student-Centered Language Arts Curriculum, K–14* (1973) and I attended miniworkshops in the Writing Project at CATE (California Association of Teachers of English); as well, I had traveled to a Zen-type writing workshop led by Moffett himself in Sacramento. He talked about mandalas and centers. I enjoyed the experience, but at the time I was lost about what I could do in my classroom with mandalas.

At the time I had tried a couple of Moffett's writing assignments and I had actually begun to enjoy teaching writing using the Moffett developmental sequences for writing. However, I wasn't entirely happy. I was stumbling around trying to teach writing using Moffett's assignments with no collegial collaboration or support. The assignments were a step beyond the five-paragraph essays I had so religiously worked with in my early teaching life.

What impressed me the most about Moffett's developmental writing program was that it began with the personal life of the writer and moved the writer and her writing outward into the world. The notion of beginning to write from the "I" and then working toward the "we" and then the "it" made sense to me. While I had intellectually accepted the notion of a student-centered curriculum, I was still practicing in a teacher-centered, controlled, content-centered mode. My students still sat in rows, I still did most of the talking, and I still taught most of my English classes in a pretty traditional, common-sense, academic way. I didn't understand that to make a change in assignments or activities in my classroom while maintaining the same beliefs about what English and what teaching English are means that little really changes. But these little changes did contribute to a reservoir of experiences from which I eventually drew.

By this time (1986) in my teaching I had developed some units that were always successful. After years of teaching I'd say that many teachers discover their successful teaching units and continue to use them. In my case, I deemed them successful because my students enjoyed them tremendously (as did I) and the projects brought out their best thinking and their best work. Equally important, as I write and reflect on them, was that I was not doing all the learning for my students. The three most successful units I developed—"how to" speeches, biographical research speeches, and the Renaissance and medieval research presentations—were *projects* rather than daily lessons or a weekly unit. These projects shared some common qualities: student choice and collaboration based on interests and experiences, flexible use of time within the project's time window (usually three weeks), sharing knowledge (the learner became the "expert"), and creative and integrated assessments (research skills integrated into the projects, which always concluded with sharing knowledge with each other).

I didn't realize it at the time, but I'd started to teach transactionally (Dewey & Bentley, 1949, Rosenblatt, 1983) with these projects. Students worked independently and together and with me in unstructured class time. We learned together from the presentations, and those presentations were about subjects students had selected that interested them. Students who loved music, for example, researched Renaissance music and often played music for us while telling us about music during the Renaissance. Budding artists researched medieval art and brought in slides or used the overhead projectors to talk about it. We learned about jewelry and dress; we played games; and we were served medieval dishes prepared in front of class by wimple-costumed maids; and so forth.

The "how-to" speeches were simple in frame: Prepare a speech of five to seven minutes demonstrating how to do something. It was amazing how creative students were. We all learned about a great many things, ranging from beekeeping to cooking projects. Sometimes the speeches took us outdoors to learn how to care for and groom a horse, or in the case of the starting varsity pitcher, how to throw the four basic pitches (complete with a demonstration in the parking lot).

Today I find Moffett's notion of student-centered learning limited as a concept for teaching and learning, for the simple reason that the term "student-centered" isolates the learner from the teacher. For me what is critical to the notion of student-centered learning is for the teacher to consider herself to be and to be considered by those with whom she works a participant, a "student." Remember the concept of languaging I introduced early in this book? That is what I am talking about. Education should not be teacher-directed solely nor student-centered solely. If education is to be transactional, we are learning together.

For the "how-to" speech projects, my classes developed their own criteria for evaluating a speech. I always gave a "how-to" speech—usually on how not to give a speech—while my class tried out the evaluation sheets evaluating me. I crammed bananas in my mouth each period while trying to talk, chewed gum while I talked, looked only at my feet, toyed with my hair, and every other word I said was a "you know. . . ." We learned and we had a lot of fun.

THE LIVED-THROUGH EXPERIENCE, BEGINNING TO UNDERSTAND

In 1991, during a conversation with Mary Barr, the former director (she followed UCLA's Patricia Taylor as director) of the California Literature Project, I learned that Louise Rosenblatt's transactional theory of reading literature formed the foundation of the CLP. Later, when I read Barr's article "The California Literature Project" in *Transactions with Literature* (1990), I realized that what I had experienced during my UCLA summer was the "lived-through" experience of Louise Rosenblatt's transactional literary and educational theory. Though we read a mix of literature, theory, and research, we did not actually read Rosenblatt's texts at the 1986 California Literature Project. However, the spirit, an essence of Rosenblatt's educational and literary theory, embued the project's enactment of her literary and educational philosophy and theory. Barr in "The California Literature Project" stated that:

> Rosenblatt's emphasis on personal response to the literary experience respects the diversity of human experience present in all classrooms. By trusting the validity of their own experiences, students learn to compare their responses to those of others, thereby widening their worlds. With the meanings of texts understood to grow out of their transactions with them, not in answer keys or their teachers' minds, we know that all students can equip themselves to engage in grand conversations about the humane values and issues only literature evokes. (1990, p. 44)

In the summer of 1992 I spent two weeks in Paris. While I was in Paris making almost daily excursions to the Louvre, the Pompidou, the Orangerie, and so on, I came to realize that my love of Impressionist painters and art was connected with the problem of retelling a life-changing experience, of trying to write the story of my experiences in the California Literature Project that you are reading in this book. Before I left for Paris I was trying to remember my UCLA experience and found that all I could muster was an impression, an evoked sense of the experience. When I gazed at Monet's paintings and looked at both the painting and its title I saw my dilemma in trying to remember the experiences I'd had in the Lit Project. What Monet sought to paint in his "Sun Rising: An Impression" reminded me of the first memories I was recalling of my UCLA experience. I could only call up impressions. Why was the CLP summer, which was such a powerful experience, one that I feel was so critical in my teaching life, available to me only in impressions, in interpretations, in generally "lived-through memory"? Beginning in retrospect, then, was beginning with impressions of experiences, remembering, writing, then reading. Later I was reading about memory and writing of experiences. I read that to write about a powerful experience is to destroy the experience from our memories. Once written, it is no longer living in our experience reservoir.

The story I remember, tell, and write about my UCLA summer experiences reading and learning begins with the remembered impressions of the experience.

THE SEARCH FOR MEANING

The stated focus of the California Literature Project that 1986 UCLA summer was "the search for meaning." It was a summer of myth and mythic searches: Anaya's *Bless Me Ultima* (1972), *Ulysses* (1961), Joseph Campbell. As I look at the journal I kept that summer I see that we were immersed in a "student-centered" reading of literature and that we teachers were the students. We teachers/learners were heterogeneously grouped (meaning that we were mixed together across grade levels, K–12). Imagine teachers of kindergarten and teachers of college prep high school English reading, writing, and making meaning together of James Joyce's *Ulysses*.

As we read together in groups, playing with text and making our own meanings, I began to experience, then to actively reflect on the idea of letting go of being responsible for my students' learning. I realized that I could not, by being the giver of knowledge, ensure that my high school students were learning anything. I was beginning to understand from reflecting on my own reading experiences how I was learning from the experience of both individual and collaborative meaning-making. I was beginning in retrospect.

I was assimilating my experiences into my existing concept of the role of English teacher: I was coming to know myself as a teacher who is a reader with personal authority, who is a learner with personal authority. This was due, for the most part, to the CLP expectation, project vision, and philosophy that honored and valued who teachers are. Exploring literature and responding to texts opened up my thinking about what reading and learning are like: They begin with lived-through experiences. This wasn't what I had experienced, been taught, and learned that good English teaching was. But the experiences struck familiar chords connected with the successful classroom research projects I'd developed. I began to redefine myself by questioning the beliefs I was holding about my profession: What is the subject English and what is teaching English? I began to question what we were learning and was concerned about such issues as, How do we teach grammar? What about spelling? What about vocabulary? Even though I wanted to stop isolating skills, I was afraid to do so. I was torn between acting on my new sense of what learning and teaching English is, and what the English Department and my students would think of my untraditional, un-common-sense

(Mayher, 1990) teaching. So there it was again: fear. This time I chose to change in spite of fear. Why? Experiences were more powerful than the fear.

The structure of that summer was not accidental: We began with the teacher as learner, then moved to the teacher as reader, as writer, and as professional/researcher, reminiscent of James Moffett's *Teaching the Universe of Discourse* (1968) structures. We experienced reading, living in and with texts, fiction, poetry, research, theory, the whole gamut. The reading experiences ranged from interviewing characters and framing prereading activities to begin with personal experiences, to dramatizing and jigsawing sections of theoretical or critical articles as well as fiction such as James Joyce's *Ulysses* (1961). For a while I was able to forget that I was a teacher and I tried them all, laughed a lot at myself, talked seriously with my new teaching friends, and was willing to see what happened. I forgot that I was a teacher and became immersed in learning.

This seems critical to think about in terms of teacher education. I was able to recognize myself, my ways of teaching, and put aside these perceptions of the "English" teacher and my notion of what is good English teaching, what the good English teacher is and does, to have some fun learning, to be a reader, to be a writer. I gave myself permission to generate and make meaning because the overall tone and theme at the project was that of searching for meaning, and I literally took this search for meaning to heart. Many teachers there that summer were not as happy as I with what we were experiencing, with the apparent lack of structure and direction.

One day while we were hiking across campus to class I said to my friend Judy as I found myself responding to those who were complaining about the lack of focus at the institute, "I love it! We get to make our own meaning of it all." I felt free to be, unconstrained by anything other than showing up and doing what was in front of us that day and learning from it. There was no right or wrong answer. We were untracked and there were no grades. What a gift! So many teachers there were utterly frustrated and angry with the chaos they were experiencing. Many teachers wanted concrete answers to teaching problems. Many saw these experiences only as new lesson plans and ideas that they could insert into their teaching program rather than an experience in changing pedagogy. I found the experience challenging and exhilarating. As I reflect in retrospect, I can see that not only was I changing pedagogy, I was changing my way of being.

I found that as a reader I was enjoying very difficult texts like *Ulysses* because we were given permission to make our own meaning. That didn't mean that "anything went," but that we could work with our own responses to the text and share them to continue to grow in our sense of the meaning of the text. We were not even expected to read the whole epic. What a concept—we could read and enjoy and wrestle with making sense of a really difficult text and that we didn't have to know it all. Following the spirit of Rosen-blatt's transactional literary theory, we responded personally to texts and built understandings and interpretations in reading communities.

We were also asked to reflect on our experiences. I don't recall ever con-sciously reflecting on my learning in educational settings before. I'd reflected on my life in my therapist's office, and around 1980 I'd begun to write reflec-tive autobiography for self-understanding, but never had I used reflection in my professional life. I would have to say that reflecting and reflection were among the most influential of my experiences that summer. I see myself in those reflections and reflective moments as a teacher in transition.

7/24/86

1. Tentative Problem: First, I must tie up loose ends, questions I've not been convinced have answers yet just based on modeling and pedagogy. The major area would be convincing myself that the litera-ture based curriculum can integrate all skills—specifically grammar con-cerns me. Casting away a grammar text is like casting away a security blanket.

Once I've experienced using the generative approach and answered that question (this will take at least a semester) I can feel more confi-dence in this approach.

2. Directed Reading—Questions: Preparing questions was diffi-cult, but also worked to reflect comprehension of the text. Many ques-tions were similar—a good thing! Meaning can be derived from asking questions based on our personal experiences but connected to the text. I enjoyed the activity. I enjoyed the activity and will use this technique in my classroom.

Directed reading asks the reader to make meaning of text (a form of comprehension) in order to read it aloud. We were making notes in the text—how to say this? who said this? Again—an excellent tool to ar-rive at meaning from experience.

Our study of literature that summer culminated in something called "As-signment to Assessment," the precursor to the integrated assessment evi-denced in the on-again, off-again (depending on who is governor) CAP (Cali-fornia Assessment Program) and framed on the writing theory of Charles Cooper of the University of California, San Diego, merged with Rosenblatt's theory of aesthetic and efferent reading (1978). The integrated CAP assess-ment more fully represented Rosenblatt's theory of literary education, testing aesthetic reading abilities of California readers, K–12. How ironic! We think that we can actually test "aesthetic" response to literature. I think not! For me an aesthetic response is the personal, the intellectual, the human, the very response of the soul. No test can approach this. It is in how we learn to live our lives as a result of the experience and of our reflections, our search for self-understanding, and the understanding beyond self in relationship to others. This is virtually untestable except in the very climate and nature of the universe in which we live. After assaults by conservative forces, CAP no longer exists as a California statewide test. This was California's attempt to match assessment to pedagogy, to truly assess the progress of reading and responding to literature in collaborative settings.

During that UCLA summer with the CLP we began the assignment to assessment phase by writing what we wanted to in response to *Ulysses*. Then we collaborated with each other in peer response, a painful experience for some of us. This experience was painful because many teachers took the traditional, common-sense teacher stance they had been taking in teaching their students: that is, they brutalized the text with razor-sharp red pencils, fixing and repairing the English rather than responding to the writer to collaborate and to help each other make meaning. My peer coach and I both apologized profusely to each other before we could find the courage to give our texts to each other to read and respond to. This experience seeded an ongoing personal and professional quest to improve my ways of reading and responding to my students' texts.

The two of us, adult, professional English teachers, were so insecure about our own writing that we had to spend time apologizing before we could let go of our work. My partner and I worked out our shared fears, but many others did not. She had been a fellow in the Bay Area Writing Project and understood writing and teacher response far better than I. I don't recall that we addressed this problem of teaching to create the "perfect" text through teachers' editing of errors in any broad way that summer in our group sessions, or that we processed the feelings of fear and pain several had experienced. I'd suggest that we missed an opportunity to look at how response affects writers and learning. I do try to work with this issue in my own classes now. I continue to reflect on my responses to texts and writers to let me know if my responses are helpful, what works and what doesn't. It is more transactional these days. The process of responding will never be done, for this is a dynamic process and each writer is unique. I am, however, developing some basic principles to work with, and my theory of languaging is at the root. Responding has much more to do with listening deeply to the writer and the text.

In the last week of the CLP we moved from experiencing literature to planning for our classrooms when we returned to them in the fall. I set about trying the generative reading approach to teaching literature we had read and discussed, and I planned two one-page plans: "Ways into Oedipus," and a reader's theater experience reading *The Odyssey*.

In the tentative plan I developed for *The Odyssey* (Fitzgerald, 1963) I wrote the following preface:

> All our lives are an odyssey—we journey, we grow wiser ourselves. I've always loved teaching *The Odyssey*. My seniors begin their quest for meaning each year with *The Odyssey*. My challenge is to create a unit pulling together as much as I feel comfortable with from the CLP to field test generative learning and collaborative learning. This unit will be refocused, "revisioned" to connect the text's meaning to their life experiences and intratextual meanings.

I knew that I couldn't change everything all at once, so I made simple changes and I took back with me, most importantly, a more positive attitude toward education, toward teaching, toward myself. I gave myself permission to make the changes I felt comfortable with and saw myself "field-testing," which meant that I was risking and I could make mistakes. I was beginning to research my own teaching and learning. I was certainly rethinking my teaching. Most importantly, I was seeing my students in a very different and critically new light: as readers, as writers, as learners, not just as students who had to learn to read and to write correctly.

It is important to reflect on our learning. It is important to reflect on our learning at many junctures in the processes we experience. Reflection needs to be a daily habit of learning. And reflection is something we need to do with greater and greater distance as our learning progresses. That is, we need to do many types of reflection in our lives and in our classrooms with our students: daily, perhaps at the end of a week, the month, midterm, and as a culminating experience when our studies end.

Beginning to reflect on my experiences as a reader, a teacher, and a learner that summer contributed to my ability to make conscious changes in my teaching. Another reflective entry that I wrote in my journal that summer is both surprising and exciting for me to see again. The questions reflect an important process of self-assessment and self-understanding, beginning in retrospect. I hope that you will take some time to respond to and reflect on your own answers to these questions:

> Why did you become a teacher?
> How did you become a teacher?
> Where are you?
> I love people and literature and I respect teachers. When I was a

child I role-played teacher. I taught my teddy bear, my cat Smokey and my dolls. I've always loved to read, to think, to share ideas. I don't remember consciously making the choice. I just remember one idea leading to another.

My training to become a teacher wasn't really how I became a teacher. I'm still working on becoming a teacher. I've learned more from watching other teachers; strangely enough a college economics professor (I was briefly enrolled in an M.B.A. program in 1984) taught me the greatest lesson—trust and care for students. I've become a teacher by listening to my students, by risking, by standing alone for the important things and showing my students how to do that by my example.

Right now I'm returning to teaching and have just completed a year of great reward after having left the profession for the last four years. I have a great sense of *possibility*.

Incredible! What happened between 1980 and 1986 that fostered such a positive sense of myself? I had not written using the language of failure, fear, and pain. Instead, I was writing with the language of joy, of possibility, of a new sense of self and teaching. I don't like to talk about this stuff, but if this autobiography means anything, I must be honest with myself. During that period I had begun to address my life and my fears by doing a tremendous amount of painful self-searching for self-knowledge in psychotherapy, primarily because I felt that the way I was living my life connected somehow to my having breast cancer.

I had had a nervous breakdown (at the time I said I had just crashed and burned) when I left teaching in 1980. The explosions in the lockers outside my classroom had proven to be my Humpty Dumpty's great fall. I went into therapy to deal with that breakdown in 1980 and here I was again, six years later, back in therapy.

I didn't want to (and still don't), I didn't like to (and still don't), but I had been telling my painful childhood stories and had been exploring my problem with relationships. I had to face the pain of the past and let go of it. I needed to face the anger I had felt but suppressed and repressed for many years and begin the process of healing. But I felt that I was betraying the people I loved and whom I thought loved me. Now I understand that I was betraying only one person: myself. Somehow during this period I had found the courage to do this: It emerged out of critical self-awareness and a desire to work on myself to lead a healthy life.

I remember that while I was recapturing these childhood stories I began to write children's stories and send them out to be published. The stories were about fearful children, a lost dog, a homeless, injured goose, a little boy going to kindergarten (interesting choice of sex) who is odd and bright. All the adults in the stories are loving, helpful and kind, understanding and nurturing.

SIMPLE, SMALL CHANGES

When I returned to my high school English classroom that fall of 1986 I planned small changes. I was beginning to recognize that embedded in one seemingly simple plan, "Ways into Oedipus," I had planned many learning experiences: reading, writing, talking to learn, social processes, and more. I had discovered not simply a strategy or an activity, but a process that might help readers read, especially if they could become conscious of what we were doing and why. That is, I tried to introduce ways of working to begin to read a text, for example, and then to help my students know that this is a practice of good readers. To help readers think about the problems Oedipus faced, I asked students to write about a time they had an experience trying to do the right thing yet ended up doing exactly what they were trying to avoid. Though they were still sitting in rows (I would experiment with small groups later), they were writing about their personal experiences, their own stories similar to one of the dilemmas of the tragic Greek hero Oedipus.

I felt that calling up our own personal experiences helped us as readers to read a text, a text I, for years, had not felt successful working with. You might recall that *Oedipus* was the same text I had struggled to teach to that group of frustrated and unhappy seniors my first year of teaching.

Even though the lesson I "planned" was on *Oedipus*, I ended up beginning the year teaching *The Odyssey*, probably because I'd always loved it. I had worked with James Joyce's *Ulysses* at UCLA, which had given me new understandings of the *Odyssey*, and I had reacquired a joyous sense of reading something tough, and a feeling that it was okay not to have all the answers or the "meaning." I began to understand how my teenaged readers felt. It could have been an unconscious desire to finally let go of the past by teaching a text I loved in a way that I had found personally and intellectually pleasurable. As I reflect on this now, I believe that I chose *The Odyssey* because of the story, the story of family, of homecoming, of growing up, of relationships—lost, wandering father, young son coming into manhood, the woman's role at home. Odysseus, Telemachus, Penelope. Story. The power of story!

I began teaching *The Odyssey* by having my classes read and talk about the text, by keeping dialectical (double-entry, note-taking/note-making) journals on the text, and by working out reader's theater presentations/readings of Homer's epic.

I had learned the dialectical journal one evening at UCLA when several of

us met in the living room of my apartment and worked with this way of responding to the Kate Chopin short story "The Story of an Hour." When I
returned to teaching that fall, I asked my junior English students, both regular classes and college prep classes, to keep a dialectical journal of their reading of that same story. For this reading experience they worked in groups to
share their responses to the story. The groups were to come to a consensus
on what they wanted to say about the story in two sentences and write their
ideas using felt-tip pens on three-by-five-foot pieces of butcher paper. We
posted those statements around the room and then shared those ideas together. I took great pleasure in seeing my students as authors of their own
ideas and meanings. I loved looking at my students' ideas and thoughts and
responses covering the walls of our classroom.

I introduced the dialectical journal (DJ) to my seniors as well. In fact, I
introduced DJs to all my classes regardless of the tracking. Though I had
experienced the power of reading and making-meaning during the UCLA summer, I found myself incredulous at my students' meaning-making in their dialectical journals. The following sample dialectical journal excerpts (which
they brought to class daily to read together, question, and explore in small
groups) in response to assigned readings in mythology show the power of
adolescent readers responding with their own questions and personal understandings of text:

Note-Taking	*Note-Making*
"The giant rabbit needed only one speck of mud. He worked with it until he made it into mountains, continents, and— finally—the whole world." (p. 131)	Who is the giant rabbit? God? Why does "one Speck of mud" sound similar to Adam's rib? Is it supposed to? Where are all the people? Are the animals sup- posed to represent us? Is that representation trying to say something? . . .
Light, spiritual, masculine forces rose to the heavens	Why is it that man is believed to be the light of spiritual be- ings? Are they better than women?
What does woman want? (Freud)	That is the question that even Freud can't answer.

Before the Literature Project I had focused on myself and my failures in
the classroom, but after that summer I began to look at what was happening
to my students while we were trying these "new" meaning-making activities.

Eventually, after I read Nancie Atwell's *In the Middle* (1987), I worked collaboratively with students to reflect on and evaluate their learning. I do hope that those experiences reading literature in that classroom that first year I was experimenting with changes helped them to begin to realize their personal lives in their intellectual pursuits.

What I can sense from that UCLA summer experience and from what I began to change in my own classroom is that my teaching began to change because I had had experiences reading literature, living experiences with literature in which I was a reader and a writer who was a teacher. When I was reading that summer I wasn't conscious of being a teacher who was an English major, who had an M.A. in English. I was becoming a reader immersed in the experience of reading: my private personal love of reading was merging with the public life I had led as the "objective," intellectual academic reader. I loved reading and my new sense of what reading could be like in English classrooms.

What I had experienced and reflected on as a reader in the California Literature Project provided the environment and support for me to make changes in my teaching. I was going to have continued connection and support for implementing what I had learned during the next two years. I was so pleased that the CLP philosophy was state-supported: I wasn't alone in A–7 at Alhambra High School anymore. I could be the odd woman in the English Department, but there were 200 other odd people in the state, men and women, who shared a common vision.

From 1986 to 1988 my cadre of CLP colleagues on the North Coast met monthly in Monterey, California, to discuss our classroom experiences with literature and with the changes we were trying. I was the first teacher to experience the CLP in my school district, and since no other English teacher in my school was using this new English Language Arts Framework and Standards, which focused on student-centered teaching and learning, this two-year follow-up period was invaluable in supporting the changes I was sometimes successfully, sometimes unsuccessfully making.

I used the unsuccessful experiences to grow from rather than seeing them or me as a failure. This was a major shift for me: from seeing only failure in my teaching to seeing teaching and learning as growth and process and progress. Teaching and learning in my English practice were becoming processes and not simply the learning of and then insertion of a new strategy or activity. In our follow-up groups we CLP colleagues shared our problems with student-centered meaning-making and learned from each other. This collegial collaboration is not something I had had nor was experiencing in my own English Department, nor had I experienced it in my English teacher preparation and education. It is something we in the profession can benefit from. It would be a powerful "reform" if schools would create something like a practicum for ongoing professional growth which could encourage teachers to read, plan, problem solve, and tell each other stories and collaborate on their educational lives.

When I first began teaching this student-centered, meaning-based literature curriculum, my students saw these experiences with literature as "fun" and seemed to think that if learning is "fun" it can't be learning. They probably remembered their own experiences in English classrooms and that was the expectation they brought. They probably bought into the classroom the stereotype and myth (the one I brought into the profession) that English is supposed to be a tough, academic subject and that teachers are the knowers. Students thought there was a "hidden meaning" in the text and they felt that if they were able to find such "hidden meanings," the class must not be English. Even though most students detested studying grammar, spelling, punctuation, and vocabulary, they viewed these isolated skills as the norm for a good English class. I began to talk with my classes about why we were doing what we were doing.

I began to ask them to reflect not just on their sense of the text, but also on their sense of what was going on with their learning and how they might use what they were learning. I did not attempt to lecture or convince them of anything. What a relief! I did share my knowledge of an author, of the text, when it seemed appropriate and useful to their meaning-making. I trusted the process. Why? Because I had experienced what I was asking them to do (and I continued to do along with them what I was asking them to do), and I knew in deeply felt ways the power of such learning.

My first experiences reading Rosenblatt began with the California Literature Project in 1986, yet I did not read a text written by Rosenblatt. Instead, I experienced one enactment of Louise Rosenblatt's transactional literary theory. In a sense my academic pursuit of Louise Rosenblatt the person who was also a woman, the theorist, evolved from the great joy I had experienced reading that summer in which the "academic" became redefined through experience. I simply wanted to know more about her and reader response. I was curious. One experience led into another.

CHAPTER 7

Reading Rosenblatt

The reading of a text is an event occurring at a particular time in a particular environment at a particular moment in the life history of the reader.
—Rosenblatt, 1978, p. 20

What role does reading theory play in the teaching of high school English? In the life of the English teacher? In 1988, after two years of experience teaching my high school English classes working with the California English Language Arts Standards and Framework, I became a teacher-leader in the California Literature Project and for the first time read the text of Louise Rosenblatt's theory while preparing for the 1988 summer institute being held at Sonoma State University. I first "read" Rosenblatt, that is, literally opened up her book *Literature as Exploration*, at the statewide leadership seminars held in Redondo Beach and Sacramento during the spring of 1988. My notes and journals reveal that we also read Susanne K. Langer's *Philosophy in a New Key: A Study in the Symbolism of Reason, Rite, and Art* (1942) and the Biblical story of Ruth. Interesting, I'd say, that these texts are by or about women, yet not specifically feminist—quite unlike my undergraduate reading experiences as a preservice English teacher and English major.

My first reading of *Literature as Exploration* was uneventful. In fact, my notes for the training workshop, April 18, 1988, on Chapter 2 (the only assigned reading) and taken on Mary Barr's introductory speech to the seminar, are sketchy: "Rosenblatt-Basis," "live circuit," "TRANSACTIONS-chains," and "Power of Reader [*sic*], Personal [*sic*] experience to text." Barr talked to us about Rosenblatt's theory as the basis for the literary experience and the project, and we were told several times, according to my journal, that we would be reading Rosenblatt at the summer institutes.

I discovered that rather than reading Rosenblatt, reading Chapter 2 of Susanne K. Langer's *Philosophy in a New Key* (1942) had made the most profound impact on my thinking that spring and summer, much more than the briefing on Rosenblatt's transactional theory as our frame.

The reading assignment we were given as homework one night was to read the Langer text: "quickly skim the whole text (my roommate and I read the table of contents aloud together and talked about what this text could be about), read Chapter 2 quickly, then select three quotations that "intrigue you, puzzle you, stimulate you." We couldn't believe the simplicity of the assignment. This simplicity was something with which many of us at first had difficulty and even disdained. As time progressed and we reflected on our reading experiences as adults and teachers and learners, the notion of keeping things simple became much more powerful. We did not know about Susanne K. Langer, that her philosophical text is dense and difficult. The simpler the assignment, the better.

My notes show that I chose several quotations from Langer's text to think about. The ones I checked, which I chose to share in our workshop the next day, are listed below as I entered them in my journal that night:

"Symbolization is pre-rationative, but not pre-rational." p. 42
"Freud. Symbolization is both an end and an instrument." p. 51
"Speech is the readiest active transformation of experience." p. 44

After sharing in our small groups the three quotations we had each selected, we were asked to write about an understanding we then had of what we'd read. I expressed my understanding of Susanne K. Langer with the phrase "symbolic transformation":

Symbolic transformation is about the idea that man and woman have a basic need in addition to realistic needs of behavior. That need is to transform the vocal into verbal communication in order to draw meaning from the experience. She feels the biogenetic theory that man and woman are higher forms of the basic amoebae is lacking—that in addition what gives us power is both a blessing and a curse—by transforming a sign into a symbol we/it fills a need to understand the experience of language. "Symbolization is both an end and an instrument."

The next day we worked in small groups to give meanings to a poem we had chosen from those given to us. My group chose the poem "My Mother Pieced Quilts" (Acosta, 1975/1979). We were not asked to interpret the poem or work out a meaning. We were asked to read the poem aloud to the group. Another simple action. What happened for me, as I can see in my journal reflections written at the time, is that what I'd been reading and wondering about in Langer's philosophy was something that I was also thinking about in terms of meaning and poetry. I include the poem for you here first so you can follow my response titled *Quick write*, which follows the poem:

"My Mother Pieced Quilts"
Teresa Palomo Acosta

they were just meant as covers
in winters
as weapons
against pounding january winds
but it was just that every morning I awoke to these
october ripened canvases
passes my hand across their cloth faces
and began to wonder how you pieced
all these together
these strips of gentle communion cotton and flannel nightgowns
wedding organdies
dime store velvets
how you shaped patterns square and oblong and round
positioned
balanced
then cemented them
with your thread
a steel needle
a thimble
how the thread darted in and out
galloping along the frayed edges, tucking them in
as you did us at night
oh how you stretched and turned and re-arranged
your michigan spring faded curtain pieces
my father's sante fe work shirt
the summer denims, the tweeds of fall
in the evening you sat at your canvas
—our cracked linoleum floor the drawing board
me lounging on your arm
and you staking out the plan:
whether to put the lilac purple of easter against the red
        plaid of winter-going-
into-spring
whether to mix a yellow with blue and white and paint the
corpus christi noon when my father held your hand
whether to shape a five-point star from the
somber black silk you wore to grandmother's funeral
you were the river current

carrying the roaring notes
forming them into pictures of a little boy reclining
a swallow flying
you were the caravan master at the ring
driving your threaded needle artillery across the mosaic
        cloth bridges
delivering yourself in separate testimonies
oh mother you plunged me sobbing and laughing
into our past
into the river crossing at five
into the spinach fields
into the painview cotton rows
into tuberculosis wards
into braids and muslin dresses
sewn hard and taut to withstand the thrashings of
        twenty-five years
stretched out they lay
armed/ready/shouting/celebrating
knotted with love
the quilts sing on

Quick write *(written after hearing several groups read poetry aloud)*
—What I learned—

We tried to make meaning of the poem to communicate our sense of it.
I learned that voices and the way they are used are a path to meaning. I
heard the same poem three times and wondered about the meaning of
"communion cotton and flannel." The inflection used, rhythm used,
and sound/tone are part of the meaning—cannot be separated. . . . We
offered a more serious reading—an epiphany as it were, for, after all,
"they were just meant as covers."

The process of reflecting privately and collaboratively about hearing different readings of the same poem helped me to be aware of the reading and
writing of meaning connected to sound. Reading poetry aloud. I began to
explore and play with the notion of "symbolic transformations" and how
sound plays an important role in our search for meanings.

After my experience reading about and creating symbolic transformations with other teachers, the next year my junior English classes worked on
making symbolic transformations, both during and after reading texts, as a
way of reading and meaning-making. For example, I had my regular junior

English classes (the Y's, and yes, we were still in full-blown tracking) read the full text of Martin Luther King's "I Have a Dream" speech using a combination of reader's theater strategies and symbolic transformation experiences.

Readers worked in small groups to draw pictures (something I now termed symbolic transformations of text) of one or two paragraphs, transforming King's eloquent, metaphorically rich text, working out meaning through images, capturing what were for them the most powerful, meaningful, provocative lines. Each group was also directed to help other members practice reading the text aloud (each member had a responsibility to read some of the text), and finally it was to all come together in a shared reading, a symbolically transforming experience for us all. Each group read aloud its assigned section of the speech (we listened to the readings in the order King delivered his speech) while we displayed around the room all the drawings that had been done on three-by-five-feet sections of butcher paper. Each group then shared with the class how and why they drew what they drew, the meanings they were making, and the questions they still had about the text.

I was able to continue to make these kinds of changes in my classroom practices because I was reflecting on and assimilating my experiences reading while making my own symbolic transformations—into my teaching. I was working toward helping my students become their own readers, hearing their own voices and making their own meaning of texts.

After the statewide training sessions we did read a selection from Rosenblatt's *Literature as Exploration* (1983) that summer at the Sonoma State University regional institute: Chapter 3, "The Setting for Spontaneity." I responded to the text by having an interior dialogue with Rosenblatt while writing in my journal. I summed up my sense of her text by saying, "Rosenblatt deals with the idea of personal experience as critical to what readers seek in literature," but I noted that she "still uses the phrase 'teach literature'" (1983, p. 59).

In a summary note, after reading 12 pages or so of Chapter 3, I restated Rosenblatt's notion that the "teachers' role is to enable primary personal response to literature and to initiate a process by which students enlarge and clarify response to the work." Then I began to wonder about Rosenblatt's suggestion that this initiates a process by which students enlarge. I asked of her text, "Why enlarge—is it a more sophisticated interpretation and appreciation?"

Then, I asked myself (and Rosenblatt), "Is it that the end is still analysis but the means is by beginning with the student's personal response rather than the teacher's personal, intellectual, academic response?" I was questioning what Rosenblatt's stance might be, what the aim of teaching literature this way might be. I wondered about her use of the word "keener" (1983, p. 77). "What is a 'keener' and more adequate perception of all the text offers?"

I also asked, "So, are *critical powers* the goal? and do readers want to enlarge 'critical powers' or is that a system-directed goal?"

I was questioning what seemed to be Rosenblatt's valuing of the reader's personal response to literature, and I was confused by what I sensed was a tension/dichotomy. I thought that I had found a contradiction in her theory of reading literature: that is, readers create a "sound vision" of the text (1983, p. 79) but there are "misinterpretations." The "key" question (I labeled it so in my notebook) I was asking of Rosenblatt's theory was, "If the text spawns an intense personal response which is not supported by the text, how is that an invalid response? It may be an invalid interpretation of text, but not an invalid response."

I also made a note to myself to read I. A. Richards's *Practical Criticism* (1929), since Rosenblatt referred to his study of college readers and the problems of their literary reading abilities in the first edition of *Literature as Exploration* (1938), which was written in response to and in consultation with Richards's research findings.

One idea continued to lead to another idea, another question, another idea. The learning was dynamic and the structure it took was of its own creation out of my experiences and need to know. Rather than it being external, I would describe what was happening as a learning that is internal and from deep inside both the heart and the mind. As I reflect on this I'd have to say that I felt free to be who I was at that moment in time in my teaching, my reading, and my life. So my experience and perceptions of the experiences in this learning environment were encouraged by the atmosphere and curricula of openness. And I wanted to know more. Isn't this what we hope education will become for our own students? That they will be so intellectually and personally invigorated in our classes that they will become lifelong learners? The California Literature Project and the magic I experienced reading that summer led me further along in my academic life and eventually into a doctoral program.

Something of major importance was continuing in my professional life, my professional reading life. Two years later, in the spring of 1990, when I was taking an educational research class at St. Mary's College in Moraga, California, I did read I. A. Richards's study, *Practical Criticism* (1929), when I launched a research project that was a historical study of reader response. I began that study with I. A. Richards. The reason I wanted to do that study was to locate Louise Rosenblatt in her historical context, in the context of reader response theory and criticism. Another more important question I had was, Where were these people and these readings in my preservice education? Why didn't I know about reader response and transactional reading theory if it had been around since 1938?

The St. Mary's historical study of reader response came after I had done some preliminary research for a project during the NYU Oxford summer abroad (the first summer of my doctoral study), a project I termed "Notes for a Candidacy Paper." I thought that Louise Rosenblatt may have been largely ignored because she was a woman, Jewish, and American. I had also been reading Terry Eagleton's book *Literary Theory: An Introduction* (1983). I had made a note that the field of literary theory had ignored the female theorist I was researching. I also noted that I did not find any other female theorist in the mainstream. That discovery annoyed and dismayed me.

THE SONOMA SUMMER, 1988

The experience I had during the summer as a teacher-leader at Sonoma State University was incredible for two reasons. First, our director, Dr. Jean D., worked with the five teacher-leaders as peers and colleagues. Jean's leadership, support, honesty with, and trust of us was the first time I had experienced a leader who worked with teachers in such a mutual, reciprocal, and collaborative way. She led by example, not by some external hierarchical authority. Jean listened and encouraged us to risk.

Both the UCLA and the Sonoma institutes ended with the CLP integration of reading and writing with literature as the base and called "Assignment to Assessment." As our summer institute at Sonoma was progressing, we teacher-leaders had been meeting daily with our leader, Jean, to talk about our daily experiences and to plan the next day's experiences (something I had never experienced in all my years of teaching high school English). When we met to plan for "Assignment to Assessment," we felt frustrated with the rigidity of the particular genre that the thing required. We discussed the possibility of changing the assignment from not just the particular type of writing mandated but from a particular genre period. We wanted to encourage people to write whatever they needed to write in whatever way they needed to write it. Jean, bless her, said, "Let's do it." And we did. We were so proud of our decision that we co-authored a plan sheet detailing how we had maintained the spirit of the writing process while opening up the possibilities of response, naming our project "The Sonoma Model." The decision to transform the statewide core curriculum in this way, to make it our own and to open it up, was powerful for each of us teacher-leaders and for the teachers we were working with. The pieces that teachers wrote, given the freedom to pursue their own interests in relationship to the text we had assigned as a core (a text in the curriculum that is required of all, regardless of ability or grade level), Jerome Lawrence and Robert Lee's *The Night Thoreau Spent in Jail* (1970) was powerful, often personal, and academic. It is from this experience that I have come to have a better idea of what "negotiating the curriculum" might mean.

You might reach back in your memories, your experiences, to think about what negotiating the curriculum means to you in your personal reading life, writing life, teaching life, life. What happened? How did it work?

Following UCLA and before Sonoma, between 1986 and 1988, I was not teaching my English classes in any way consciously connecting Louise Rosenblatt's transitional theory with my pedagogical changes. When I finally did read the theory, after two years of living in it as a way of reading literature, reading Rosenblatt gave me a theory with which to discourse, to have a conversation, to think about teaching literature, and to question the aims of teaching literature. I did consciously plan reading experiences for my classes that would explore the connections between their lives and what they were reading. Both I and my students often used the phrase, "As a reader responding . . ."

One Friday in late fall, we were completing Homer's *The Odyssey* on homecoming day. I asked my seniors to brainstorm as many ideas as they could to compare the homecoming celebration the school was experiencing that week with Odysseus, Telemachus, and Penelope's journey home. We had a wonderful discussion about the text, and since this was their last year at our school, their feelings were high. We had an incredible discussion in which these young people made amazing connections between the events of school, their lives, and the homecoming Odysseus and Telemachus experienced.

By this time I had begun to reflect on my teaching and my students' learning much more, and I found myself asking (still in conversation with Louise Rosenblatt's theory), What was the goal of such a discussion? Valid textual analysis? Valid textual interpretation? Hardly, if valid textual interpretation means that we were intent on getting a meaning validated in the text, as Rosenblatt had suggested. What I think we did was a valid textual interpretation in the sense that we talked about the text truthfully for our lives in relationship to the lives we'd experienced reading *The Odyssey*, and we moved beyond the text in our thinking about revenge, coming home, growing up, faithfulness, and reconciliation.

In the same fall 1988, Rosenblatt came west, to Long Beach, California, from her home in Princeton, New Jersey, to address the leadership academy sponsored by the California Literature Project. This academy brought together about 200 CLP cadre members from 1985 to 1988. At this academy Rosenblatt delivered the body of a "technical" paper she had recently written called *Writing and Reading: The Transactional Theory* (1988). After her paper was delivered to our academy, we went off to work in groups to symbolically represent (Langer still lived in our experiences) in some way our sense of what Rosenblatt had said. My group came up with a poem we titled "Portrait of a Lecture as a Young Poem." Cadre colleague Ann Smith and I read our group-constructed response in front of the full academy.

"Portrait of a Lecture as Young Poem"

Efferent
Yield. Yield. Yield.
And that again is another speech.
I haven't time for the reminiscences.
    (She's the perfect grandmother).
50+ what? I'm not going to tell you.
I don't object to scholarship—
    sometimes I do.
Again, subversive.
Response is not the end, it's the
beginning.
Again, subversive.
I really read William James.
At ten months—give him a cat.
Smoooth [*sic*].
Fishing in the stream of consciousness.
Some interpretations are more acceptable
    than others.
Again, subversive.
Aesthetic experience—the elegant solution.
Heaven help the fate of literature if
    it's only used to teach basic skills.
We live through the making of meaning.
Does it have a white stripe?
What color is the horse?
Who cares?
Again, subversive.
The observer is part of his own observation.
Re: Hirsch—VICTIM OF HIS OWN BOOK
We are really—
Real readers in imaginary gardens.
Again, subversive.

I remember the feeling of shared experience I felt when we read this poem to that audience, for we all had listened to Rosenblatt's remarks, a core experience. We'd made meaning and communicated our sense of Rosenblatt's talk using her words and our contexts. In Susanne K. Langer's sense, we had "symbolically transformed" the text of Louise Rosenblatt. That line we used, "Real readers in imaginary gardens," was part Rosenblatt and part our group, merged in the languaging of our sense of reading with Rosenblatt's. Rosenblatt seemed overwhelmed by the responses teachers shared with her that day.

In 1988 I was enjoying teaching my English classes, but I was frustrated with my principal and my department. As a mentor teacher for the district I was having more success implementing the California English Language Arts Frameworks and Standards in the school district working with K–8 teachers than I was working with "new" concepts in my own department. I was dangerously near burnout again.

In the spring of 1988 I found myself teaching high school English, serving as English Department chairperson, and working as a mentor teacher leading the District's model curriculum standards and English language arts framework implementation. I was also serving on the Contra Costa County English Language Arts implementation committee, and in my not so spare time, working as a CLP consultant facilitating workshops in Oakland, San Francisco, and Alameda counties. The journals for this period of my teaching and learning life reflect a woman who was overworking herself again. This is part of the profession we don't hear about or address in teacher education or preservice education. Teachers' lives are sucked dry to the very marrow if we let it happen to us. Stop reading this right now and take a quick inventory of your professional life. Write it all down, jot it down. What are your major and minor responsibilities as a teacher? Don't forget to list the emotional and psychological ones in addition to the actuality of the day—the life lived is an equally critical component. Once you have this inventory, select one of two that you can change. Not easy, I'd guess. Yet we take ourselves to the edge of burnout over and over because we "can't face ourselves honestly." This was in part much of my problem.

It was a struggle to keep a balanced life. Then my friend Jayne died of breast cancer in April. We had become good friends because of my own fight with breast cancer three years earlier. Jayne had been my inspiration: while she lived, I believed that we women with breast cancer survive. I remember being angry with her for leaving me, for reminding me that I could die from cancer. I saw my own death in hers. I remember feeling pain, anger, and fear. Another moment of epiphany. I decided I needed to change my life, both personally and professionally. This fear and anger needed to be turned into action. I began to again reflect on what was happening in my life, both personally and professionally. I began to transform fear and anger into action, to make changes.

It was spring and again, as I had had to do three years earlier, I had to confront the very real possibility of my own death. I had been overmedicating, mixing prescription antidepressants and alcohol. I had to finally address the unmanageability of my life when I drank alcohol on a daily basis. I did not drink before school, I did not drink during school, but I did drink every day when I arrived home. I was tired, I had worked hard. I deserved it. However, I clearly read that one doesn't drink and take antidepressants at the same time, and I thought that I could. And I did so. I realized that I was killing myself in another way.

Not only did I want to live, but I wanted to live a better life, a more sober life. I began exploring ways to change my professional life, entertaining the idea of pursuing a Ph.D. in psychology. I also began to accept my own spiritual emptiness and to seek another personal recovery, the recovery of my self. I had sought solace for the unmanageability I was experiencing, numbing it away with alcohol. I made a decision to change that and began group therapy for a sober life, a life that would eventually restore to me some degree of peace that I had always been searching for. Much of the fear that I experienced began to disappear. My emotional life was finally turning the corner.

I had been sober for one year when I began a 12-step program for recovering alcoholics, where I began to experience, practice, and read the simple ideas of a spiritual life based on personal honesty and responsibility, faith, love, and tolerance. How many of you in the educational life have experienced anything in your teacher education or English major curriculum that addressed the heart and soul of the teacher, the reader, the writer? Few, if any, I'd guess.

During these personal and professional crises I turned to reading for solace, for help, for understanding. As I did in my childhood and in my adolescence, I turned to reading when my life was unbearable. This time, though, I was reading as if my life depended on it. During a three-month period I read so many books I'm astonished by the list. I feared death so much that in my personal reading I was reading to save my life: *Feel the Fear and Do It Anyway* (Jeffers, 1987) and *Love Is Letting Go of Fear* (Jamplonsky, 1988) as well as many "New Age" texts such as Herbert B. Puryear's *The Edgar Cayce Primer* (1982) and *The Course in Miracles* (Singh, 1986). Reading a good book always salves my soul. What do you read personally to salve your soul? How do we encourage our students to read to "salve" their souls? Though rhetorical questions, they are real questions we need to address in education, particularly English education.

During the same time period my professional teacher reading included rereading sections of *Literature as Exploration* (1983) and *Philosophy in a New Key* (1942). For the first time I was reading the CLP selections *Eye of the Heart* (Howe, 1976), *Roll of Thunder, Hear My Cry* (Taylor, 1976), *Wilfred Gordon McDonald Partridge* (Fox, 1989), *The Night Thoreau Spent in Jail* (Lawrence & Lee, 1970), *The Stone Cutter* (McDermott, 1975), and *What's Whole in Whole Language?* (Goodman, 1986). All of this in addition to the literature I was teaching in my English classes. I couldn't read fast enough. My life and my marriage were on really shaky ground.

I had a personal reading life with literature as well. I was reading and rereading James Joyce's "The Dead" (1967). I was fascinated with it. I think I wanted to figure out my own marriage by reading about Gabriel and Gretta's. What is love? What is death? She seemed so intelligent and sensitive, and he seemed so unable to understand love in any other terms than domination. Joyce's language seduced me: "His soul swooned slowly as he heard the snow faintly falling, like the descent of their last end, upon all the living and the dead" (Joyce, 1967, p. 215).

Reading Joyce's text caused me to think: We in life are in the midst of death and dying. I made notes on each of the characters, especially focusing on the uneasy relationship of Gretta and Gabriel and the eventual frost, snow, death that settles on him. Just as he thinks he's "overmastering" her, she sings a song and his lust turns cold. What an incredible piece of writing, I thought! My marriage felt so like this marriage, incredibly cold.

I was planning to begin peer support groups for teachers of seniors at our school. Many of us teachers who taught seniors were angry and frustrated with our principal for listening to student complaints and not supporting us. We formed an ad hoc group to support each other and talk with our principal about our concerns.

Somewhere I had read that people caused their own cancer, that our attitudes and the way we lived our lives—if we were unhappy—led to our cancer. So, there I was reading Bernie Siegel's *Love, Medicine, and Miracles* (1986), asking myself, Do teachers as a group fall prey to cancer—the result of suppressed and repressed hostility and anger?

As the end of the year approached, with eight weeks left in school, I was overworked, like most of my colleagues, and continued to contemplate changes in my life. I thought to myself, I'm running hot. I'm overdoing it with teaching, workshops, department chair, mentoring, and I'm flying to L. A. for the weekend for CLP training. I went to Jayne's funeral. I grew more desperate. I wanted to live the joy of life each day—not wait for it not to happen. What stress! I was doing too much of what I liked to do (professionally). I had lost Pat again to everything outside her.

I had no time for my husband, Neil, and my family. My husband was right once when he took my inventory, listing my priorities: teaching, Cara, the cats, and him (in that order). I didn't look at this at the time; I was working so hard and feeling so overwhelmed and unloved by him that I thought he just didn't understand. He was entirely right about my priorities. These have changed dramatically today, though not without a great deal of work.

When Jayne died, I grieved for my friend and for myself. I wrote a poem for Jayne to set my aching mind to rest, but I could not seem to rest. The poem was really for Pat. And for us all facing loss.

The poem for Jayne

Her spirit hovers above me
She is a shade
The living dead
Her spirit soars
To celestial beds.
All imagining
Cannot bridge
the living to the dead
Odysseus tried
But Failed.
Theseus' joy out of sorrow . . .
Not now . . . maybe tomorrow.
Visions of life
After death
Visions of death
in life
Resurrection.
I cannot will disembodiment
and return.
I see my own death.
Is life one or another?
There is peace for the living
There is peace for the dead
But, not for both.

Thinking about death and making choices for life became my almost obsessive concerns. Though I was three years cancer-free, I knew in a deep way that life is short and that mine might be shorter than I expected. After years of denial that my life wasn't okay, of expecting and accepting my husband's anger at me for my choices, I decided to make some dramatic changes, to move toward life rather than to continue along a path toward self-destruction. I took Siegel's suggestion to heart: Make your choices based on whether you're going to die in a day, in a week, in a year.

READING ROSENBLATT, 1988

At the same time that I was undergoing this personal and professional crisis, I finally realized that I was always doing too much as a teacher, "carrying others' responsibilities." Even with my Literature Project experiences, teaching English was still an assessment and grading nightmare. If anything, because the logs and journals my students wrote were so important to read and respond to, I was buried in papers. The work never felt done. From the beginning of the school year until the last day I could not relax and rest, not at the end of the day or on the weekends or even on the breaks at holidays. Something inside me told me that I should be working on school all the time. I know now that I am not alone in the feeling, but for many of my teaching years I felt that way. How can we in teacher education address this issue with teachers? We certainly need to do so, and it begins in retrospect, in examining our lives critically.

Because we had begun to become conscious of the whole of teaching English, one question many other teachers and I began to ask about at CLP meetings was, "What about assessment?" When will we work to match our assessments to our notions about teaching literature?

As I finished teaching during the spring of 1988 I wrote, but did not send, a request for a leave of absence. It was as I contemplated leaving the classroom for a year that I began and continued to read Rosenblatt on my own, both textually and experientially, during and over the next seven months. I was reading her text and consciously checking my teaching pedagogy against my understanding of her educational theory and philosophy of teaching English.

At that CLP fall leadership academy in 1988 at which Rosenblatt gave her technical paper I stood in line to get Louise Rosenblatt to autograph my copy of *Literature as Exploration* (1983). At this point I had not read more than three or four chapters of the book.

One year later at the NCTE convention in Baltimore (1989), I again met Louise Rosenblatt (at an NYU reception), and I was able to talk with her briefly. I remember telling her the story of how I was teaching Hawthorne's *The Scarlet Letter* that fall. My juniors and I were keeping dialectical journals recording our personal responses to the text. We were working in small groups to explore those responses and to continue to work toward interpretations of the text.

Finally, when we finished the text, I assigned my student readers to create a visual symbolic transformation symbolization of something they found important in the text. Then, using their symbolic representations, they were asked to write a more finished response/analysis to the book. Along with the symbolization and responses, these projects involved oral sharing with the large group. After I finished narrating this way of working with my high school juniors to Rosenblatt, she encouraged me to write something about that experience. I was quite surprised, for I thought that many others probably were teaching literature the way I described it. I recall that Louise Rosenblatt commented something to the effect that I had effectively translated what she advocated in *Literature as Exploration:* that is, personal response as the beginning response, followed by interpretation, an extension of the responses they initially had to the text. She felt that she had, regardless of criticism to the contrary, described what teaching literature could look like, but that most people just didn't understand that *Literature as Exploration* truly had a teaching paradigm in it. That personal encouragement had a great deal of influence on my teaching. Someone I respected as an authority in my profession, and a woman, had listened to me and encouraged me to continue my way of working as an English teacher. Her encouragement drew me further into reading more by Rosenblatt about teaching in connection to reading literature.

I am very fortunate to not only have read Rosenblatt but to have had the opportunity to meet her, share my classroom work with her, and receive her encouragement. I can say that reading Rosenblatt is a complex web of experience. What and how we read or write a text is a confluence of the moments we have lived, the moments we are living both inside and outside the text, and the present moment. We need to consider this when we teach literature, when we are "reading a text."

CHAPTER 8

Theorizing the Reader, the Teacher, and Personal Knowledge

I began my first serious study of the theory of Louise Rosenblatt during the 1989 NYU Graduate Study Abroad Program in Oxford, England. After the dynamic experience of reading theory at UCLA in 1986, I wanted to really read theory and study. Reading the theory of Louise Rosenblatt became a central focus in my obsession with the reader. So, here we are. It's summer. It's 1989 and I'm off to England.

I left my angry husband, again (this time we had negotiated my decision, but he was still angry), to go to England to study while our daughter Cara, again, went to Texas to study with the Joffrey Ballet. Leaving my family for the summer to study abroad in a foreign country with strangers was frightening, freeing, and exciting. For me, choosing to study abroad was an action toward change, not just a postmodern mental commitment to read and think about change.

I was beginning to take action in the sense that Bernie Siegel had suggested in *Love, Medicine, and Miracles* (1986): I was living change, not just reading or talking about it. I didn't go to UCLA or to England to escape from my husband, to reject him, to punish him, to leave him. I went to adventure and to study English education. My husband Neil always felt that I was abandoning and rejecting him. Whether it was UCLA, Rohnert Park (Sonoma State University) or Oxford, England, I always hoped Neil would work with me so we could be together and I could follow my love of education. Putting my happiness and my love of education before my husband has caused me (and him) tremendous pain in our relationship, yet putting my love of education first has given me the greatest joy for my relationship with myself. This is an ongoing struggle, but not one I/we alone experience. Brown and Gilligan in *Meeting at the Crossroads: Women's Psychology and Girls' Development* (1992) found that this is a critical struggle for women and girls: establishing and maintaining a relationship with oneself in a "web of relationships," staying in connection with herself.

So, when I made my travel plans to England, I made travel plans for my husband Neil to fly to England during our study abroad group's one-week study hiatus so we could be together. I didn't want to give up my need to study and travel, and I wanted him to know that I loved him and that I was there studying, not leaving him. I do not believe that he understood this, but it was not for a lack of trying on my part.

When I arrived in England, I remember flying into Gatwick Airport, then taking the bus to Oxford. I could not believe that I was going to be studying abroad, in Oxford, England, no less. I felt free and happy even though I knew no one. This was to be the first of four summers studying in both England and New York, which would culminate with my earning a Ph.D. in English Education from New York University. I could not believe I was actually doing what I had only dared to dream about.

Twenty-four of us, not counting the instructors, spent that unseasonably dry English summer reading, writing, and talking about language and learning: *Language and Learning* (Britton, 1970), *From Communication to Curriculum* (Barnes, 1988), *How Texts Teach What Readers Read* (Meek, 1988), *Teaching Literature Nine to Fourteen* (Benton & Fox, 1985), *Cymbeline* (Shakespeare, 1955), and *Oranges Are Not the Only Fruit* (Winterson, 1985). I continued focusing my thinking on literature and literary response, reading more theory, extending my concern with reading literature in English classrooms and meaning-making. At that time I intended to write my dissertation on something to do with assessment. I brought my concerns about standardized testing and traditional letter grade evaluations, which my teaching and learning experiences told me were totally inadequate in describing learning, to England. Grading was and still is a continuing source of pain for me. I still agonize over being honest, useful, and encouraging when I work alone to evaluate my students' progress and work. When I work in collaborative communities I am not alone, and the despair and frustration are minimal.

That summer in Oxford I read a Wallace Stevens poem, "The House Was Quiet and the World Was Calm," in two of our assigned texts: Louise Rosenblatt's *The Reader, the Text, the Poem* (1978) and Michael Benton and Geoff Fox's *Teaching Literature Nine to Fourteen* (1985). At the time Stevens's poem seemed to capture the experience and the vision I had of what constituted reader response. Stevens's reader represented my ideal reader. Wallace Stevens gave language to my pleasurable experiences reading: As a reader I "became the book," alone in a solitary lived-through event. At the moment of "becoming the book," what Louise Rosenblatt calls the transaction of the reader with the text, "there was no book," there was only the "poem."

I thought of reading literature in the language I had learned reading Rosenblatt: as a transaction, that is, a juncture of the being of the reader with meaning-making—and the event was active and dynamic. This romantic image of a reader transacting with a text represented my goal in teaching literature: to empower students to read like Stevens's reader, to become the poem. I loved the notion of the totally existential moment of reading and being one with the poem. I wondered, How can I help my own students know this?

READING LITERATURE AND RESPONSE THEORY

The recognition of the role of the reader in reading was not such a new notion for those in literary theory (but it was for me), for I. A. Richards (1929) and Louise Rosenblatt (1938) began the first modern theoretical and research-based discussions of the role of the reader in literary interpretation.

In the 1960s, about 30 years after Louise Rosenblatt's *Literature as Exploration* (1938), theorists again looked at the role of the reader. This time, however, I studied literary theory focusing on the role of the reader, reader response. Norman Holland's *The Dynamics of Literary Response* (1968) and James Squire's *Response to Literature* (1968) rekindled interest in the reader. In the 1970s and 1980s reader response theory and criticism was a major area of continuing theoretical debate within the reader response camp, as well as within other literary camps such as the Formalists and New Critics.

Reader response critics and theorists disagreed on what constituted the reader: their descriptions of a reader ranged variously—a super reader (Riffaterre, 1966/1980), a mock reader (Gibson, 1950/1980), three readers—real, virtual, and ideal (Prince, 1973/1980), a competent reader (Culler, 1975, 1980), an implied reader (Iser, 1974/1980), an optimal reader (Fish, 1980b), and a self-constructing reader with an identity theme (Holland, 1968/1980).

Response critics and theorists also disagreed on the degree to which the reader played a role in reading of the text. Georges Poulet (1972/1980) described the reader as a "victim of the text," while Walker Gibson (1950/1980) characterized the reader as "accepting a role to be assumed and directed by the text." Gerald Prince (1973/1980) and Michael Riffaterre (1966/1980) both placed meaning in the text and indicated that the reader is directed by the text toward a meaning in the text. Other response theorists placed meaning in the reader (Fish, 1980b; Holland, 1968/1980) while two of the major theorists, Louise Rosenblatt (1978) and Wolfgang Iser (1976), placed meaning in the "transaction" or "interaction" between the reader and the text, in the event of reading.

That Oxford summer I openly and fearlessly questioned and explored readers and literary theory. Who is the reader and what role does a reader take in the literary event?

What I learned from literary theorists by exploring the relationship of the reader and the text is that most major reader response theorists, except Louise Rosenblatt, focus on the *act* of reading as a solitary act (even if there is an interpretive community or social/cultural acknowledgment of what a reader brings to a text). A reader like Wallace Stevens's reader, regardless of her reader role, is somehow "becoming the book," a private event. Rosenblatt viewed the reading event as a "self ordering, self creating process, shaped by and shaping a network of interrelationships with its environing social and natural matrix" (1978, p. 172).

When I began my exploration of reader response theory during that summer at Oxford, following my historical overview research at St. Mary's College the previous spring, I was looking at the teaching of literature. I focused on the problem of the autonomous and solitary reader in my own reading experiences and the readers I worked with as a teacher in my high school English classroom. It was during that summer in England that I began to consciously rethink things. Reading Douglas Barnes's *From Communication to Curriculum* (1977), a text in which he advocated the importance of how we talk in groups, helped me to be tentative in my questioning of theory while reading and working in groups. I questioned not only the reader and the text, but also the role the teacher played in classroom literary transactions as well as the nature of the language we use when we work with students and with each other in groups.

How do we teachers work with readers of any age? I argued in the response papers I wrote that summer (responses to Britton, Smith, Probst, Meek, and Benton and Fox) that "teaching" literature needed to change. In arguing for a change, I was actually writing to give myself authority to change my own pedagogy. I was struggling to give language to, to name for myself, to redefine in a sense, what it is to teach: "how to move my classroom toward empowering the reader to read literature so that she, the reader, becomes the text" (Schmidt, 1989b). I questioned the notion. How could I take Margaret Meek's advice, "Lessons are taught by the text. . . . Let them read" (1988)? Further, I asked, how can we describe what readers know, what lessons they've learned? Are the only "lessons" those in the text? Assessment was still very much on my mind and surfacing in these questions.

What I came up with was a theory, not about reading literature, but about ways of being as a teacher—that teachers needed to quit "teaching" and see themselves and their students as readers together. I was redefining my own role as an English teacher. I wanted to find ways "to empower the reader to become the book, to know the quiet that is part of meaning, to finally step away and watch 'the reader leaning late and being there'" (Stevens, 1965/ 1985). The notion of stepping away, freeing the reader to read when the "lesson" is finished: to become a lifelong reader.

All that summer I stumbled with my language. That is, I tried to talk, but none of my language seemed to fit and I felt awkward. I was in between languages. Now I realize that sometimes the reason we can't say what we want to say is that we're in the process of change and we don't have the new language yet to describe what it is we know. Sometimes when we are appearing confused, we are in the midst of real confusion, not defective thinking.

At the encouragement of our NYU professors I began to make notes for my candidacy paper. The subject I chose was learner response, for it occurred to me that reader response is more than that, it's about language and learning.

I was exploring and questioning language and learning issues in the candidacy paper notes I was preparing. Reading was at the center of my thoughts. Jimmy Britton's *Language and Learning* (1970) served as the frame for my notes. I was interested in Britton's "gap," which he described as "our total response to what confronts us and any formulation we can make of what was there and what took place" (1970, p. 277). I read Britton's remarks as meaning that language cannot adequately express learner response to the experiences of any given moment, regardless of the type of experience: "the processes grow more difficult to 'pin down,' until we give in to a sense that the rest must remain unexplained" (1970, p. 277). I tried to marry Britton's language and learning discourse with my sense of reader response theory and criticism.

In my notes for my candidacy paper, I wrote using the language of each theorist, trying to assimilate their terms, "The shift reader response theory gives to literary theory is to place the spotlight on the transaction (Rosenblatt) or interaction (Iser) between the reader and the text, between Britton's language learner and the world, rather than on the aesthetics of art and artist" (Schmidt, 1989b).

I was fascinated with the distinction Rosenblatt made terming what happens when we read a literary work a "transaction" and Iser's phenomenological term "interaction," which is what he calls what happens in the act of reading. Rosenblatt described reading as an event (something that happens), and Iser described reading as an act (something readers do). At the time I was making meaning of all I had been reading that Oxford summer by trying out meaning. That is, I was playing with what one writer might be saying in terms of what others were saying. Imagine a shuttlecock whizzing back and forth between the text and the reader, connecting, dynamically weaving meaning. The meaning is not on either end, but somewhere in the middle. In reader response theory it lies somewhere in the whizzing, the dynamic happening, in the transaction, in Britton's language/learner "gap" (Schmidt, 1989b, p. 3).

HOW DO WE ASSESS THE MYSTERIOUS GAP?

I was going to connect all of this reader concern with many a conscientious teacher's nightmare: assessment. Given readers' lives and the importance of recognizing that meaning-making is inseparable from the reader's life and the expectations the reader brings to the reading experience, how do we assess what readers know? How do we know what exists in the mysterious gap? How do we assess learning? No one can read a poem for us. Then it seems to me that the point of the standardized testing honors not what the reader knows and experiences, but precisely the opposite of what is powerful in the reading experience. We continue, however, to teach reading and literature for these tests. We need a revolution! Now!

I reasoned that Rosenblatt offered teachers an "acceptable," grounded view of assessment: that meaning must have a "defensible linkage with the text." As a high school English teacher still seeking the approval of my own "interpretive community" of English-teaching colleagues, this return to the text for "validity of interpretation" suited me. I could now justify, citing authority and research, what I was doing in my classroom. I was unhappy with the idea of the return of meaning, of authority for meaning, to the text. My questioning of the idea that the "validity of interpretation" lay in returning to the text was now two years old. I wanted to know, What happened to the virtual meaning created in the transaction between the reader and the text? Rosenblatt calls that meaning "the poem." Using Frank Smith's language (Smith, 1988) (I'd been reading him, too, that summer), I wanted to know, How do we measure the deep structure, that which is in the mind, and then assess it? In retrospect, these questions about readers, readers' lives, readers' meaning-making, and what we are assessing in our assessments foreshadowed my dissertation research. I was asking, "How do we know about and use knowledge that the reader gains in reading? What does the reader know?" Do the assessments we use value the beliefs we have about reading, teaching, and learning? Ask yourself these questions about assessing readers' reading and spend some time thinking about your answers.

My answer to my own question in 1989 was to state my belief about the teacher's role through my understanding of Frank Smith's "feeling for the primary role of the teacher," that "teachers need to ensure that readers have adequate demonstrations of reading being used for evident meaningful purposes, and that teachers need to help readers learn to fulfill such purposes themselves" (1989a, p. 5).

I became adamant about evaluation, redefining evaluation so that measuring and assessing meaning-making would be done in such a way as to honor the learner, the reader. I asked, How do we best do this? What would be the purpose of assessing meaning-making? I concluded that "The purpose needs to change from that of a political, social measurement of knowledge to a learner-centered tool for improving learning and language use" (1989b, p. 6). I found that Rosenblatt was arguing for literary understanding that in turn would help us to understand ourselves better in a democracy. I was exploring something similar, but my focus was now on personal knowledge and language and learning rather than on the students' literary understanding.

We concluded our Oxford experience by writing a self-assessment. I wrote mine in the form of a reflection, though our professors had devised a format for us. I just couldn't respond in the format they'd given to us, so I wrote my own assessment in my own language. I was afraid that my resistance to using their form would be costly. Though I was trying to trust the two instructors, who insisted that the assessment was for us, I was having a hard time believing them, for I knew I was going to receive a letter grade evaluating my work. It is risky to challenge authority, but only if you think the others have it and you don't.

Reflections of a Learner, Oxford, 1989:

This has been the most humbling experience I've had in my learning and writing. It has been painful, uncomfortable, agonizing, and I'm grateful for it all. Though I'm not a learner who waits until the last moment to work on a project, I'm painfully aware of how hard it is to "process" even when I don't feel ready to do so. Good as it may be to stop and pull together my thoughts I let myself get caught up in destructive thinking: I'm a "doctoral" student so this must be perfect, it must be more than it needs to be for *my* purposes. When I saw Eve's use of Jerome Bruner's thought about reflection it gave me pause to accept my work where it is: truly in process, open to mistake and refinement, and ongoing:

> Much of the process of education consists of being able to distance oneself in some way from what one knows by being able to reflect on one's knowledge. (Bruner, 1986)

This is what I haven't given myself permission to do: reflect. So, I've come from Wallace Stevens' image of the reader totally immersed with the text to the notion that the transaction or pure reader response isn't enough—that there is an environment and social context—to the awareness that I need to re-read Rosenblatt and Smith and Iser. Instead of forging on, I need to re-read and reflect.

I closed my narrative reflections of that Oxford summer experience with

> It is 1989 and those questions have been transformed and are continuing to transform. They are transformed and transforming by three years of reading, teaching, learning, collaborating, and reflecting. (Schmidt, 1989b)

So, I say I was evolving. What did my teaching look like? When I returned to my English classroom in 1989–90, I experimented with a more student-centered, meaning-centered classroom: groups, collaborative experiences, group and independent learning.

The previous spring, my last semester as English Department chairperson before being fired from the position by my principal, I had been everywhere but at school teaching my classes; instead, I was doing workshops and presentations for teachers. I still had no sense of personal or professional boundaries: I was English Department chair, mentor teacher for English language arts for my district, a teacher leader for the California Literature Project, and presenting workshops everywhere. I was wearing thin again.

I had successfully lobbied for heterogeneous grouping for incoming freshmen and -women at our high school. The decision was hard fought. The department vote was 5–4 in favor of heterogeneous grouping. Three of us in favor of this major change from the department's four levels of tracking also volunteered to teach the ninth grade English classes. We reasoned that for such a program to be successful, it needed to be taught by those of us who believed in it. In addition, we sought and received administrative support. We received released time to collaborate on the curriculum, to coordinate major goals and expectations for all students, and to communicate with the community. In 1993 the department voted to expand heterogeneous grouping (except honors English, of course) to include sophomore English. Initiating this change in our department curriculum in 1990 is one of my proudest accomplishments in teaching. Ninth graders would have a chance to start again in their academic lives rather than continue along irretrievable paths. Some of those academic walls that divide young people into cliques might become less rigid, less stereotyped, less discriminatory, and people might begin to see themselves and each other as human beings rather than "college prep" or just "general." As I have taught and observed tracked classes over the years, I noticed two things: that students rarely, if ever, moved up; and that kids were placed more on behavior than on their abilities. Our communication classes were almost entirely male, and both discipline and attendance were the major problems. Could the problem be with the curriculum and the pedagogy, not just the kids?

When I began teaching heterogeneous groups of freshmen and -women, I shifted my role as teacher to what I can best describe as facilitator/teacher. I also changed the organization and structure of my classes and classroom into workshops for learning. The central theory and pedagogy driving the classroom workshops was Nancie Atwell's *In the Middle* (1987). Atwell's approach is student-centered, interactive learning in which teachers and learners work in partnership on specific, defined content areas of reading and writing. Her workshop approach in the classroom really appealed to me. I feared the reaction of my department and the community at large. There is that word again: FEAR. I also felt that this would work because I believed in what I was doing and I had experienced the power of this way of teaching and learning and reading myself. And it did work. Because students were progressing on individual levels and because I was keeping individual folders on each student's progress as well as holding individual consultations on reading and writing, the reaction to this pedagogical change was positive and supportive.

While much is important in Atwell's work (the valuing of the individual learner to construct her own writing and reading assignments and the processes of workshopping), the separation of reading and writing as distinct areas of learning may be a failure (at a basic theoretical level) to address the importance of integrating language activities. Atwell understood the importance of reading and dialoging about what we read (the dinner table notion of talking to each other as readers about what we read), and she understood the importance of a workshop for authors of texts with an audience beyond the teacher, but the activities of reading and writing were separated language contents. The next step, if I were to transform Atwell's reading and writing workshops, could be a "languaging" workshop, which would be a workshop with language at the center. That would be a critical pedagogical and epistemological leap: from English as subject, with literature and grammar and composition as content, to a language workshop.

The workshop approach freed me to be the kind of teacher I have been all along yet was afraid to be, but who I am still becoming: a person who was able to work with students individually, conferencing with them about their writing, their reading, and their learning. It also allowed me to free my students to take responsibility for their learning and to come to know and assess their own learning through self-evaluations each quarter. Teaching and learning English was a shared experience, and I enjoyed that year, especially with those three classes of ninth grade English, tremendously. All these young people were being given a chance for a fresh start in their education, and I felt satisfied that the struggle and pain of change within the department had resulted in a powerful change for kids. I feel that the way I chose to work with learners valued them all at wherever they were in their learning and allowed me to teach in connected ways. I finally felt at home, myself actually, teaching English.

For me, however, being a part-time doctoral student wasn't satisfying. I decided to devote my life and my energies to my studies and stop fragmenting myself, trying to make everyone else happy. With the help and encouragement of my New York friends from Oxford, I applied for a teaching fellowship at NYU. Since our daughter was now 17, I felt my major mothering role was pretty much complete and that, again, I could risk what has always brought up great pain and anger in my marriage, leaving my husband Neil to do what I love—teach and learn. This time I left with a deeper attitude than I had ever left with: I knew that I loved him profoundly and that I was not leaving him because I was rejecting or abandoning him. I could tell him this and I kept telling him this: I love you and I need to do this.

Fear can surface in many forms. The next chapter of this life story deals with something we all struggle with, but teachers particularly: doing the right thing in spite of fear.

CHAPTER 9

The New York Stories, 1990–1992

Risk. Fear. I feel incredibly small and New York City is overwhelming, I thought to myself as I arrived at La Guardia Airport to begin my New York life and doctoral studies. My Oxford/New York friend Diane told me how to get here, but I'm so scared.

(Pat Schmidt, *Journal*, 1989a)

INTERIORS: THE BLUE LAMP

I stepped off the Carey at Grand Central Station, hailed a taxi, and we sped off to Third Avenue and Ninth Street. I'm on Mr. Toad's wild ride for real, I thought. Preparing to move for the past few weeks had been a flurry of wrapping, packing, and shipping fragments of my life east. I looked at Alumni South, the building where I was going to live, and I stared up at the purple and white NYU flag hanging in front. I was surrounded by the typical New York East Village homeless, filth, and clutter, and I seriously questioned my sanity. Then I remember thinking, my friend Diane came from South Dakota and she made it. I can do this, too.

Pat, who fears heights and hates (claustrophobic) elevators, was going to live on the 14th floor and use an elevator (unless I was willing to walk up and down those 14 floors several times a day). The gray walls of the hall looked like an endless void, and my apartment was at the end. I had moved to New York a little earlier than most graduate students and my whole hall was deserted. I was afraid that a mugger lurked everywhere on that lonely hall, even though it was well secured by an ubiquitous network of closed-circuit cameras. I dumped my luggage that day, and I ran to find Diane. My body had arrived, but my life packed in boxes hadn't. Seeing Diane calmed me down. Another Oxford friend, Zoey, came, and we three went to dinner. I can only describe feeling small and shaky, of somehow being crazy for coming to New York. And I possessed an intense FEAR.

I felt numb. Leaving my husband Neil, none too happy with another separation, and our daughter Cara for the unknown life ahead of me in New York was an experience that had exhausted me. The first thing I noticed about my new, barren apartment was that there was no light besides the small light on my desk. Something in me feared staying in such a dim, dark room located at the end of a deserted hallway that first night. I remember so well how my friends Diane and Zoey walked me to Conran's to find and buy the lamp. I needed to feel and see light in the New York City night.

To this day, when people ask me about my experiences in New York, I tell the story of my blue lamp. The story is not an elaborate or complex one. It is, however, a critical story. I needed the lamp for my apartment, and while I kept my friends waiting with much thinking and visualizing of what I wanted my room to be like, I finally settled on a cornflower blue lamp. That first night in New York, sirens were wailing up and down Third Avenue. All I, this middle-aged, middle-class California teacher woman, had up there alone in my 14th-floor apartment was the cornflower blue lamp and myself. I see myself alone in my room with the blue lamp, full of equal parts of hope and fear. I felt a bit more secure with that lamp that night. That day and night marked the beginning of my life in New York, promising a full, exciting, rich life. Fear permeated my entire being those first few months in New York.

When I left New York in May 1992, I was alone again in my room with the same cornflower blue lamp. That last night I had dinner with a friend, happily went alone to the Joe Papp Public Theater on Lafayette Street to see García Lorca's *Blood Wedding*, walked home to Third Avenue, and felt wonderful and alive. I walked down the same gray hallway, happy to be alive, to have lived alone, to have conquered my fear of just living life.

Today, in retrospect, I think, how appropriate. The last night was again Pat and the blue lamp. And fear was gone. The last person I said goodbye to the next morning was my friend Diane. I gave the lamp to my roommate when I left. I no longer needed it.

I'm not sure why the lamp story is so important to my New York story, to this teaching life study, but it is. Buying a simple, rather inexpensive blue lamp meant a great deal to me. I only know that I couldn't tolerate darkness, so I bought myself that lamp. It was my room, my lamp, my life. If I were afraid of being alone, then I needed to seek to change my condition.

During the first year of doctoral study in New York I continued to struggle with many issues in my teaching and learning and my personal life. The fear of the darkness in my apartment metaphorically described the fear I carried around with me generally of my relationship with my husband Neil, of my ability to do doctoral work, of my ability to teach at the university level, of the New York streets. What if they discover that I'm not the person they think I am? What if they discover that Pat is not good enough for the doctoral program or to be a teaching assistant? I still distrusted my own authority to do and to know.

Ironically enough, my first doctoral seminar was reminiscent of those literature survey courses I took as an English major: one book a week and little time to really read and think about my reading. I felt that reading was again like the process of pouring sand through a sieve. We worked in discussion groups to share our readings of texts, but George, our professor for the "Writing Theory and Research" doctoral seminar, and sometimes James (another professor in the English Education Department), had a habit of talking to the group, usually at the end of seminar. They seemed to be explaining the text to us. I felt insulted by what I perceived they were doing to us. I wondered why they were telling us their interpretation of the text. Didn't they trust us to make sense of the text? Were they trying to ensure that we knew *the meaning* of the texts we had been studying? I knew one thing: I was uncomfortable with this way of working. James did this to a lesser degree in the "Language Acquisition and Development" class, a class I was taking from him that fall. I could only challenge this practice of transmission in my log, and I used a fake humility to do it: something like, "Am I mistaken or is this commonsense teaching?" I was afraid to directly confront authority, and I wanted these professors' acceptance and approval (old good girl stuff).

In retrospect, I wonder why George and James didn't state their concern with our readings so we could reflect on our own processes and, at the same time, why they didn't reflect with us about their own constructs and assumptions about our readings and our needs as readers. My reading was that George's and James's enactment of the principle that we would learn collaboratively from our reading, writing, talking, and listening together wasn't working, so they decided that we were going to receive their authoritative readings. I remember telling my roommate Barbara that I was frustrated with what I saw as their authoritarian reading of texts, and I mentioned my observation in my learning log, but at the time I was unable to openly voice my concern in class or directly to either one of them. I have to ask myself, Would this have been different if instead of George and James, the professors were named Susan and Beverly? Perhaps.

At the same time, I was teaching my first NYU Writing Workshop I class and working as a writing consultant in the NYU Expository Writing Center, and I found myself enjoying the experiences. I continued the workshopping paradigm I had worked with à la Nancie Atwell. However, I found that I was very concerned with the nature of my response to student writing. I was asking myself, my colleagues, and my students, What is the most useful way to respond to text? I began to read, question, and think about how I and my class talked about and respond to text and to each other, both in conversation and in writing, reflecting on *Response to Student Writing* (Freedman, 1987). I was very conscious of the language I used while teaching my classes. I responded to text in ways my own English teachers and professors had not: I languaged with the text. A sample of my response to a student text is below. The student read the first draft of the text to the group. All members of the class wrote a mirroring response to the text and shared that response with the author (in mirroring, the "readers" hear the text being read and say to the author what we hear and don't hear in the text).

In my responses to student text that fall I was consciously trying to work with writers in a "collaborative problem-solving mode" (Freedman, p. 6), which was based on a Vygotskyian developmental notion of response. This problem-solving mode frees learners to work more and more independently. The following is an example of my response to a text written for Writing Workshop I during the fall of 1990:

> I heard a paper that speaks about an idyllic group of memories associated with Incarnation Lake. We are on a canoe ride enjoying the lake then you begin to narrate your reflection of the experience at the lake over a period of three years. I hear about how you came to know immortality but I don't know what prompted that issue. I hear about Lookout Pt. and the vastness of the sky but I don't hear you talking to friends. The description of your father's visits seems important but I never hear him speak. How do you hear him and actually picture him there with you? I'd like to see him as you do. What would he have said, what did you say?

Though by this time I had evolved into thinking about language issues rather than the transactional literary theory of Louise Rosenblatt, I was not aware of the change. I continued to focus on writing my candidacy paper about Rosenblatt's transactional theory of the literary experience for my doctoral work. It seems that changes occur before we can know or name them.

READING ROSENBLATT, 1991

When I returned home to California after my first academic year at NYU, I took a photocopy of the 1938 text of Rosenblatt's *Literature as Exploration* (the first edition is out of print) home with me. I was considering doing a comparative reading of the two texts, the 1938 and 1983 (fourth revised) editions. This reading and study were similar to the project I had begun when I read John Fowles' *The Magus* (1965) for my M.A. in English in 1979: I would read the first edition (1965) and compare that with a reading of the revised edition of *The Magus* (1977). I was working in a traditional interpretive academic mode.

When I was reading Fowles, I planned to compare the changes as I read them with what Fowles said he was doing. I guess I could characterize that as checking my sense of truth with the author's. Is what an author, the authority of his/her own text, doing what he proposes to be doing? If not, what can we say about the author's authority regarding his/her text? What place does a reader's response, my discoveries of synchronicity and dissonances, have in relationship to the authority of the author (his/her intentions), the text? I was still wrestling with Wimsatt and Beardsley's Intentional Fallacy. Dr. K. would appreciate my long-time effort to end my confusion.

I had spent a great deal of time reading Fowles's two editions, making hundreds of notes and emendations regarding the changes. I felt lost in a morass. The study probably was more suited to a doctoral dissertation. I found it too unwieldy and eventually abandoned it (but not the work itself) to write about romance parody in *The Magus*.

The study I wrote of *The Magus* was connected at the time to my study of Chaucer and my interest in "The Miller's Tale," definitely inseparable from what was going on in my personal life: my continuing search to define relationships and personal authority in relationships. It did not seem accidental that both the male and female protagonists bore the same names (Alison and Nicholas) as those of Chaucer's protagonists (Nicholas and Alisoun); nor did it seem accidental that Nicholas was an Oxford scholar in both texts and that descriptions of Alison in *The Magus* seemed to come from Chaucer's text. Beyond the similarities in characters, I felt that Chaucer's "eke men shall not make earnest of game" was descriptive not only of the foolishness men make of romantic love in pursuing the ideal woman in medieval romance, but that this notion also seemed to be in the spirit of Fowles's existential romance.

I was quite happy with my thesis and sent it to John Fowles through his publisher. He read it and replied to my letter, responding that, alas, he had never read Chaucer. I did not believe him, for I knew that he had a B.A. with honors from Oxford in French and was schooled in the British system. It seemed incomprehensible to me that he had not read Chaucer. It was akin to being an English major in American literature who had no knowledge of *Huckleberry Finn*.

Fowles had written a book called *The Ebony Tower* (1974) in which he translated the *lais* of Marie de France, which meant that he was knowledge-able in medieval literature. I felt like writing to Oxford to ask for a copy of his studies there. He was known to play with academics and scholars in terms of his truthfulness, much like his character Nicholas Urfe in *The Magus* played with truthfulness in relationships, testing our willingness to capitulate to authority, to play the "god game."

A year or so later I continued my correspondence with Fowles because I was researching an article focusing on the three epigraphs introducing the major sections of *The Magus*. Fowles was generous, this time writing to me on his personal stationery from Lyme Regis, England. The epigraphs were from the Marquis de Sade's *Justine*. I sent the French translations I had made to Fowles. His response regarding why he had used de Sade as well as the corrected translations were very encouraging: The epigraphs were intended to set the tone of a black comedy. I did not finish the article. At the time, my return to teaching in my English classroom took precedence over writing the article.

All of this prefaced and set the context for me to study the two editions of Rosenblatt's *Literature as Exploration*. Without realizing it, I think I was continuing to define the nature of authority and relationships in the context of teaching and reading about teaching literature. In addition, so far in my NYU studies we had not read Rosenblatt, other than an article in the summer study abroad in Oxford. I found this ironic, since Louise Rosenblatt founded the English education program at NYU.

When I began to read Rosenblatt in the summer of 1991, I was wondering how 50 years had changed her thinking and if a close reading of her text might reveal those changes. I was trying to discover what changes in one's pedagogy by studying someone else. There must be something hiding in the text for me to discover. If I could discover it and tell others what this might be, I was doing academic research. No matter that this would contribute nothing in terms of helping us teach and learn in English classrooms. It would be continuing the practice that I was critically questioning.

Instead of studying Rosenblatt to discover a theory of pedagogical change, I chose to study myself. This was now the only way I felt I could read or study Rosenblatt. The writing of my dissertation became the ultimate alternative to standardized testing and traditional research as sources of knowledge. I wanted to get as close as I could to the knowledge of the learner. Critical, reflective autobiography as assessment. Radical theory! Yes!

For me, understanding individual change, transformation, and evolution in terms of personal knowledge demanded a self-study rather than the study of another person. Rosenblatt would have to tell her own story, for I couldn't do that for her. I'd been studying other people through reading literature for most of my life. I'd been studying my husband and trying to change myself to be in the relationship. I'd been trying to be the good teacher for others' approval and acceptance for most of my life. It was time to look at myself and find a relationship with myself.

This, too, became a way of answering the questions about assessment I was raising in Oxford: How can we know what the reader knows? If reading transforms lives, how can we know what transforms? I have had powerful reading and learning experiences, but none of the standard or traditional assessments comes close to measuring or describing the deep, personal knowledge learners have. I have watched the transformations in my students' lives and I know this deeply in my own life.

A CLOSE READING

I began to closely read the 1938 *Literature as Exploration* that summer. As I think about it now, my initial plan to write a comparative study seemed like another effort to write in the English academic research paradigm: scholarly research meant doing a study of text. The text was still the authority of its meaning, along with the author's intentions (was I still working out the "Intentionalism and Intentional Fallacy" confusion?).

I felt that Rosenblatt was making some important statements regarding the issue of change, writing the following in my notes:

> The key to what L as E [*Literature as Exploration*] offers is what R [Rosenblatt] herself states: "In short, this book seeks to present a philosophy for teachers who desire to help young people gain the pleasures and understanding that literature can yield." (1938, p. vii)

I viewed Rosenblatt's philosophy (and I still do) as an intensely radical one.

> At the core of R's philosophy is the belief that the literary experience and the teaching and learning experience are a living experience, a very personal experience. What does this mean? What does this look like? R. tells us. This is a very dangerous and radical book. From my experience people do not know what to do with her philosophy of living, teaching, and learning, for it requires a change in what it means to "teach." Is it enough to describe what this philosophy is? How can we as teachers, learners, experiencers of literature experience this? (Schmidt, 1991)

As I reread and write reflectively about the above response to the 1938 text, I realize that for me naming my philosophy of life is inseparable from naming my philosophy of teaching English. What I also realize is that for many years I was not able to teach in a manner that matched my philosophy. Writing this autobiography questioning and reflecting on my teaching and learning life helps me, and I hope others in the profession, to gain insight and perspective on the processes and experiences that influence how we teachers teach English.

The tension I had felt while teaching English before the California Literature Project was greatly due to the dissonance between what I believed and how I viewed myself, how I related to myself, and my perception of the authority I had to act on those beliefs. While I believed in the value of the student's ability, that all students are capable of learning given a good teacher who believes in them, and that teaching English meant teaching literature, for reading literature could open the world to us, I taught young people in a way that destroyed the pleasure of reading (purely an intellectual exercise) and left the learner out of the transaction of reading and learning experiences. I remember thinking and saying quite clearly for years, I want my students to be able to think critically. How could they if I did most of the thinking for them? I so tightly controlled and directed the classroom that there was little or no room for them to experience and explore reading literature in the context of their own lives.

However, by teaching English the way I was taught and by accepting everyone else's authority (English Department colleagues, prior English teachers as models, my college English methods instruction, and New Critical and Structuralist theory), I could not accept my own personal authority. Yet I felt totally responsible for my students' successes and failures. Experiencing learning other than in isolation (CLP, Oxford, New York) helped me to begin to shed that sense of total responsibility and to seek ways of pedagogically enacting a shared authority and responsibility for learning.

Personally, 1991 was a hard summer, for my husband Neil was again quite angry with me for choosing to return to New York for a second year of study. Our now 18-year-old daughter Cara traveled to Seattle that summer to dance with the Pacific Northwest Ballet professional training program. I both missed her and worried about her. She had been traveling away from home to study ballet professionally since she was 12, when she went to San Antonio to study with Robert Joffrey and the Joffrey Ballet. During the school year her life was filled with school and the San Francisco Ballet. My husband and I were left to ourselves. Tensions were tight in California.

Periodically, out of total frustration, I would confront Neil on these issues. I don't quite understand why I kept trying to work this relationship out when it seemed that for things to work out in relationships, whether they are professional, family, or personal, people have to be willing, to be open, and to be honest with who they are, as well as value and accept the differences they may have. Perhaps this is another sense of what I'm trying to get at when I write of my notion of languaging based on the Chaucerian notion of sovereignty: shared understandings while valuing differences. It's accepting who people are, what their experiences are, and sharing our own experiences in the hopes that some connections are made that will help us both to learn. This is my sense of a spiritual connection with the world. That I am eight years in recovery and continuing to work on a spiritual program to live my life may have a great deal to do with trying to match beliefs and actions in working with others: the paradox of being selfish and yet not being self-centered. I continue to learn that to do this one must work on openly listening to others and valuing oneself. While this understanding is easy to comprehend, it is not as easy to live.

This is the setting of my life in which I sat down that 1991 summer to read and journal my response to Louise Rosenblatt's 1938 *Literature as Exploration*. I wrote a 15-page, single-spaced response, but what I'm including here is my reading and response to Chapter 3, "The Setting for Spontaneity." To continue to write and read my learning life as a reader and teacher, I'll be sharing another reading of Chapter 3 that I wrote in 1992, shortly after my return home from New York, since that chapter was the first chapter of her text that I read in 1986. This allows us to study the journey of a learner, of a reader, of a teacher, of a woman over time.

The following section is entirely from my reading/writing journal. I include this journal response now as inseparable from the rest of this text, for my sense is that I can't tell the dancer from the dance. Should I? Join my dancing reader's mind as I write and think aloud with you about Louise Rosenblatt's *Literature as Exploration* (1938).

LITERATURE AS EXPLORATION: June 1991

> *Part 2   The Human Basis of Literary Sensitivity:*
> *Ch. 3, The Setting for Spontaneity*

This section of Rosenblatt's text begins with an example of Indian children reading restoration comedies. The idea that they could make something of such a foreign experience. In this section she sets the relationship between teacher and student. Comprehension: Student has been able to demonstrate by means of verbal definition the scenes, actions, and personalities. This often does not awaken the personal response. Also characteristic of a literary experience is the teacher pointing out what others have seen that make it significant. Students have two experiences: he or she memorizes the ideas about literature that his teacher or the literary critic presents to him as being the traditional ones; and he or she reads, and has a personal experience that he or she may never express or even recognize. Our experience with literature is felt when we actually live through the experience. The motions of teaching are empty unless the experience has a direct impact upon the experience of the student (1938, p. 71). She feels that students are taught literature but do not experience literature, they have knowledge about, but not experience with, of. Teachers often never glimpse the personal experience of students with the book. Acknowledges the problem of the "unbridged gap" between the experience of the student and what the teacher thinks the student should notice (1938, p. 74). Students are transmitted (my term) to and think there is a "right" way to read a text. The blight on our educational system exists in seeking the teacher's approval and/or good marks rather than knowledge for its own sake (1938, p. 76). She looks at I. A. Richards' study of student responses: they were left without a critical or professional stance and did not even know how to mount a personal response. Basically, they were unable to think for themselves. (She) Avoids a paradigm of teaching but rather suggests important concepts necessary for learning. States the importance of the teacher's stance, love of literature. Let students have a primary response: what a work means to him and does for him. Let him freely express, not contingent upon form. Let the response take the form dictated by what he has lived through in reading the book. Then there needs to be a setting of informal discussion, the primary criterion should be honesty and sincerity of ideas and reactions he expresses. The class should be a friendly group come together to exchange ideas (1938, p. 83). Work on listening with understanding and to express their own ideas in relevant terms (1938, p. 83). Teacher participates as one of the group. We choose books on literary tradition and students' intellectual and emotional needs. Footnote states that ultimately students will select their books. Literature is not a body of knowledge but a series of experiences.

This text seems to agree with Richards, use his research to acknowledge and look at the problem of literary response and offer solutions to improving student response to books: Primary response is free. Students then look at what in them and the book brought about this reaction? This is phase one of student's response. Phase two is to clarify and enlarge the response: increased self-knowledge and increased understanding of the work. This is a critical awareness of his own reaction. They go simultaneously and work off each other (1938, p. 89).

BEGINNING IN RETROSPECT: READING ROSENBLATT, READING A LIFE

When I finished reading the entire 1938 text, I remember thinking that I preferred this to the fourth edition (1983). Though this edition (1938) wasn't as finely honed in the writing, was less tight in its construction, I enjoyed the tone, the language, which I felt spoke more directly to Pat the teacher.

When I returned to New York for the second year of my doctoral study, I was poised to write my dissertation proposal to do a study of my reading of Rosenblatt. My research question was, How does reading theory influence the teaching of English? I began to write my proposal and managed to write a pretty rough draft to continue working on in the second semester in "Dissertation Proposal Seminar."

That fall, 1991, in addition to my graduate courses, I was working as a consultant in the Expository Writing Center. My work consisted of one-to-one consulting with writers from all disciplines and collaborative biweekly staff meetings. And I was teaching a preservice teachers' class, "Reading with Adolescents," in my own department, Teaching and Learning. I was also teaching a course in a collaborative "writing across the curriculum" project with the NYU History Department, the "History of Western Civilization." If that weren't enough, I was taking my third doctoral seminar, educational linguistics, and a class in narrative. What a crash course I was on, and, indeed, I eventually crashed. I still didn't know how to take care of myself in some sort of reasonable or balanced way. Now I believe that education and the teaching profession do not encourage us as teachers to take care of ourselves. I have two friends who after 15 years of teaching just burned out. I would guess that this happens somewhere between 10 and 15 years (another research project?).

Though I loved my family, I had returned to New York. I couldn't imagine that living in California could begin to provide me with the experiences I needed and valued in my education and in my life. Fear had been replaced with a sense of safety. I risked the end of my marriage, but I trusted that I would be okay, whatever happened. Some have viewed my pursuit of a Ph.D. as selfish, especially since I left home and lived apart from my family for two years; I think that it is more selfish to deny one's spirit, my desire to learn. The following journal entries capture the internal life, the one going on while I was reading, writing, teaching, and learning in New York. Today I encourage my students in literature and linguistics to read, write, and learn about others and themselves in this same manner. No one can read a poem for us. No one can read a life for us.

10–24–91

It's time to find the space for myself.

Since I've returned to New York I've found myself more relaxed, more talkative, and, I hope more receptive. Feel more vulnerable and safer.

I'm concerned about the future but try not to be obsessed about it. I wonder about next semester but it will just happen. I do the footwork and God does the rest.

Spanish test tomorrow. I'm not worried one way or the other. Hope I pass. Perhaps next semester if not this time.

Returning to the dissertation proposal is what I'll do next weekend. Stand back a bit. Perhaps Sunday if I complete the other work. Bakhtin. Halliday. I want to read *Orlando* a bit. Time to enjoy literature. Take time to thank James for the aesthetic element in our class—the novels. Yes! Still want to read Calvino—also Atwood's *The Edible Woman*.

Today I was okay. Talked to Mary—the nightmares we all share, the freeing of the self. I raised my hand today to try to get out of self will and self fear. To live in God's will and be willing. Make me a channel of your peace. Yes!!!

I love this journal for writing. The size and gloss are wonderful.

Thanks for your grace in my life today.

10–25–91, *Friday*

It was a good day. Last night I finished the papers I needed to read before the weekend. I want to enjoy Sundays without weights and chains. As my good friend Zoey says, "it's a time for change and a time for boundaries." I wonder if I should buy a Scott Peck copy for NY. Had my hair cut by Bruce. Think I'll see Albert in a month for a highlight, lighter, reddish blonde. I feel good about my hair for the first time in probably a year. It's about time.

Took the Spanish exam. I hope G is good for his word when he reads my exam. It's in God's hands now.

The evening and meeting with Zoey were good. I'm riding subways with less fear these days.

Also time to work on the dissertation proposal again. Halliday will be quite useful. He defined language as a social semiotic.

I guess I still want to teach, love working with people, just abhor the politics of academic life. Do potters have political hegemonies? Probably. Stick to what you know!

10–31–91

Halloween! I'm totally exhausted today. Wednesdays always exhaust me. Hectic dysjuncture [*sic*] and I'll look at them as important to establish my reality. . . .

My proposal needs much more work than I'd thought. It seems insurmountable but it will work itself out. Perhaps I'll be able to get to the issues now that I've written my story. It's time to go meta on this.

Neil—a twinge of sadness for this man. Somehow he seems so

sad—alone in himself. I guess if I could withdraw into alcohol, he could withdraw into another form of silence. I need to let go. It's all in God's hands and I'll be fine (after the pain). After the pain. The pain is fleeting. It's a part of life.

So, is it a phenomenological study of dialogic pedagogy? What is that?

THE FEVER THAT BURNED ON THROUGH THE NIGHT

As in 1985, when I discovered I had breast cancer, illness preceded crisis (out of which, in my case, come the actions toward change). Illness played a role in my teaching and learning life (I believe that I will continue to experience these life lessons until I get them right). By the next week I had become very sick. My head pounded, and I was coughing violently with nothing coming up or out. I began hallucinating (and I was leading a sober life now), and I experienced fever and cold sweats. I was quite ill.

I struggled for two weeks, thinking I had something bronchial. I tried to take good care of myself by resting, staying in bed. Two of my friends came to my apartment and took me to the NYU Health Center to see a doctor. I didn't see a doctor. I saw a screener who sent me home, advising me to take cough syrup and get a humidifier. I remember saying to her that I knew what the flu was like and this wasn't it.

Finally, I became so sick that I challenged the screener I had seen at the NYU Health Center who, four days earlier, had diagnosed me as having the flu. I acted on the authority of my illness rather than on what she had told me was the source of my illness after only a cursory exam. I saw a doctor. I had pneumonia.

My biggest concern was that I was sick and I couldn't teach, couldn't go to class. I couldn't walk to my own bathroom a few feet away without feeling weak. I was incredibly ill, but I worried about my classes. I feared that I was failing as a teacher and as a student. Good teachers and good students don't get sick. They go to class whether they are sick or not. There was my stinkin' thinking again: "Good girls should . . ., Good teachers should . . ., Good wives should . . ., Good mothers should . . ., Good academics should . . . ."

I wrote about my illness that fall. Thank God my friends and colleagues did not share the same belief I had about good teachers and sickness.

11–4–91
A poem in Progress

I eased into the
steaming

water, burning with a fever
They were coming
I'd forced them back in
For years, but they were
coming
my mouth formed a
strained scream, a
silent scream
Then I saw
A small girl sitting
in her mother's lap
hurt and in pain
being comforted
wrapped in her mother's
arms
Loved
They came, the
tears oozed onto my face
blended with the hot
steaming water
and then the burning image vaporized
And, I knew that
though my mother
didn't hold me in her lap
she would have
if she'd known how.
The fever burned on through the night.

It was November 25 before I was able to return to teaching my Western Civ section and even then I had to take life easy: that is, I could only venture out in the world for two to three hours at a time.

You might be wondering: How did an English teacher end up being a teaching assistant for the History of Western Civilization? Good question. Another story.

INTRICATE CONNECTIONS

In the spring of 1991 I had been an instructor in The Copse Project at NYU (we wanted to name it the Copse and Dana Project to honor the dual leadership), a collaborative teaching and learning project using writing to learn in

World Mythology, a course in the Religious Studies Department. That experience led to the Western Civ project. Like the cascading of a stream as it moves along, one experience flowed into another.

I loved the experience teaching and learning in the Copse Project: writing, telling, and listening to stories, our own and each other's, helped me to think of and write my candidacy paper as the story of my thinking. My role was to "lead" the group of undergraduates with which I worked, but I led the group by working to share authority: I risked sharing my stories, my life, my responses to required texts with my students, and I worked with them to help them tell their own stories. Our common goal became to tell our stories, to listen mythically (what resonates?). Then we began to tell the story of our stories. For me, the contents of the course and of our lives became inseparable.

During the Copse Project, late in the spring, Professor Copse took leave from the course to begin hospice with his wife, who was dying of breast cancer. This really affected me. In my own life I had had breast cancer and survived it. I had returned to teaching part-time while I had undergone nine and a half weeks of daily radiation. I taught in the mornings and had breast radiation in the afternoons. All those feelings came up again for me, and I remember at one point telling my story to Jim as we stood at the corner of Washington Square Park. He was wrestling about what to do—either continue teaching or stay home to care for his wife in hospice. I told him that he might think more about staying with his wife, that education was not best served by a personal sacrifice that denied him caring for his wife in her final days, and that we as a group could carry on with the class. Eventually he chose hospice with his wife. I have no idea whether what I shared had anything to do with his decision. And it really doesn't matter. I needed to say that to him for myself. Teachers are expected to be self-sacrificing. We as human beings need to maintain a spiritual, physical, and emotional balance. Choosing to be with a loved one who is dying supersedes being expected to show up for a class.

When Jim left lecturing and telling stories, attendance at the lectures, which usually numbered about 130 to 150 students, fell off. Jim Copse was a professor of mythic proportions and students not in the small groups (about 50 out of the class) chose not to come. Many students equated learning as emanating from one powerful source, in this case Copse. They seemed to reject the possibility of learning from small groups, from each other, from graduate assistants of "lesser" stature, or, God forbid, from and with each other. As instructors we were very painfully aware of the students' sense of loss when Jim left the lecture sessions, and we planned a variety of experiences to offer for the remaining lecture sessions: a movie, small-group discussions of texts one week, and writing and telling our stories as well as reflecting on our stories and processes.

I don't remember that attendance in our small groups fell off. My small group elected to have extra sessions because we had more stories than our once-a-week, one-and-one-half-hour meeting could handle. This was powerful for me. They chose to meet, and it had nothing to do with me or my "charismatic" teaching, but rather with their need to work together. They had experienced the power of sharing lives and stories and knew deep inside, without naming the experience, what I now call languaging.

A most reliable and engaged student, Peter, disappeared. Peter had been on a medieval quest. His sense of myth came from the pleasure he found in telling his own story in the language of the mythic knight's quest. His quest changed dramatically and so did his story.

Peter found me outside class one day during the last week of class to tell me in a stunned state that his father had died unexpectedly. We cried together and I told him, "Don't worry about a thing. Just do what you need to do and we'll talk later." Jim's wife, Peter's father. My friend Jean.

I am coming to know the fragility of life for us all, teachers and students, and it is in writing, telling, and listening to stories that we can come to know ourselves and each other, giving ourselves the authority to "do life." Jim had published a book on death, was an "expert" on the theory of death. Peter was living in an ideal world. Both were confronted with deaths, with loss, with grief, a reality that cannot be abstractly theorized. Jim later told us that though he was considered an expert on death, he realized that he knew nothing about death.

That spring I can say that I worked hard to language, to share and question, what my philosophy, my way of being and of working, was. I constructed a statement that appears in three states of evolution: one in a collaborative set of statements produced by a study group in my writing practicum, one that appeared as the final statement in my candidacy paper, and one that appeared in my reflections for a doctoral seminar in curriculum that spring, which I called "Constructing a Philosophy of Learning":

> When we work together with each other as co-learners in our class-rooms and among ourselves as professionals, not in some hierarchy based on myths of intelligence and power as authority which in turn demands a "perfect" text, when we devise a curriculum whose vision we share openly and which is negotiable, then we can hope to begin to learn with each other all the languaging processes, transacting together, mutually, reciprocally, respecting difference.

THE HISTORY OF WESTERN CIVILIZATION PROJECT

So I became a member of the Western Civilization Project in the fall of 1991 as a continuation of the work with Barbara Dana and the Copse Project. I was not an authority in the field of history, but I felt entirely comfortable with who I was as a teacher and learner. This collaborative project proved to be personally, socially, culturally, and politically difficult, for the two professors and the eight teaching assistants (4 history, 4 writing) set about our work diametrically opposed to each other, and things pretty much stayed that way.

As we did in the Copse Project, we met as a staff once a week to collaborate on our work in small writing sessions as well as to make suggestions for Professor Jamesson's lectures. From the beginning the history grad assistants felt that we writing folks did not have authority because we were not knowledgeable in history, and they acted on these beliefs in the efforts we made at staff collaboration. They did not respect our knowledge about teaching and learning or writing.

We instructors from the Writing Center found that our beliefs about the collaborative process were tested to the limits: at some point in the experience, actually during the time that I was recovering from pneumonia, I began to view the history folks as great political scientists working in a Machiavellian mode. They read us well and seemed to use what they knew about our beliefs in working together collaboratively and democratically to destroy efforts to value learners and learning. They viewed the whole enterprise as a game, a sort of war to be won or lost: We writing folks were the enemy and the history folks were the only true authorities. On one level they were correct: We writing folks were not experts in the subject of history, but we were knowledgeable about the language and learning issues ubiquitous in all disciplines. What they valued was the notion that knowledge was finite and absolute and that none of us writing folks had any comparable experiences to theirs in history. We had not experienced "thinking" historically (a phrase we spent endless meetings thrashing about among ourselves and with our students). No, we had not experienced thinking historically, but all the knowledge and experience we brought to the project were effectively silenced (not that we didn't have heated discussions).

Lines were drawn. Ego, pride, pettiness. We often lost sight of what might be in the best interest of learning, of thinking historically. I finally told myself that I couldn't respect what was happening, but that I had to accept that I could not change the history folks. This insight came while I spent four weeks in bed with pneumonia. I came to a sense that I could believe in myself rather than look to the history folks to accept what I/we writing folks might contribute to our focus to use writing to learn. I decided to focus my energies on doing the best I could do with my writing section, and continue to work with the history folks in the best way I possibly could. When I spoke (which was rare), I tried to keep the focus on a simple principle that honored learning and learners. It didn't matter if I "won" with the group. I found peace within, knowing that I believed in the learner and raised questions based on that principle, though the experience was anything but enjoyable. Somewhere in my reflections I realized that we history and writing people were living in different experiences and different languages and, at best, I could continue to articulate mine, question theirs, and let go of the notion of changing them. It is amazing how life goes when we have principles we believe in and actually try to live in and with and by.

A journal entry I made in late November tells part of the story. I had been paired to work with history grad assistant Karen, whose goal was to "nail it," meaning to teach the perfect small-group session while Professor Jamesson observed. I was annoyed with this attitude because she wasn't concerned with learning or with the students' work, thinking, progress, and so forth, but with her performance. I would now say that I lacked compassion for Karen, since she was young and had little experience with other than traditional academic paradigms. I keep learning about myself and others in writing this.

11–25–91

Today was my first day returned to teaching and I enjoyed my group. I was reminded of those history folk—stuck in themselves. Victoria's lecture, which Pamela and Karen love, was so ridiculously ego-centered. I am sure she learned a lot but it was so twisted—Henry VIII a great king. Bullshit! Karen and Pamela withdrew Pamela's visit probably because Karen couldn't "nail" it (Karen's language). This is a real lesson about working with people for whom I have to acknowledge I have no respect—they are so closed they think they are better. Just acknowledge it, let them be and keep centered on my group's learning which is the important issue.

This is the real world. Luckily, Copse project may balance this tension-filled project. A great deal. As Diane would say, the pain of learning.

Time for another Tylenol with codeine—my coughing is returning along with the pain. Only a few more days. As I look back I realize how seriously ill I've been I'm incredulous. It's as if my body belonged to a stranger. The weekend was Pat's movie escape—three diverse movie experiences—Friday—*Beauty and the Beast*—wonderful; Saturday, *La Belle Noiseuse*—incredible; and Sunday, *Meeting Venus*—enjoyable, mostly for the Wagner. Sunday I simply told Neil straight forwardly that I was f—ing pissed with him for not caring about me during my pneumonia.

Remember this, Pat: He did not once call, write or express (even when you called him) any more a concern than a wish (once) to "get well." Just remember that.

After the turmoil of the Western Civ Project, I looked forward to the Copse Project coming up in the spring and to collaborating with my friend Diane on a course we would be teaching as adjuncts in the English Ed Department. Since I was leaving New York to live at home again after this second year, I had to write and have my dissertation proposal accepted during the spring term. So I enrolled in "Dissertation Proposal Seminar," a course designed to help doctoral candidates write dissertation proposals. If I thought I had experienced turmoil with Western Civ, I was in for a surprise.

DRAINING SWAMPS

I was most anxious and fearful that I might not complete my dissertation proposal before I moved home to California, and while I was experiencing this proposal writing process, I found myself philosophically questioning everyone as well as the dissertation proposal paradigm itself. There's that fear thing again. Ubiquitous. I was just recovering from pneumonia, from anger at my husband for not having the basic human decency to care about a sick person he said he loved, and I was feeling tremendous pressure to complete my dissertation proposal and review before returning home to California.

2–19–92

Well, it's been a long week. The sessions with G and M have been painful. It's so ironic that we're encouraged to experiment, to "construct" our own meaning and here we are falling into predictable paradigms. And, into critical stances where there were none before. Rites of passage. So, Pat, go within. Do not overreach—go with the instinctual side of me. Just sit down and write a letter to myself about what this is—what questions it raises and how I'm going to do this.

At one point I found myself in my doctoral adviser's office, asking him if I could drop the dissertation proposal seminar, take an F, whatever. In my heart it felt as if I was being emotionally abused. I was willing to risk an F or a failure because I felt so strongly about what I was willing to go through. I don't remember ever dropping a class (I had always suffered through them and complained): this was one of the hardest visits and requests I have made during my educational life. I was willing to risk not being a "good" girl, good student, etc., rather than accept an unacceptable situation.

I wanted out because I felt that what I was experiencing was antithetical not only to everything I professed to believe in—sharing, nonhierarchical, mutual, reciprocal teaching and learning—but that I was trapped in an emotionally abusive situation. The professor for the seminar, an expert in the field of ethnography, told me in the first sentences of our first discussion of my proposal that my writing was incomprehensible. She appeared to feign innocence, saying that she was a simple reader. She said that she felt embarrassed to be saying this to me "since you're a writing instructor at EWP." A simple "I can't read this. Let's talk" would have been a more honest approach. Her words seemed couched in a false humility to cover what she had planned to say, knowing that it would be a painful message for her receiver. I felt that I was being emotionally manipulated, but I stuffed all my feelings until I left her office. I spent about 40 minutes or so listening to her remarks, left her office, and burst into tears in the elevator. The experience brought back all the feelings I'd had as a young girl, stuffing tears so as not to appear weak in the presence of authority, an authority who seemed to want to humiliate me and take over my proposal.

Why on earth would it be embarrassing to her when she was telling me, the "writing instructor," that she could not comprehend what I, a "writing instructor," had written? Her manner, her tone, her language said to me that writing instructors are supposed to be good writers and anything less was "bad." As a writer and as an EWP writing instructor I had failed to write traditional academic comprehensible text in the traditional academic motif: My topic sentences failed to properly introduce each of the requisite parts of a proposal: problem statement, research question, and so forth. I had tried to write a phenomenological proposal. That is, I was doing what I was proposing. On one level I had failed to write for an academic reader's expectations and I knew that. I had also received several other readings of the text, all of which were positive. I was baffled by her judgment of incomprehensibility, which to me meant that it was a mess and that nothing made sense. This professor called herself a transactionalist, but we had very different notions of what a transactionalist might be.

What happened to the process of negotiating with writers, with transactional teaching and learning, of sharing experiences? Instead, the message I read was that I had failed, I had failed to write comprehensibly, and I was certainly not worthy of being a writing instructor if I couldn't write comprehensibly for another academic reader. This was my response to her reading and criticism. I had no idea of her intentions.

I went to my adviser, James, because I decided enough was enough, I wanted to draw some boundaries for myself. I wanted no part in what for me was destructive "help." I was willing to negotiate difference, but I was not willing to submit to hierarchical demands for some "perfect" text directed by only a particular reader. It felt like I was reliving my father's demand for perfection, Dr. K.'s demand for a perfect text, my calculus failure, the Western Civ Machiavellians, my first year seniors, and my relationship with my husband in her office that day. FEAR again!

James advised me to remain in the seminar, and I did. It wasn't anything in particular that he told me that influenced my decision. At the time I was so upset about going to him (though he had never given me any reason to think so, I thought he would think I was being weak and selfish), I only remember him saying, "It wouldn't be wise, Pat."

Why did I stay in the class? James listened to me and heard my feelings. That helped me decide that staying in the proposal seminar was a reality I needed to face and work through in a healthy way. The academic world was not going to always language with me, and I had shared my fear with James and others. I wasn't alone.

Each week when I went to the proposal seminar I had to work hard to maintain my dignity as a writer and learner and to keep my focus. I took the advice that was useful and helpful and let go of the rest (in fact, it was my seminar colleagues who helped me most with writing my proposal). I can remember that the seminar professor was shaking her head, saying that my proposal wasn't ready up to and right through the review process, but I focused on getting my work done.

From this comes the swamp story. It's a simple one my wise friend Betty told me to help me through the situation: "Remember that when you're up to your ass in alligators, your purpose is to drain the swamp."

So, each week I went to seminar and focused on draining the swamp. Another lesson in simple principles to work by. I kept writing. I tossed the "incomprehensible" proposal and began again. I met with my colleague in the writing center, Lisa Berns, on a weekly basis. We worked together to write a clean, clear text. One day as I was wandering down MacDougal Street in the Village I saw and purchased a plastic alligator with teeth bared, which I placed on top of my printer. It was a reminder that as long as I focused on draining the swamp, the alligators did not hold power over me, and they were harmless. With the help of a friend and confidante, I used an alligator story to help me literally and metaphorically deal with the emotional, intellectual, and spiritual aspects of living through the proposal process. I finished the course.

Most importantly, I drained the swamp: I wrote my dissertation proposal and it was accepted. For me the times were indeed frightening, not only in dissertation proposal seminar but also in the world.

5–1–92

Tonight is frightening. The Rodney King verdict has touched off national riot syndrome in L.A., S.F., and now New York City. The sirens, the helicopters, the news reports. It's frightening. My friend Roy lives near Tompkins Square and called earlier this evening to tell me a hostile group gathered in T. Square. Bottle throwing and broken glass. Just heard that people are injured at 8th St. and University. Demonstrators are out and vandalizing the area. It's very unsafe. I've tried to call home but there is no answer. I wish I could talk to Neil. No answer.

I've finished my proposal and am just now working to clean it up. The biblio is a bit messy still but I can clean it up later. I'll decide tomorrow if I want to give to the printer or clean it up a bit more.

It's pretty frightening here. And, it's violent at home. Safety is hard to come by in our country. As long as the Reagans and Bushes (and, God forbid, Dan Quayle) govern us things will not get better. As in learning, violence/pain are what bring about change.

I returned to my family and my home in Walnut Creek on May 21, 1992, to begin work on my dissertation, eventually to become this book. Yet another story.

CHAPTER 10

Educating the Spirit: Reflections on English Education

I love the notion of putting together realities and a phenomenological reading experience. This notion looks like writing and reading our lives as we experience life and reading. The boundaries between life and reading, personally, professionally, and academically, have become one for me. In this reading life that I'm describing, we become one with the text, live in it, experience it and ourselves, know it and ourselves. At the same time, we can stand outside looking in in a meditative, metaphysical stance, reading and writing, living in and watching ideas. So, my notions of reading and writing continue to evolve. Join me inside a reader's heart and mind.

READING ROSENBLATT, 1992

I sat down to read Rosenblatt this morning and chose to read *Literature as Exploration* (1938/4th ed., 1983), Chapter 3, "The Setting for Spontaneity." I've just finished reading and taking notes on the chapter. As I peruse my notations in the text, I'm struck not only by my thinking, but also by the way I am reading. The first phrase I read and noted was ". . . parroting of empty words and phrases to satisfy a teacher's demand" (1983, p. 57). Rosenblatt had been telling the story of Indian reservation readers struggling with Restoration comedies, raising the question of what young readers might make of such texts in terms of "understanding." I underlined the above phrase because I am interested in the teacher's influence on readers and reading. Over and over I noticed that Rosenblatt is concerned with the control of meaning, structured by teachers who are influenced by academic and critical circles, circles that value understanding outside the reader's personal experience, thus rendering the text meaningless.

The teacher can structure the setting for spontaneity, but what influences the teacher to do so is complex. I realize that my sense of what influences change is tantamount to a spiritual conversion, something that takes place not only in the intellect but also in the soul, the spirit of a person. That is, a teacher needs to not only set the scene for spontaneity, but she also needs to value the literary, the educational experience as a vital personal experience for herself and others. It goes beyond words and into living a self-examined praxis, for teachers a questioning of what Rosenblatt calls "habitual attitudes and academic practices" (1983, p. 61).

Academic practices encourage "close readings." Readers learn that what is rewarded in an English class is a "sophisticated interpretation" and the "accepted judgment." Many teachers like myself, who often teach a text for years, expect student readers to meet their expectations of a text's meaning, forgetting the human joy and pleasure that is the reason for reading in the first place. Teachers also fail to realize that students reading a text for the first time couldn't possibly read a text with the same understandings and interpretations of which they, members of an elite academic community, are capable.

Rosenblatt states that what most often influences teachers is "what can be systematically taught and tested" (1983, p. 65). The social, cultural, and political influence of parents and administrators, academia, and students themselves pressures teachers to teach what can be justified. Yes, that describes my experiences teaching high school English and trying to make changes in my English teaching. What it doesn't include is what in me, in many of us teachers, transacted with this influence, and that was self-centered fear.

Rosenblatt is careful not to prescribe a formula for teaching literature, but rather suggests "general considerations that should influence practice." This may be why people miss her "paradigm." She states and describes general principles with which those teaching literature can work, then she suggests ways of working with those principles. First, she suggests that a general principle is that the teacher herself needs to value the literary experience, and, most critically, that ". . . any definition of the ideal relationship between the student and the literary work applies also to the teacher" (1983, p. 65).

Rosenblatt's suggestion here and my response to it are part of the reason why I chose reflective autobiography, beginning with my reading of the texts of Louise Rosenblatt. Through the reconstruction and critical reading and reflection on my experiences we can begin to know and understand what some of the primary influences have been for us as readers who teach literature. Teachers must recognize and liberate themselves, as well as the students they work with, from the "self-defeating" practices to which Rosenblatt refers.

During the summer of 1992, Chiyo Masuda, my collaborative teaching partner, and I worked with a group of K–12 teachers we were teaching in a CLP graduate seminar at UC Berkeley. I've included the course outline for "The California Literature Project, Graduate Seminar, 1992" in Figure 2. For

Figure 2. *California Literature Project, University of California at Berkeley.*

California Literature Project   June 22-July 2,1992   Chiyo Masuda   Pat Schmidt

EXPERIENCING LITERATURE

June 22 Monday

> A.M.   Experiencing Literature: The Integrated
> Lesson
> "Last to Go"

> P.M.   How We Became Readers: Autobiography of a
> Reader
> The Act of Reading: How Texts Teach What
> Readers Learn

June 23 Tuesday

> A.M.   The Act of Reading (continued)
> How Texts Teach What Readers Learn
> Experiencing Literature: Making Meaning
> in the Presentational Mode--Poetry

> P.M.   Creating Literature: Collaborative Reading
> and Writing

June 24 Wednesday

> A.M.   Responding to Literature: Theory
> "The Literary Transaction: Evocation and
> Response," "Dialogue with a Text"

> P.M.   Response to Literature: "Grady"
> Experiencing Literature: Entering a Text
> Chronicle of a Death Foretold

June 25 Thursday

> A.M.   Experiencing Literature: Visioning the Text
> Griffin and Sabine
> Black and White

> P.M.   Talking to Learn: Theory
> "Honest Questions and the Teaching of English"
> Developing Response to Poetry

June 26 Friday

> A.M.   Talking to Learn: Observing, Reflecting,
> Doing

Figure 2. *Continued.*

P.M. Experiencing Literature: Metaphors to Make
      Meaning--"Thinking About Thinking"
      Reflecting on the Week

June 29 Monday

A.M. Writing to Reflect and Explore Meaning
      Chronicle of a Death Foretold

P.M. Formal Assessments: Matching Theory with
     Practice
     CAP Integrated Reading and Writing Assessment

June 30 Tuesday

A.M. Writers at Work: Peer Response Groups
      Reflecting on CAP Assessment

P.M. Assessment: Classroom Practices
      California Learning Record
      "Interview: Mary Barr on Assessment"

July 1 Wednesday

A.M. Assessment: Classroom Practices
      Portfolios--"Portfolios and Self-assessment
      by Students"

P.M. Planning and Implementation: Grade-alike
    Groups
          K-3 (Paula Crivello)
          4-6
          7-12

July 2 Thursday

A.M. Reflection: Self Assessment
      Portfolios: Making Connections
      Evaluation of Seminar

P.M. Dining to Learn: Lunch and Conversation

Figure 2. *Continued.*

California Literature Project   June 22-July 2,1992   Chiyo Masuda   Pat Schmidt

BIBLIOGRAPHY

Albritton, Tom. "Honest Questions and the Teaching of
     English."
Bantock, Nick. Griffin and Sabine. ($16.95)
California Learning Record
Dias, Patrick. Developing Response to Poetry.
Garcia Marquez, Gabriel. Chronicle of a Death
     Foretold.($5.95)
"Interview: Mary Barr on Assessment."
Macaulay, David. Black and White. ($14.95)
Meek, Margaret. How Texts Teach What Readers Learn.
Pinter, Harold. "Last to Go."
Priestly, J.B. "No School Report."
Probst, Robert. "Dialogue with a Text."
Raines, Howell. "Grady's Gift."
Rosenblatt, Louise. "The Literary Transaction: Evocation
     and Response."
Thomas, Lewis. "On Thinking About Thinking."
Tierney, Robert, et al. "Portfolios and Self-assessment
     by Students."

a sense of the transformations in my teaching and pedagogy, look again at Figure 1, in Chapter 3, which was the "Lesson Plan" for my first year of teaching English in 1969.

We began our experiences in the CLP Graduate Seminar reading literature by writing and reflecting autobiographically. We began with the experience and life of the learner, the reader, the writer. We wrote and told our stories and we reflected on our lives, both individually and collaboratively, as readers, writers, teachers, and learners, as a community of learners.

Chiyo and I consciously chose not to tell these teachers that they needed to change their pedagogy to match their beliefs or ours; instead, we chose to continue to frame experiences while we continued to reflect on those experiences, raising questions and exploring differences. Most important in this was that we all spent time sharing our personal responses to the content and the processes we were experiencing: concerns, reactions, observations, realizations, questions, and so forth. We were encouraging teachers to make choices, to change their teaching out of their sense of who they were, and out of their current experiences in transaction with their past experiences reading, teaching, and learning. This shared, critical, reflective autobiographical process is a dynamic process.

CONNECTING THEORY AND LIVES: TEACHERS' CRITICAL REFLECTIONS

At the end of the two-week intensive seminar (we had asked teachers to keep a portfolio of their experiences in the course), we asked the group, including ourselves, to write a critical, reflective self-assessment. What follows are excerpts from their self-assessments, which evidence (to a degree) how the experiences in the course and with the reflective process influenced these teachers' thinking about reading, about education, and about themselves:

> *J.S.*—I will take much more away from this course because we have taken the time to relate what we are learning to the experiences we bring to the classroom. This has an implication for my teaching. I plan to build many more opportunities to write about and discuss with a partner or a small group what we are learning. . . .
>
> I know that much of the meaning I get from what I read depends upon the background I bring to it. I approach what I read with the expectation that it will make some sense and include some resolution. I'm afraid I need to improve my tolerance for ambiguity. . . .
>
> I believe that we are not just teaching reading and writing. We are also teaching what reading and writing are. . . . I want to change some things about my teaching and also to retain some of the things I am presently doing.

> *A.M.*—The literature I've experienced this week and last has affected [me] deeply. It has shaken up many of the beliefs, assumptions and classroom practices that I have used as guides in my teaching. Even though I have used many of the strategies we read about and experienced in class, its [*sic*] an attitude change—what Pat, Chiyo & Rosenblatt call stance—about looking at myself and my students as all learners, readers, & writers. It's a freeing, yet frightening feeling at the same time. For me, it's a lot about "letting go" of beliefs (which have served me to some degree) and control of my students' learning. Pat wrote that she also experienced this burden of responsibility (often reinforced by the

beliefs of administrators and parents in my opinion) before she experienced the Lit Project. . . .

It's strange because as a result of this class, I now have a clearer picture of what I don't know but need to find out in order to feel whole again as a teacher—both for the kids and me. I've also found that it's important for me to get connected to a larger community that believes the way I do.

This perhaps is a very important lesson for me because I feel that I stopped growing as a teacher and started listening to the school malcontents at the same time. I've discovered that I need to be with people who regard themselves as learners, not victims of the "system."

D.W.—In looking over and rereading the contents of the enclosed portfolio, I have come to the realization that I respond well to and enjoy being able to approach literature and responses to literature from *my individual needs.* That is to say, I found that in being allowed to approach the literature through a wide variety of response choices, I remained "open" to each new piece of literature we experienced. About myself as a reader, I have discovered that I like sharing my feelings (good and bad) about a text with other people. . . . I found that I learned more from a difficult text (Rosenblatt) when I was able to discuss it with a partner and I shared the reading out loud. . . . I am excited about the possibilities for putting more consistent and meaningful actions behind my beliefs. . . . Each day as we encountered different texts and wrote, discussed, and shared with different (sometimes the same) people, I learned many new ideas and ways of looking at things from them. . . .

S.C.—I found it really interesting that my last paragraph on the Metatext already began dealing with my beliefs as a teacher. I think that my subconscious took over because this was at the heart of what we were doing this week. I know that I have always loved literature, but I realized this week why I seek out more "pleasure" novels for light reading than turning to classics at this time in my life. I was feeling somewhat guilty for making some of the choices that I do in choosing books, but now I understand why I have been doing this. So much of my reading is reading for efferent meaning in doing research for my teaching that I choose to read for sheer enjoyment the rest of the time. I use this type of reading as an escape so that I can get caught up in make believe stories and just have fun with the text. No pressure—my life has too many of them already. . . .

Metatext: . . . I feel that these last two weeks have given me a chance to reflect and think about the joy that I experienced in learning to read. I know that I will be reflecting for a long time on how best to put this wonderful philosophy into classroom practicality. At the root of my classroom activity I will first ask myself, "What is the purpose of this activity?" Then I will ask myself are the students experiencing the aesthetic as well as the efferent value of the text. If I can answer both questions positively, then I will feel that I am getting to where I want to be as an educator. I am also realistic enough to know that I will make many mistakes along the way. However, when I have gotten stuck in the past, my philosophy has always been to go back to the kids. They have so many great ideas and can teach us so much.

N.X.—My own serious reading is limited—by time and lack of a safe place for dialog. I read the newspaper daily and find that I'm not even a very good reader as judged by my ability to read for details. I get a general picture, but often find that I can only parrot limited opinions, I can't abstract and describe patterns. My reading of literature continues to be a source of great pleasure to me—an escape and sometimes a re-fueling, but here, too, I find that I often don't have words to describe my sense of the book. I can describe my response, but I don't do the re-reading and discussing that Meeks suggests in her article. I think that at some level I do have an understanding, a communion with the text of a book that has moved me and yet I still don't have the words to describe my ideas. I'm interested in this preverbal—averbal???—kind of knowing.

MORE ON TEACHERS FACING THEMSELVES

Just this small sampling of reflective self-assessments written by English/language arts teachers participating in a teacher education seminar in which teachers return to seeing and knowing themselves as readers and learners evidences the influence of self-critical reflection on our personal experiences reading, teaching, and learning in teacher education. The influence, in turn, of such reflections on ourselves as readers and learners, in our teaching beliefs and approaches, can be seen in the change in thinking that may eventually be enacted.

Rosenblatt suggests that the first step is not to impose a preconceived notion about the proper way to react to any work. She states that youth need to be given "the opportunity and the courage to approach literature personally." Teachers must value students' responses to literature and help the student realize that that's what is valued. Initial responses should be free of concern for form; the requirement should be that the response be genuine and honest, un-self-conscious and spontaneous. As an example, Rosenblatt decries the traditional "book report."

Again, I notice how Rosenblatt discusses unexamined practice. Those practices influence reading. Daily assignments, devices for evaluation, and classroom methods may drive how readers read, rather than the reader having a personal transaction with the text. Rosenblatt believes that anthologies constrain meaning-making, too. I continue to be amazed that she conceived of this in 1938!

How do we break the chains of academia and faulty pedagogy? Rosenblatt tells us to scrutinize all practices to ensure that the initial response is a personal crystallization of the work. I wonder what her sense of "crystallization" is. Is crystallization an overall emotional feeling that describes the response? Is crystallization a sense of what it means? Is overall emotional feeling also a sense of what it means?

If teacher education courses addressed the need to scrutinize our teaching practices in the context of valuing personal experiences, the influence on teaching and learning would be profound. If English literature majors could experience literature in the informal, friendly, explorational exchange of response atmosphere Rosenblatt suggests, followed by critical self-examination of those responses, the sense of shared lives and shared authority, the languaging of the two disciplines, English and education, could take place. Surprisingly, it hasn't happened at New York University, where English majors are still educated separately from English teachers: Two completely different disciplines of English and English education. The practice continues still in the California state university system.

Imagine undergraduate English majors working in collaborative communities exploring literature, learning and possibly teaching together while reflecting on their lives, their learning, their sense of the human condition, rather than focusing on literary devices, themes, trying to write papers that regurgitate a professor's expert knowledge. Imagine English education students reading as much literature as they do theoretical and/or research-based text. What a brave new world! Imagine English majors knowing themselves as authoritative readers and meaning(s) as plural. Imagine English majors and preservice English teachers writing free, open, and explorational responses to texts, perhaps even being tentative in their understanding and willing to listen to other possible ways of reading and writing about a text.

My experiences, explorations, and reflections tell me this means that teachers need to actively participate as learners, raders, and writers when they teach "English." It means that they share the making of meaning with other readers. In Rosenblatt's words, "There is no formula for giving students the assurance to speak out" (1983, p. 70). Instead, she suggests that it is important for the teacher to place the discussion in the conceptualization, the notion of personal response as the center and the beginning.

Rosenblatt states that teachers are not passive in classroom interchanges and defines their role; their role is to draw out, to help readers clarify, to extend, to help elaborate on ideas. I would add to this that teachers need to clarify, to extend, to elaborate on their own personal evocations of a text *with* their students in a classroom setting. To be able to do this in our classes, we need to be open and honest about ourselves first, and we need to have experienced reading, teaching, and learning in open, supportive, critical, collaborative ways ourselves.

After 10 years (those following my reading, teaching, and learning experiences in the California Literature Project in 1986) of what I describe to be a consciously evolving pedagogy, I realize that Rosenblatt's suggestions that readers will benefit in two important ways is what I was becoming aware of when I began my California Literature Project experiences. First, when a reader examines the personal responses he or she experiences with literature, we each need to consider why we responded in a certain way, and in that process we do learn to read more richly, simultaneously learning to value and understand our lives and the lives of others. Integral to that understanding is the personal meaning, the sense of connection to our lives that we experience when we read literature. Second, when readers experience free exchange, helped by a teacher who works with them to extend their experiences, we can also develop the ability to listen with understanding and to respond appropriately.

I realize now that a person's language ability grows with lived-through experiences with literature and life, but that reading literature is only one of several influences on our language ability.

I am reminded that what Rosenblatt advocated in the late 1930s is neglected today by the majority of "English" teachers and educators teaching English methodology.

SOME THINGS CHANGE, BUT MANY THINGS REMAIN THE SAME

My nineteen-year-old daughter was taking an "intro to literature" course at our local junior college. She is an avid reader and has been since early childhood. Her experience with literature at the college level is the height of absurdity. She is lectured to about the form of short story, of poetry, and so forth. Her responses are limited to answering the questions that follow the selections in the literature anthology, and there was no spontaneous class discussion of the literary experience.

The first paper she was assigned to write was an essay comparing two

Faulkner short stories using a literary criteria of "best" story. This was not the instructor's originally authored writing prompt, but one in the anthology. The class did not discuss the assigned texts until after the papers had been turned in. Her paper was returned with a B and the instructor's comments to her that "You have chosen the wrong story as the 'best' story by literary standards and you do not know how to structure an essay."

While my daughter enjoys reading literature and is widely read for her age, this literary experience has given her second thoughts about becoming an English major. She's leaning toward anthropology now. I've tried to tell her that I don't think it would be much different in that discipline. She'll have her own alligators and swamps to deal with. Her experiences echo mine when I was a junior college freshman.

The sad part of all this, past and present, is that my undergraduate college experience was nearly 30 years ago and nothing much seems to have changed in terms of the education and experiences of English majors who then go on to become English teachers. In 1929, I. A. Richards's study of college English majors' reading abilities and deficiencies primarily attributed the paucity of rich literary response to the then current literary tradition of studying the history or life of the writer, which precluded focusing on the study of the text. Out of that study emerged what has dominated traditional English studies, New Criticism, the close reading of text. Decades later the discipline of English is still complaining that readers of all ages are incapable of making and writing sound literary interpretations. If the state of students' ability hasn't changed in this century using traditional methods, why isn't the discipline examining its pedagogy and methods? Instead, the profession faults students, the advent of television, the electronic media, the lack of standards, and so on.

Of the four classes my daughter was enrolled in at our local junior college, only one offered the kind of experience Rosenblatt suggests. It wasn't an English class.

Chapter 3 of *Literature as Exploration* (1983) reflects a scholar asking herself the questions peers would ask, critically examining her own proposals. Rosenblatt asks something to the effect of, "Isn't there more for the instructor to do?" The last part of this chapter addresses the critical importance of selecting books for readers that are suited to their interests, maturity, linguistic abilities, aspirations, and general backgrounds.

It strikes me as odd, even ironic, that Rosenblatt includes a sort of "beware" of letting it all get too personal, lest we loose sight of our literary aims, which are "to develop literary understanding." Literature is art and affords us an emotional release, but we need to ever be striving for enhanced understandings.

I find myself troubled by the phrasing Rosenblatt uses toward the end of the chapter: "Yet all of this, as great an achievement as it represents, only means that the obstacles to real education have been eliminated" (1983, p. 75). What is "real education"? Rosenblatt defined real education as acquiring the "mental habits that will lead to literary insight, critical judgment, and ethical and social understanding" (1983, p. 75). I sense the shadow of the literary establishment here, yet Rosenblatt completes this by suggesting that the real education continues with self-critical reflection. Rosenblatt suggests that the reader needs to reflect upon her responses, asking, Why did I respond this way? What in the work produced my reaction? Do I need to modify it? Accept it? Reject it?

Without using the words, Rosenblatt describes a reciprocal relationship between readers and texts, and most importantly, between readers, students among students, and teachers along with their students. This is the nucleus of Rosenblatt's transactional pedagogy.

What I realize now is that Rosenblatt, who is well known for the theory of the literary transaction, should be better known for transactional pedagogy, a term not currently used to describe her theory of education.

REVISITING MADAME CURIE

Along with reading Chapter 3 of Rosenblatt's *Literature as Exploration* (1938/ 4th ed., 1983), I decided to revisit Marie Curie's life. I wanted to know what in it, what about it, touched me. Though faint, why was it so powerfully etched in my mind and heart? I drove to the public library and checked out *Madame Curie* (1937), written by her daughter Eve Curie.

I sat out in the warm California Indian summer day, sunning, sipping morning tea, and began to read the book I had loved as a teenager. I had been puzzled by my book report (finding it and reading it for my research was a complete surprise) and my continuing memory of this as my favorite book, so it seemed important to reread *Madame Curie* again after all these years.

I opened it and began. . .

> Deep silence invaded the school building in Novolipki Street on Sundays (1937, p. 3).

The Sklodovski children are intensely playing at war. As I read the first few pages, I wondered why this book was so unforgettably etched in my reading memory. Expecting something monumental, I felt nothing for the text. By the time I had completed reading the first 29 pages, I closed the book and openly wept. It was a complete sadness that I felt. At that moment reading evoked a "spontaneous overflow of powerful feelings" (Wordsworth, *Lyrical*

Ballads, Preface). I began to understand why I have mentioned this book over and over as my most memorable reading experience, one that I took great pleasure in and loved, and why even in writing a traditional high school book report about it, the experience of reading such a powerful text could not be destroyed.

Eve Curie, Marie Curie's daughter, wrote her mother's biography, and the tone of this text is one of understanding and love, romantic in its narrative of a life lived. Manya Sklodvska (Madame Curie) lost both her oldest sister, Zosia, and her beloved mother at an early age. She was intellectually precocious and very much loved by her family. As I think about my adolescent life at the time I was reading this biography, I remember that I had moved from a safe life in Arizona, where my intellect and my femininity were not assaulted, to a Central Valley farm in California. My mother had suffered a breakdown and my parents decided that being near my mother's family would help her feel better or so we were told. My younger sister was also emotionally fragile: She couldn't adjust to the move and attending a K–8 country school. I remember that she would be picked up from school in the morning, crying and unable to continue in class. It was only years later at a moment of stress that my father told me the truth about our family's move. He had tried many occupations over the years, beginning with being a drill instructor in the army, then a policeman in Pismo Beach, California, then a mechanic, then a gas station owner, an iron worker, and finally, in the return to California, a farmer. We all struggled.

I tried to be a strong one in the family, like my father. I was angry and upset about the move, for it meant that I couldn't enroll at Arizona State University, which is where I had always dreamed of going to school. Instead, because of financial problems, I attended a local junior college 30 miles away from my farm home by school bus.

The love I felt Eve Curie had for her mother as I revisited that book that day brought me to tears again. My mother was physically alive in my life but emotionally missing, like the white-haired image of the inexorably lost mother in O'Neill's *Long Day's Journey into Night* (1995). I don't remember, but I imagine that I probably wept when I read *Madame Curie* as a teenager. Like Manya's mother, who was ill and did die, my mother disappeared into her medications and her depression. Like Manya's mother, mine seemed lost to me forever, and like Manya's prayers for her mother, mine went unanswered.

During those adolescent years, my spiritual faith faltered and, eight years later, left completely when, begging God to take her, my grandmother died. I felt that she had committed suicide by God. Her life was hell with my cantankerous grandfather, who had blacked her eyes just shortly before her death. God was beyond my comprehension, and I had no way to question or understand a God who would answer a prayer to die, a form of suicide for an otherwise healthy 62-year-old. Rereading *Madame Curie* brought back all these feelings. Talk about a personal evocation of a text! Is this living in the text and with the text a valid interpretation? It is for me.

After writing about this reading of *Madame Curie* and my response to the book, I realized that what I had been doing during this reading experience was what I was reading about the aesthetic experience described in Rosenblatt's "Setting for Spontaneity" chapter. That is, I was not only responding personally to the text and to my experiences with it, but I was also exploring why I was having the response I did. The response I found myself having had to do with the web of my life experiences at the time I first read the text, layered today with the 30 years of experiences in between.

What I felt at the core of the reading experience was a sense of shared lives, of shared sadness, though the details of our lives were very different. There was something in the reading experience that went beyond words, beyond intellectual description, and connected with my heart and mind. It is a spiritual reading, in a sense. I'm not referring to spiritual in a religious sense, or to any particular doctrine of spirituality. By spiritual I mean that it connected with my feelings about being a young female with intellectual precociousness and losing one's mother—only for Marie Curie this happened in a kind, gentle, loving family. I felt the love in their lives. I was touched by that love: it was a heart-to-heart matter that occurred in this reading experience.

Have you thought much about how you read and what is happening to you/with you as you read? Have you questioned what is going on in your life, your experience that calls up the particular reading you give a text? It is really revealing to begin this process, this way of reading a text.

As a reader, as readers, I am, we are, the culmination of the matrix of all reading experiences I/we have had, personal, academic, professional. Now I can say, though, that I read texts, whether they are *Madame Curie* or *Literature as Exploration*, by beginning with the personal making of meaning and the questioning of that meaning. I record my responses, asking, What is happening as I read and why is this happening? When I name these experiences, usually through writing, I can begin to understand not only why I had that response, but I may also be able to put it aside long enough to consider how what I'm reading can extend my thinking about the world and ways of being in the world. Perhaps this is what the act of reading has evolved to be for me: It is a way of questioning who I am and what I believe in relationship to the world, not just for literary understanding.

PRESENT MOMENTS OF READING AND WRITING

Reading, then, for me is an act of meaning, of making meaning of the text I'm experiencing by shuttling back and forth not only with my knowledge of words, of culture, of social phenomenon, but also drawing from the reservoir of my own experiences.

I just finished reading a memoir by Eva Hoffman, *Lost in Translation: A Life in a New Language* (1989). Hoffman's experiences with language, both her native Polish and her English, left me with the sense that our ability to language is greater than the sum of the parts of language, and the greater part is the particular human being's sense of self, a self that connects with the world through the language we possess; written, spoken, unspoken, seen, felt, sensed, and heard. "Human beings don't only search for meanings, they are themselves units of meaning; but we can mean something only within the fabric of larger significations" (1989, p. 270).

For me, reading literature has been an active search for meaning, for a key to living life in a world that often eludes my comprehension. Hoffman found her connectedness with her friend Miriam. Her description of what that friendship means describes my feeling about what reading means for me, what it means for me since I have begun to seek a friendship with the world, a sense of connection with the world when the real world of my life was disconnected.

> We've woven intricate designs for each other, and have subjected them to close mutual investigation. To a large extent we are the keepers of each other's stories, and the shape of these stories has unfolded in part from our interwoven accounts. (Hoffman, 1989, p. 279)

To a young girl in a family of nonreaders, of black-and-white thinking about the acceptable way to be and live in this world, books have offered me, and still do, a way to keep and investigate my story with those of others.

What I am writing now in response and reflection as it tumbles out of my fingers is that the act of reading is the inside spiritual experience, that felt sense of shared connection with living stories with which we construct ourselves.

I began this autobiography with two research questions: What influences the teaching of English? How does reading theory influence teaching English? I focused the research on four strands—my reading, my teaching, my reading of theory—primarily the literary theory of Louise Rosenblatt—and my personal life—in hopes of understanding more fully how these areas of experience influenced my teaching of English.

What I have found is that personal and educational experiences with authority, with unhealthy perceptions of authority, and the way I worked in relationship to authority were the primary influence on my teaching, but not on my theoretical pedagogy.

SEEKING SHARED LIVES

When we work together with each other as co-learners in our classrooms and among our-
selves as professionals, not in some hierarchy based on myths of intelligence and power as
authority (which in turn demands a "perfect" text), when we devise a curriculum whose
vision we openly share and which is negotiable, then we can hope to begin to learn with
each other. We can begin to learn with and from each other when we begin to tell, to lis-
ten to and to write our stories as women and men, teachers and learners, languaging
our worlds.

—Pat Schmidt, 1993

It is the winter of 1993. I sit at home in Walnut Creek, California, making notes to begin to work on this autobiography. I have been doing a great
deal of reading: it is reading without the context of teaching, and I have a
strange feeling. I have found it very difficult to read most theoretical texts I
used to read voraciously while in New York: sitting on my pile of newly published unread English education texts are books by James Moffett and Gordon
Wells, as well as Italo Calvino's novel *If on a winter's night a traveler* (1979/
1981).

My book buying has not abated, just my tastes and pleasures have shifted.
Take away an addictive personality's addiction and she will find another. Reading is not an addiction that I will die from doing too much of, thank God.

Feeling alone, isolated from the educational community I left in New
York, I have found myself seeking the company of women, of women writers'
lives, their fictions, their stories. Sitting on my desk are the novel I finished
yesterday, Barbara Kingsolver's *Animal Dreams* (1990), and the fruits of my
visit to the county library last week along with my current pursuit, reading
women's lives: *Ever Yours, Florence Nightingale: Selected Letters* (Vicinus & Nergaard, 1989), *Letters from Egypt* (Florence Nightingale, 1987), *A Feeling for the
Organism: The Life and Work of Barbara McClintock* (Evelyn Fox Keller, 1983),
"Cassandra" by Florence Nightingale (included in *The Norton Anthology of Literature by Women*, 1985), and *Blackberry Winter* (Margaret Mead, 1972).

What all these women have in common, which reminds me of how I felt
when I read Carolyn Heilbrun's *Writing a Woman's Life* (1988), is the sense I
share with them of my own life, the struggle (sometimes great, sometimes
not) to become, to be a woman with aspirations, with a profession in a culture
that resists such pursuits by women. Yes, I can identify with Hillary Rodham
Clinton. I'd suggest that on one central level we all should: as individuals, we
need to value each other's gifts regardless of gender or race. Isn't this what
multiculturalism is all about? Caring compassionately about each soul we
meet.

Reading these women's lives encourages me to continue my work here in California. I have very few conversations about my work these days. Once in a while I call a friend who is teaching and talk about their schools and their students with them, but I find myself working in relative isolation. It is a mixed blessing. I've tried unsuccessfully to connect with my doctoral friends and professors in New York, but their lives go on and I'm not there to be in their immediate circle of experience. I find that I really don't enjoy this isolation and would prefer to be teaching at least one class while I write. I miss the sense of community I enjoyed in New York. Ironically, I rejected the suggestion that I teach while I write this. I could not see how to do both without losing Pat again.

Two weeks ago, just before Christmas, my father-in-law, Peter Schmidt, died. It has been a hard holiday season, and I feel alone in my grief for Peter's death. Our family talks about Peter as he lived, but not about our feelings of grief. So, as I did when I lived on the farm as a teenager when I felt lonely and isolated, I seek connection with lives through my reading, and my reading today is consciously and unabashedly about and by women. I'm also much more aware today of why I seek the company of women. This is not because I reject or resent men. It seems to come from an inner need to language the journey with those who have also experienced the struggles. Their stories help me to continue to write my own, to believe in the worth of my story, as unimportant as it is in the larger scheme of the world.

I hope to continue to make the discoveries of my life: a sense of Pat, of myself as a person/reader/learner/teacher. I hope to share that understanding, fleeting as it is, to inform the me of the teacher I am becoming, to know and understand myself and to accept myself, to nurture a compassionate heart for us all. I used to read to literally save my life; now I turn to writing to literally know my life, to accept the parts of it I cannot change but at the same time to change the things I can. And, to continue to seek the wisdom to know the difference.

CLAIMING AUTHORITY: LANGUAGING

Writing this autobiography of my reading, teaching, and learning life has helped me to realize how much of my authority of self I (and a great many other girls and women) freely gave to others, thinking that this is what good girls, good women, good teachers, good readers, good learners all do. This is what a great many learners who desire approval and acceptance in their academic fields also do. Much of my evolution as a teacher comes out of a need to redefine myself as a woman, a teacher, a reader, a learner, to resist redefinition by others, for that is what happened in my early years of education, of life.

In all my years of reading and writing about my reading, I do not remember beginning any paper with my own language, my own ideas, in words I had chosen to represent my experience and knowledge. It was accepted, encouraged, and safer to cite the words of others to frame my discussions. I clung tenaciously to the text so that I could be characterized as having correctly read the text and having acquired the meaning it held, in a sense Louise Rosenblatt's "valid interpretation." I thought that my reading would be considered by academic standards a poor reading if other authorities did not accept my thinking. I used a great many crutches, the words of others, to state my ideas. Part of this way of working came out of fear, part of it came from my training to read texts as objects whose meaning was to be unearthed, part of it came from my experiences in education and life.

Part of me loved and reveled in the language others used, but part of me defined myself as authority, as an authoritative reader and writer, by demonstrating that I had literally read the text and could facilely use the author's words, the language of the text I was reading. I found that I unconsciously followed this pattern throughout my undergraduate and graduate work as an English major, even into the formal papers I wrote as a Ph.D. student at NYU in two humanities courses. My candidacy paper began with a few lines from a Wallace Stevens poem, and three sections of my dissertation proposal cite authorities in my reading, Lionel Trilling (1970), Susanne Langer (1953), and Jerome Bruner (1990).

I begin this section with my words; all of them are mine. The words are the language of my experience. Yet they are the words of others, too, for I have experiences that tell me that language is socially and culturally constructed (Rose Budding). Writing my beliefs about teaching and learning in my own language, the language of what I see, what I understand, think, feel, and believe—growing out of my experience and my reflections on those experiences—is a step toward knowing and accepting my self as an authority. Yet when I place my statement first in this section of my autobiography, I do not feel that I am an isolated authority. This is why.

I finished my candidacy paper, "A Developing Theory of Languaging: How Transactional Response Transforms Language and Learning" (1991), by almost totally citing my own text. Almost all of that closing statement is in my own language. At the time that I literally sculpted the statement, I spent hours choosing and thinking about each word as well as the whole sense of the meaning of the statement. The last 12 words of my original statement were the words of Louise Rosenblatt, taken from *Literature as Exploration*, ". . . points of growth in the social and cultural life of a democracy" (1938, p. ix). I wanted to impress my readers with my ability to construct my own belief about teaching and learning, but I also wanted to let people know that I wasn't alone in this belief by incorporating Rosenblatt's words, an authority in my fields (and a woman), into my own statement.

When I state my beliefs entirely in my own language, it is not a rejection of the authority of others but an acceptance and assertion of my own authority to know what I know and to say what I know as equal in authority. I am doing my best to language my experiences.

Beginning this section with a statement of my beliefs in my own language is frightening and freeing. I'm out in the open, no longer hiding behind the authority of others or using them to shield my own fear of criticism or inadequacy. My statement is the best representation of what I believe, but those beliefs will continue to evolve.

I believe that this notion of languaging, of sharing our personal, our teaching and learning, our reading lives with others, is critical to thinking about what we do in education. Each word in that 97-word philosophical statement is a story. I had to read and write and tell many stories to make that statement. Each word is informed by past lived experiences and what is happening in my life today.

When I chose to become a teacher, I thought my teacher education prepared me to be a teacher and that when I completed the course work, received my credential, and secured a job teaching English, I was a teacher. I had to experience a great deal of personal and professional pain before I could begin to transform my concept that becoming a teacher was "a done deal." I had thought that once I *became* a teacher, I *was* a teacher. "Good" teachers were supposed to think of themselves this way. I know now that I was a teacher as a child, in spirit. Then I worked to become a teacher—taking a major detour from my self along the journey.

Having written this autobiography, my stories, and listening to the stories of others while I continue to write, I can say now that I am a teacher becoming. For me, being a teacher now is being a teacher becoming. I will continue to tell, to write, to share stories of my reading, my writing, my teaching and learning, and my carefully wrought statement of beliefs will continue evolving. It may take years to change even one word, but I know words and meanings and understandings will continue to change out of my experiences. I ask you to reflect on these questions. How did you become a teacher? Were you a teacher before you became one? Are you open to changing your vision of yourself from having become a teacher (done with it) to becoming a teacher? To a teacher who is becoming?

In a sense, Lionel Trilling made a crucial statement about what may influence teaching when he said, "The experience of the teacher proposes the possible experience of the student" (Trilling, 1970). What teachers do with their experiences, not just in the context of the informed reading stance that Trilling proposed for teachers of literature, influences what and how they teach.

We teachers need to critically explore our experiences by telling the stories we carry around inside us. We need to challenge and question ourselves, and work with others to help them also challenge and question. For many of us in education our experiences and the stories of those experiences constitute our authority and inform what we do in our classrooms. We need to tell them and become conscious of what we do and why we are doing these things. Pamela Grossman called this "principled practice," or the integration of theory and practice, in *The Making of a Teacher* (1990). Freire calls it *praxis* (1990), and bell hooks calls it "engaged pedagogy" (1994). When we tell stories to ourselves, to each other, we begin to free ourselves from the existential prisons in which we find ourselves teaching and learning. Sartre's *No Exit* (1946) is what I have in mind. His characters were trapped by their own thinking and failed to take action to leave. The door was open, but they failed to take the steps to free themselves, to exit. We can trap ourselves as persons, as teachers, as readers, as learners, but the door is always open.

For me, authority is neither completely external to us nor is it completely self-contained, internal. It is shared, something that is both inside us and outside us. Like the Good Wyf of Bath in Chaucer's *The Canterbury Tales* (1963), whose personal transactional philosophy of life and education caught my imagination in the early 1980s when I reread and wrote about her tale for a weekend seminar, I've explored my relationship with others in my personal/professional life (alas, only one, not five, husbands). The Wyf taught her husbands and me about "sovereignty," the idea of recognizing the authority of self in relationship to the authority of others and the joy of reciprocity. For me sovereignty carries a spiritual notion of acceptance and unconditional love for those with whom we work and live. It is an honoring and valuing of each person's humanity. It behooves us all to ask, How are our current pedagogy and curricula enacting such principles?

This notion of languaging that I have tenaciously held forth on for four years is the active verb I need to name my experiences for you; the word is my best way of capturing what happens *sometimes* in my teaching and learning. It is a concept I'll continue to wrestle with and to write about.

In 1968, when I first began to teach, I had a sense of what I valued and believed, but no way of looking at and understanding what I was teaching in the context of those beliefs, the chaos of authority. Writing these stories and constructing the narrative of my reading, teaching, and learning life enabled me to examine my life and the chaos that I was experiencing. Critically writing about and reflecting on these experiences with others, with my committee, has helped me to understand the influences, the changes, the evolving nature of becoming a person and a teacher. I truly feel that I have begun, am beginning in retrospect, constructing and reconstructing my life.

What influences the teaching of English? Virtually everything in the life of a teacher. It is in the socially and culturally constructed languaging processes of self-reflection and self-understanding, of understanding and examining what we believe and what we do with those beliefs, that we as teachers and learners may continue to learn and grow, to evolve personally and professionally.

CHAPTER 11

Beginnings in Retrospect: Self-Understanding and Education

We understand that even the most seemingly objective scholarship in every field reflects an implicit interest in preserving the patriarchal status quo, including certain notions of canon, authority, and tradition from which the contributions of women and others have been excluded.

—Christ, 1980, p. xi

Picture your Self (please note that I will be using Self with a capital "S" to indicate the importance of a being inside the teacher, the reader, the learner) walking forward down the street looking backward. In a sense, writing this retrospective feels like that is what I am trying to do here—strolling forward in life while looking and being mindful of the past, and at the same time writing to make some sense of one woman's life. I'm struggling with trying to look back while continuing in the present.

I set out to write my autobiography in order to answer what now seems like rather presumptuous research questions: What influences the teaching of English? How does reading theory influence teaching English? My questions seem presumptuous in that they are so general and broad to explore. And it feels Self-absorbed to present experience and internal personal knowledge as evidence to explore and understand the evolving life of the English teacher. In some way the research and theory I had read had already named the major, abstract influences on the teaching of English (Britton, Shafer, & Watson, 1990): social, political, and cultural. It is also highly personal.

Initially, I sought to know how the life lived as experienced by the teacher in these contexts influenced the teaching of English. To hold my research together on some focus, I chose to tell the stories focusing on my reading life, reading literature and theory. I believe Jerome Bruner's notion of autobiography as acts of meaning (1990). More specifically, I chose to tell the story of my experiences reading the transactional literary theory of Louise Rosenblatt over time to explore the intertextuality of reading theory and experiencing teaching consciously. After one year of reflective writing and storytelling, my research question has, I see, become less presumptuous: What influences one teacher's teaching?

In the "Prologue" section introducing *Stories Lives Tell*, Carol Witherell and Nel Noddings (1991) both celebrate and author the power, the authority, of narrative and story in the lives of teachers and students. They tell us that "the narrator of a story has a story, one that is embedded in his or her culture, language, gender, beliefs and life history. This embeddedness lies at the core of the teaching-learning experience."

Writing as honestly as I could, reconstructing, telling, and reflecting on my life experiences, I sought to disembed my story, with which for many years I sat alone in silence.

Anita Plath Helle, a professor of English working in women's studies, comments in her article, "Reading Women's Autobiographies," in *Stories Lives Tell* that "There is a relationship between lives lived, lived in process, epistemology and pedagogy" (1991, p. 54). As I look at the life I have lived, that I am living, I see a woman who is a teacher searching to bring together the parts of herSelf, seeking wholeness of Self, but at the same time, like strolling forward while looking backward, constructing mySelf while helping others to construct themselves. Though it wasn't evident to me in the beginning of this work, the center of my wholeness is coming to know mySelf as a woman in patriarchal social, political, and cultural contexts. I am a woman who is a reader, a learner, and a teacher.

Though I initially focused my research to critically explore and understand what influences the teaching of English on four areas of experience, the reading life, the reading of theory life, the teaching life, and the personal life, I assumed that these four areas were all inseparable. I learned that though I separated them and parts of mySelf to write about the parts of the teaching life, they are inseparable. Sometimes we have to read it in black and white to SEE it.

The thread holding the fabric of my research together was my love of reading. I thought that my experiences reading influenced my teaching and my life. I had it backwards. My experiences reading influenced my life but to a much lesser degree my teaching until I began to critically reflect on experience. The educational experiences I had at UCLA and with the California Literature Project offered to me at a critical moment in my life a new way of working and thinking about teaching English. They would remain unconscious, like my early teacher education, without the practice of Self-reflection and critical reflection.

In looking back while strolling forward, I see that there may be many ways of talking about the evolution of my epistemology and pedagogy. At the center of this influence on my teaching is my life being female. When I began to experience new ways of reading and enjoying literature in 1986, I was given the opportunity to reflect on my teaching and learning. At the same time, I had begun psychotherapy, telling the stories of and reflecting on my experiences as a woman struggling to be in relationship to others, family, students, parents, authority figures. In 1988, when I chose sobriety, I filled a deep, dark soul hole with critical, Self-reflective practices called daily inventory, a way of searching for and making amends for any behaviors that need correcting that have harmed or injured others. I learned to include mySelf in this process.

The process of redefinition emerged from moments of personal and professional crisis. Most of my life I struggled with but submitted to authority, to the "procedural languages of the dominant culture" (Helle, 1991). I wanted to be the "good" girl, then the "good" student, then the "good" teacher, and finally the "good" wife and mother.

My ways of knowing, my development as a woman, generally follow the epistemological categories described in the research of Belenky, Clinchy, Goldberger, and Tarule in *Women's Ways of Knowing: The Development of Self, Voice, and Mind* (1986). Without knowing me or my life, Belenky et al. accurately characterize the narrative of my "Self, voice, and mind" that I construct in my autobiography. In some ways this astounds me. I am not alone in my experience. My experiences as a woman in education, with my family, and in relationships have previously been researched and valued.

My early life experiences and most of my educational experiences, in Trilling's sense, did construct my pedagogy, a pedagogy that had been constructed out of my experiences with and views of authority. Belenky et al. (1986) describes how experiences with authority influence women. With my family, my mother, my father, my husband, my principals, the police, my teachers, over the years I struggled with what Belenky et al. terms "wordless" authority, that is, an authority that expects one "to hear and to obey." To survive, I hid in silence and retreated into mySelf, exhibiting external "good" behaviors. To deal with these experiences, I became a "hidden multiplist" (Belenky et al., 1986, p. 67). A hidden multiplist stills her public voice and is reluctant to share her private world.

As I progressed in my formal education, seeking my teaching authority through yet higher and higher education, I was experiencing and embracing "separate knowing." I sought the voice of reason as my authority. My admiration and unquestioning acceptance of the discipline of English and its definition of knowledge and truth, of the Dr. K.s' voices of reason, continued to reinforce my distrust of my Self while reinforcing the power of external authority. I'd suggest that this tension transcends the personal and is, rather, endemic, systemic tension that is part of the educator's life.

CRITICAL MOMENTS, TURNING POINTS, AND CHANGE

The moments of clarity when I knew that things needed to change were pre-cipitated by personal crisis. Whenever I hit the emotional bottom (a break-down, cancer, alcoholism, redefining mySelf in my marriage and family), these moments brought me to my knees and I began to ask for help, to seek connection. Belenky's studies found that points of change in women's lives occur when we keep journals and use the processes of Self-examination, when we begin to redefine ourselves, when we begin to reconceive truth and knowl-edge, when we walk away from the past, and when we make choices. "The New York Stories" tell the stories of my pain in leaving home yet again to pursue my education, the pain of relationships in teaching and learning, as well as the sense of joy which, for me, matches the depth of the pain of my stories. The blue lamp story is not the only story I have told about being alone with a piece of furniture.

Many years ago I wrote a sing-songy piece, "Alone in a Room With a Chair," and no one but mySelf is there. The New York version, the full-circle blue lamp story that ends my stay in New York, expresses a sense of joy and connectedness in stark contrast to the loneliness and despair of the chair poem.

> Alone in a Room With a Chair
> And,
> No one but my Self is there
> Alone
> In a room
> With
> A Chair.

Carol Gilligan's *In a Different Voice* (1982), while describing women's psy-chological/moral development, suggests that the transformation of moral judgments corresponds in change in the view of Self. I would argue that con-comitant with that notion, the transformation or evolution of epistemology and pedagogy corresponds in change in view of Self.

The last "way of knowing" that Belenky et al. discuss is constructed knowing, the "integration of voice." The constructivist thought is that "all knowledge is constructed and the knower is an intimate part of the known" (1986, p. 137). Characteristic of the constructive knower is a woman who is becoming and staying aware of the working of her mind, stretching the boundaries of her consciousness—making the conscious unconscious, some-one who consults and listens to the Self, voices the unsaid; someone who lis-tens to others, and someone who tries to imagine herSelf inside the poem, the idea or the person that they want to come to know and to understand. In my developing theory of languaging, the story of my education with Rose Budding, we two women at that moment were experiencing a silently shared authority, both of us working together a constructivist stance. She wanted to know and understand me and I wanted to know and understand her. We knew and understood, though verbally unlanguaged, through the stories of our lives that we told each other, that we were writing our lives together.

LANGUAGING OURSELVES

Carol P. Christ in *Diving Deep and Surfacing: Women Writers on Spiritual Quest* (1980) speaks to many of the issues I have written about in this book, and Christ offers us a transforming hope for women (and men) who are questing for the Self. Christ gives us a particular emphasis on women's experiences as expressed in literature. She characterizes women as questing for both social and spiritual knowledge of themselves, "two dimensions of a single struggle" (Christ, 1980, p. 8). Christ defines the social quest as one in which women concern themselves with "the struggle to gain respect, equality, and freedom in society—in work, in politics, and in relationships with other women, men, and children" (Christ, 1980, p. 8). Women's spiritual quest is a "woman's awakening to the depths of her soul and her position in the universe. A woman's spiritual quest includes moments of solitary contemplation, but it is strengthened by being shared" (Christ, 1980, p. 8).

Christ's description of the process of questing follows a pattern: nothingness (emptiness in our lives—in Self-hatred, in Self-negation, in being victim, in relationships with men, in the values that have shaped our lives); awakening, a coming to Self that often occurs in community with other women, in which we identify and gain insight; and naming, which reflects a new orientation of the Self, a movement to overcoming dualisms (dichotomies, black-and-white thinking) through experiencing the powers of being (1980, p. 13).

If you have joined me along this journey of being and becoming, you have begun in retrospect. Carol Christ characterizes this as a "new naming." Naming the experiences I have had in my reading, my teaching and learning, and my professional and personal life are, for me, an occasion for celebration, a celebration of the teacher as Self. It is an active and searching naming of the experiences of the Self. I am still evolving: from New Critical reader to Transactional teacher to languaging theorist; from teaching English to languaging with people; from rows and lectures to teacherless small-group discussions; from questions with answers to questions with more questions and a great many "maybes"; from teaching skills and literary understanding to reflective teaching and learning with language in its diverse "subjects" at the center.

Many of us chose to teach English because we "loved to read." For a great many of us, reading literature and loving to read, both in and out of school, is a meaning-seeking process. As a mature reader, I seek aesthetic pleasure, Self-understanding and acceptance, and knowledge of the world and with the world through reading. Many of us do. Somewhere along the journey I became all tangled up in fear and enmeshed in the cultures and canons and theories. Many of us do.

The quest for Self-understanding and Self-acceptance does not work in isolation (the manner in which many of us are taught and experience reading, learning, and teaching), but in connection and feeling connected to the world. It is a crucial issue not only in English classrooms for English teachers and those of us in English education, but for all of us committed to education. Because we are told and taught in academic life, not just as women, that Authority is outside us (in the text, in the teacher, in the principal's office, in the curriculum, in educational and literary theorists, in research), we learn not to trust our perceptions, our own minds, who we are. We learn this, and when we go into teaching we usually teach this without understanding our own losses.

Self-understanding and Self-awareness are the beginning to understanding and compassion for ourselves and others, particularly for teachers (Jersild, *When Teachers Face Themselves*, 1995); this search for meanings in our lives is a basic principle of my belief in the overarching purpose of education. This is the highest challenge for education. Who are we as individuals and how are we learning to value ourselves, to be true to ourselves, while in relationship to others, negotiating relationships within society and culture, community and canon? How can we work to know ourselves as readers, teachers, learners, while in relationship with the culture of our discipline?

Years of authoritarian educational and reading experiences are difficult to overcome. The change I needed to make as a teacher was to work toward restoring the sovereign human spirit to my curriculum. To do this I had to initiate the process, seeking new experiences, telling the stories of my experiences, and critically reflecting on the teacher I was to inform the teacher I am becoming. In a sense, I am still talking about the importance of strolling forward while looking backward.

In many ways this autobiographical narrative has been a mythic quest, telling my story, a return to and a restoration of Self as a sovereign being, a female, a teacher, a reader, a person in her culture. Epistemology and pedagogy are not a matter of authority now, but of sovereignty.

Arthur T. Jersild studied hundreds of teachers in the early 1950s and concluded that teachers need to have intimate and personal meaning in what they are doing, for the teacher who understands and accepts himself or herself is the most important requirement in any effort he or she makes to help students to know themselves and to gain healthy attitudes of Self-acceptance (1955, "Foreward"). "Without Self-examination, what one sees may be distorted and what one does may be without much meaning" (Jersild, 1955, p. 131). He further states, "The ultimate test of the meaning of what we teach is its implication for the individual person. Meanings may be shared, but they are realized as a personal experience by one person, and by him or her alone" (Jersild, 1955, p. 134).

Pursuing a doctorate in English education has been a God-given act of courage I did not know I had the heart for. Writing a Self-critical autobiographical dissertation of my reading, teaching, learning, and personal life has been another God-given act of courage. Publishing this book is truly a gift of grace.

Throughout this journey some things have not changed. My desire for the kind of life on which I am journeying was expressed in my high school book report on Madame Curie. I admired so much her searching mind, her loving family, her ability to combine a life's work with a loving relationship with her husband Pierre: "Madame Curie is not a story of one person discovering a substance vitally important in the world today, but of the person of a Polish girl—shy and brilliant who came into fame through the family, husband and world."

Many years later, when I had chosen to leave my family, my husband and daughter, to journey to New York to continue my very precious doctoral work, I found that I, like Manya Curie, struggled with my identity as a woman in conflict with conventional cultural expectations for women. Pursuing my doctorate in English Education and writing this autobiography were in many ways acts of meaning (Bruner), a conscious act toward Self and identity: It is now a consciously feminist act (Heilbrun, 1988), for a reading of what this all might mean requires a feminist psychology because the stories are the stories of a woman's life (Belenky et al., 1986; Brown & Gilligan, 1992; Heilbrun, 1988).

As a reader, a teacher, a learner who is a woman, I am emerging from underground and silence. I do not think, however, that what we can learn about what influences teaching when the study focuses on the life teacher who is a woman is limited to female readers only (though my guess is that few men save my university readers will read this text). I have avoided the word *feminist* in describing my work or my languaging theory, for in our culture feminist carries a tremendous pejorative and limiting shared meaning.

Somehow feminism has become a soundbite of negativity: feminists are generally stereotypically deemed strident, man-hating, unfeminine bra burners. In my first doctoral seminar my study group happened to be comprised only of women. Somehow we were labeled "the feminists." We weren't burn-ing bras during seminar, nor were we stridently anti-male. We were a strong-willed group who cared about the human condition, primarily the female condition, and we happened to be female. It seemed natural to focus on educational concerns with the female experience.

My work is feminist in that it is of the feminine nature. It is an acknowl-edgment of mySelf as a woman whose life has evolved in the company of other women's stories and theories, ways of knowing, and who believes that education is the cultural context in which these evolutions can be constructed (I guess I am still a romantic idealist).

I have been redefining myself as female, as feminine.

As a young girl and a young woman I felt torn about my femininity. I was definitely a tomboy, and I saw as a young girl that men and boys had power. I loved playing baseball, shooting baskets, running track, swimming, constructing roads and towns in cool dirt in my mother's geraniums. I resisted my mother's efforts to "femininize" me with makeup, lipstick, frilly dresses. Yet I was always self-conscious about my looks, and while I wanted to be equal with the boys I still wanted to have boyfriends. I struggled with being smart and female. Once I dated a young man who became incensed when I opened my own door on our date. I had the audacity even to help him locate a parking place, bruising his masculinity with my help. It has been a struggle to be fe-male without being femininized into submissiveness and obedience and help-lessness or labeled a "feminist" because my work addresses gender.

So, I now think of myself as female in the loveliest sense of the word, multifaceted, strong, still becoming, loving, intelligent, compassionate. I am concerned with the lives of women and teachers and students, male and fe-male, in relationship to educational and literary cultures. "Whatever their form or medium, these stories have formed us all; they are what we must use to make new fictions, new narratives" (Heilbrun, 1988, p. 37), to stroll for-ward while looking backward.

References

Acosta, T. P. (1979). "My Mother Pieced Quilts." In *United States in literature* (Medallion ed.) (p. 7). Glenville, Illinois: Scott, Foresman. (Original work published in 1975 by University of Southern California)

Anaya, R. (1972). *Bless me ultima.* Berkeley, CA: Tonatiuh—Quinto Sol International.

Ashton-Warner, S. (1963). *Teacher.* New York: Simon & Schuster.

Atwell, N.(1987). *In the middle.* Portsmouth, NH: Boynton/Cook Publishers.

Atwood, M. (1969). *The edible woman.* New York: Warner Books.

Balzac, H. (1914). *Eugenie Grandet.* Boston: D.C. Heath.

Barnes, D. (1977). *From communication to curriculum.* London: Penguin Books.

Barr, M. (1990). The California Literature Project. In E. Farrell & J. R. Squire (Eds.), *Transactions with literature* (pp. 39–45). Urbana, IL: National Council of Teachers of English.

Belenky, M. F., Clinchy, B. M., Goldberger, N. R., & Tarule, J. M. (1986). *Women's ways of knowing. The development of self, voice, and mind.* New York: Basic Books.

Benton, M., & Fox, G. (1985). *Teaching literature nine to fourteen.* Oxford: Oxford University Press.

Bradley, S., Beatty, R. C., & Long, E. H. (Eds.). (1962). *The American tradition in literature* (Vol 1). New York: W. W. Norton.

Britton, J. (1970). *Language and learning.* London: Penguin.

Britton, J., Shafer, R. E., & Watson, K. (Eds.). (1990). *Teaching and learning English worldwide.* Philadelphia: Multilingual Matters.

Brown, L. M., & Gilligan, C. (1992). *Meeting at the crossroads: Women's psychology and girls' development.* Cambridge, MA: Harvard University Press.

Bruner, J. (1986). *Actual minds, possible worlds.* Cambridge: Harvard University Press.

Bruner, J. (1990). *Acts of meaning.* Cambridge: Harvard University Press.

Burke, K. (1957). *The philosophy of literary form.* New York: Vintage.

Burnett, F. H. (1987). *The secret garden.* New York: Oxford University Press.

Calvino, I. (1981). *If on a winter's night a traveler* (W. Weaver, Trans.). San Diego, CA: Harcourt, Brace, Jovanovich. (Original work published 1979)

Capote, T. (1965). *In cold blood.* New York: Random House.

Chaucer, G. (1963). The Canterbury tales. In A. C. Baugh (Ed.), *Chaucer's major poetry.* Englewood Cliffs, NJ: Prentice-Hall.

Chopin, K. (1984). The story of an hour. In S. Gilbert (Ed.), *The awakening and selected stories.* New York: Modern Library.

Christ, C. P. (1980). *Diving deep and surfacing: Women writers on spiritual quest*. Boston, MA: Beacon Press.

Culler, J. (1975). *Structuralist poetics*. Ithaca, NY: Cornell University Press.

Culler, J. (1980). Literary competence. In J. Tompkins (Ed.), *Reader-response criticism* (pp. 101–117). Baltimore, MD: The Johns Hopkins University Press. (Original work published 1975)

Curie, E. (1937). *Madame Curie*. New York: Doubleday, Doran.

de Sade, the Marquis. (1965). *Three complete novels*. (R. Seaver & A. Wainhouse, Trans.) New York: Grove Press.

Dewey, J., & Bentley, A. F. (1949). *Knowing and the known*. Boston, MA: Beacon Press.

Dostoyevsky, F. (1980). *The possessed* (A. MacAndrew, Trans.). New York: New American Library.

Durrell, L. (1957). *Justine*. London: Farber & Farber.

Eagleton, T. (1983). *Literary theory: An introduction*. Oxford, UK: Basil Blackwell.

Elbow, P. (1990). *What is English?* New York: Modern Language Association.

Ellison, R. (1952). *Invisible man*. New York: Random House.

Fish, S. (1980a). *Is there a text in this class?*. Cambridge, MA: Harvard University Press.

Fish, S. (1980b). Interpreting the 'variorum.' In J. Tompkins (Ed.), *Reader-response criticism: From formalism to post-structuralism*. Baltimore, MD: Johns Hopkins University Press. (Original work published 1976)

Fitzgerald, R. (Trans.). (1963). *The odyssey*. Garden City, NJ: Anchor Books.

Foundation for Inner Peace. (1975). *The course in miracles*. Tiburon, CA: Author.

Fowles, J. (1963). *The collector*. New York: Dell.

Fowles, J. (1965). *The magus*. New York: Dell Publishing Company.

Fowles, J. (1969). *The French lieutenant's woman*. New York: The New American Library.

Fowles, J. (1970). *The aristos* (rev. ed.). Boston, MA: Little, Brown.

Fowles, J. (1974). *The ebony tower*. Boston, MA: Little, Brown.

Fowles, J. (1977). *The magus: A revised version*. New York: Little, Brown.

Fox, M. (1989). *Wilfred Gordon McDonald Partridge*. New York: Kane-Miller Books.

Freedman, S. W. (1987). *Response to student writing* (NCTE Research Report 23). Urbana, IL: National Council of Teachers of English.

Freire, P. (1990). *Pedagogy of the oppressed* (M. A. Ramos, Trans.). New York: Continuum.

Freire, P., & Macedo, D. (1987). *Reading the word and the world*. New York: Bergin and Garvey.

Gibson, W. (1980). Authors, speakers, readers, and mock readers. In J. Tompkins (Ed.), *Reader-response criticism from formalism to post structuralism* (pp. 1–6). Baltimore, MD: The Johns Hopkins University Press. (Original work published 1950)

Gilligan, C. (1982). *In a different voice*. Cambridge, MA: Harvard University Press.

Goodman, K. (1986). *What's whole in whole language?* Portsmouth: Heineman.

Greene, M. (1988). *The dialectic of freedom*. New York: Teachers College Press.

Grossman, P. L. (1990). *The making of a teacher: Teacher knowledge and teacher education*. New York: Teachers College Press.

Hawthorne, N. (1962a). The birthmark. In S. Bradley, R. C. Beatty, & E. H. Long

(Eds.), *The American tradition in literature (Rev.) Vol. 1* (pp. 490–496). New York: W.W. Norton.

Hawthorne, N. (1962b). The minister's black veil. In S. Bradley, R. C. Beatty, & E. H. Long (Eds.), *The American tradition in literature (Rev.) Vol. 1* (pp. 480–490). New York: W.W. Norton.

Hawthorne, N. (1962c). Rappaccini's daughter. In S. Bradley, R. C. Beatty, & E. H. Long (Eds.), *The American tradition in literature (Rev.) Vol. 1* (pp. 511–535). New York: W.W. Norton.

Hawthorne, N. (1962d). Young goodman Brown. In S. Bradley, R. C. Beatty, & E. H. Long (Eds.), *The American tradition in literature (Rev.) Vol. 1* (pp. 469–479). New York: W.W. Norton.

Heilbrun, C. (1988). *Writing a woman's life.* New York: Ballantine Books.

Helle, A. P. (1991). Reading women's autobiographies. In C. Witherell & N. Noddings (Eds.), *Stories lives tell.* New York: Teachers College Press.

Hirsch, Jr., E. D. (1989). *A first dictionary of cultural literacy: What our children need to know.* Boston, MA: Houghton Mifflin.

Hoffman, E. (1989). *Lost in translation: A life in a new language.* New York: Penguin.

Holland, N. (1968). *The dynamics of literary response.* New York: Columbia University Press.

Holland, N. (1980). Unity identity text self. In J. Tompkins (Ed.), *Reader-response criticism from formalism to post-structuralism* (pp. 118–133). Baltimore, MD: The Johns Hopkins University Press. (Original work published 1968)

Holland, N. (1988). *The brain of Robert Frost.* New York: Routledge.

Hollander, J. (Ed.). (1968). *Modern poetry: Essays in criticism.* Oxford: Oxford University Press.

hooks, b. (1994). *Teaching to transgress.* New York: Routledge.

Howe, B. (Ed.). (1976). *The eye of the heart.* Indianapolis, IN: Bobbs-Merrill.

Iser, W. (1976). *The act of reading: A theory of aesthetic response.* Baltimore, MD: Johns Hopkins University Press.

Iser, W. (1980). The reading process: A phenomenological approach. In J. Tompkins (Ed.), *Reader-response criticism from formalism to post-structuralism* (pp. 26–40). Baltimore, MD: The Johns Hopkins University Press. (Original work published 1974)

Jakes, J. (1990). *The bastard* (Reissue ed.) n.p.: Jove Publishers.

Jamplonsky, G. (1988). *Love is letting go of fear.* New York: Bantam.

Jeffers, S. (1987). *Feel the fear and do it anyway.* San Diego: Harbrace.

Jersild, A. T. (1955). *When teachers face themselves.* New York: Teachers College Press.

Joyce, J. (1961). *Ulysses.* New York: Modern Library.

Joyce, J. (1967). The dead. In *Dubliners* (pp. 175–223). New York: Penguin.

Keller, E. F. (1983). *A feeling for the organism: The life and work of Barbara McClintock.* New York: W. H. Freeman.

King, M. L., Jr. (1992). *I have a dream: Writings and speeches that changed the world.* New York: HarperCollins.

Kingsolver, B. (1990). *Animal dreams.* New York: HarperCollins.

Lakoff, G. & Johnson, M. (1980). *Metaphors we live by.* Chicago: University of Chicago Press.

Langer, S. (1942). *Philosophy in a new key: A study in the symbolism of reason, rite, and art.* Cambridge, MA: Harvard University Press.

Langer, S. (1953). *Feeling and form: A theory of art.* New York: Charles Scribner's Sons.

Lawrence, J., & Lee, R. (1970). *The night Thoreau spent in jail.* New York: Hill & Wang.

Martin, N. (1991). Conversation: National Council of Teachers of English Convention, Indianapolis, IN.

Mayher, J. (1990). *Uncommon sense.* Portsmouth, NH: Heinemann.

Mead, M. (1972). *Blackberry winter.* New York: Simon & Schuster.

Meek, M. (1988). *How texts teach what readers read.* Bath, UK: The Thimble Press.

McCarthy, M. (1963). *The group.* New York: Harcourt, Brace & World.

McDermott, G. (1975). *The stone cutter.* New York: Penguin.

McNeil, L. (1986). *Contradictions of control.* New York: Routledge.

Melville, H. (1962). Billy Budd. In S. Bradley, R. C. Beatty, & E. H. Long (Eds.), *The American tradition in literature (Rev.) Vol. 1* (pp. 895–961). New York: W.W. Norton.

Miller, J. E., de Dwyer, C. C., Hayden, R., Hogan, R. J., & Wood, K. M. (Eds.). (1979). *United States in literature: America reads series* (Medallion Ed.). Glenville, IL: Scott, Foresman.

Moffett, J. (1968). *Teaching the universe of discourse.* Boston, MA: Houghton Mifflin.

Moffett, J. (1973). *A student-centered language arts curriculum, grades K–13: A handbook for teachers.* Boston: Houghton Mifflin.

Nightingale, F. (1985). Cassandra, excerpts. In S. M. Gilbert & S. Gubar (Eds.), *The Norton anthology of literature by women* (pp. 804–813). New York: W.W. Norton. (Work originally published 1928)

Nightingale, F. (1987). *Letters from Egypt: A journey on the Nile 1849–50.* London, UK: Barrie & Jenkins.

Noddings, N. (1989). *Women and evil.* Berkeley, CA: University of California Press.

O'Neill, E. (1955). *Long day's journey into night.* New Haven, CT: Yale University Press.

Orenstein, P. (1994). *School girls.* New York: Doubleday.

Orwell, G. (1949). *1984.* New York: Signet.

Poulet, G. (1980). Criticism and the experience of interiority. In J. Tompkins (Ed.), *Reader-response criticism* (pp. 41–49). Baltimore, MD: Johns Hopkins University Press. (Original work published 1972)

Prince, G. (1980). Introduction to the study of narrative. In J. Tompkins (Ed.), *Reader-response criticism from formalism to post structuralism* (pp. 7–25). Baltimore, MD: Johns Hopkins University Press. (Original work published 1973)

Progoff, I. (1975). *At a journal workshop.* New York: Dialogue House Library.

Puryear, H. (1982). (Richard I. Abrams, Ed.). *The Edgar Cayce primer.* New York: Bantam.

Richards, I. A. (1929). *Practical criticism.* New York: Harcourt Brace.

Riffaterre, M. (1980). Describing poetic structures: Two approaches to Baudelaire's "les chats." In J. Tompkins (Ed.), *Reader-response criticism from formalism to post-structuralism* (pp. 26–40). Baltimore, MD: The Johns Hopkins University Press. (Original work published 1966)

Roark, P. (1968). *Intentionalism and the intentional fallacy.* Unpublished paper.

Rose, M. (1990). *Lives on the boundary.* New York: Penguin.

Rosenblatt, L. (1938). *Literature as exploration.* New York: Appleton-Century-Crofts.

Rosenblatt, L. (1978). *The reader, the text, the poem: The transactional theory of the literary work.* Carbondale, IL: Southern Illinois University Press.

Rosenblatt, L. (1983). *Literature as exploration* (4th ed.). New York: Modern Language Association.

Rosenblatt, L. (1988a, October). *Writing and reading: The transactional theory.* Paper presented at the meeting of the California Literature Project, Long Beach, CA.

Rosenblatt, L. (1988b, January). *Writing and reading: The transactional theory* (Technical Report). Berkeley: University of California, Center for the Study of Writing.

Rouse, J. (1978). *The completed gesture: Myth, character and education.* New Jersey: Skyline Books.

Salmon, P. (1988). *Psychology for teachers.* London: Hutchinson.

Sartre, J. P. (1946). *No exit.* (Stuart Gilbert, Trans.). New York: A. Knopf.

Sauer, E. H. (1961). *English in the secondary school.* New York: Holt, Rinehart and Winston.

Schmidt, P. (1980). *Romance parody in John Fowles'* The Magus. Master's thesis, Holy Names College, Oakland, CA.

Schmidt, P. (1986). Feminism in the "Wife of Bath." Unpublished manuscript.

Schmidt, P. (1989a). *Journals (1989–94).* Unpublished writings.

Schmidt, P. (1989b). *Notes.* Unpublished writings.

Schmidt, P. (1991). *A developing theory of languaging: How transactional response transforms language and learning.* Candidacy paper, New York University.

Schmidt, P. (1993). *Statement of philosophy.* Unpublished writing.

Schon, D. (1983). *The reflective practitioner.* New York: Basic Books.

Secondary English Editorial Staff. (1965). *Adventures in American literature.* New York: Harcourt Brace Jovanovich.

Shakespeare, W. (1955). *Cymbeline* (J.M. Nosworthy, Ed.). London, UK: Routledge.

Sheehy, G. (1976). *Passages: Predictable crises of adult life.* New York: Bantam.

Siegel, B. (1986). *Love, medicine, and miracles.* New York: Harper & Row.

Simmons, J. S., Shafer, R. E., & Shadiow, L. K. (1990). The swinging pendulum: Teaching English in the USA, 1945–1987. In J. Britton, R. E. Shafer, & K. Watson (Eds.), *Teaching and learning English worldwide* (pp. 89–130). Philadelphia, PA: Multilingual Matters.

Sizer, T. (1985). *Horace's compromise.* Boston, MA: Houghton Mifflin.

Smith, F. (1988). *Understanding reading: A psycholinguistic analysis of reading and learning to read.* Hillsdale, NJ: Lawrence Erlbaum Associates.

Spark, M. (1961). *The prime of Miss Jean Brodie.* New York: New American Library.

Squire, J. (1968). *Response to literature.* Urbana, IL: National Council of Teachers of English.

Stegner, W. (1971). *Angle of repose.* Greenwich, CT: Fawcett Crest Books.

Steinem, G. (1991). *Revolution from within.* New York: Little Brown.

Stevens, Wallace. (1985). The house was quiet and the world was calm. In M. Benton and G. Fox (Eds.), *Teaching literature nine to fourteen* (p. 93). Oxford, UK: Oxford University Press. (Original work published in 1965)

Susann, J. (1966). *Valley of the dolls.* New York: Simon and Schuster.

Tannen, D. (1990). *You just don't understand: Women and men in conversation.* New York: Morrow.

Taylor, M. (1976). *Roll of thunder, hear my cry.* New York: Dial Press.

Thompkins, J. (Ed.). (1980). *Reader-response criticism from formalism to post-structuralism.* Baltimore, MD: The Johns Hopkins University Press.

Trilling, L. (1970). *Literary criticism.* New York: Holt, Rinehart, and Winston, Inc.

Vicinus, M., & Nergaard, B. (Eds.). (1989). *Ever yours, Florence Nightingale: Selected letters.* London, UK: Virago.

Warriner, J. E. & Griffith, F. (1963). *English grammar and composition.* New York: Harcourt, Brace & World.

Welch, N. (1993). Resisting the faith: Conversion, resistance, and the training of teachers. *College English, 55(4),* 387–401.

Wiggington, E. (1986). *Sometimes a shining moment.* New York: Anchor Press.

Wimsatt, W. K. Jr., & Beardsley, M.C. (1954). The intentional fallacy. In *Verbal icon: Studies in the meaning of poetry.* Lexington, KY: University of Kentucky Press.

Winterson, J. (1985). *Oranges are not the only fruit.* London, UK: Pandora Press.

Witherell, C., & Noddings, N. (Eds.). (1991). *Stories lives tell.* New York: Teachers College Press.

Wordsworth, W. (1882). *Lyrical ballads,* Preface. In E. M. Beck (Ed.), *Bartlett's familiar quotations* (14th ed., rev.) (p. 511b). Boston: Little, Brown. (Original work published 1800)

Wright, R. (1964). *Native son.* New York: Signet.

Zinsser, W. (1987). *Inventing the truth.* Boston: Houghton Mifflin.

Index

About the Author

Patricia Schmidt taught high school English in northern California for seventeen years, teaching all grades and levels of English. She holds a Master's degree in English from Holy Names College in Oakland, California, and earned a Ph.D. in English Education from New York University in 1993, specializing in Literature, Reading, and Media Education. Part of her doctoral work included studying English curricula and classrooms in British schools in Oxford and London, England. She has been a lecturer at both New York University and Sonoma State University in California, teaching courses in both English and Education as well as working with student teachers. During most of her doctoral studies at New York University she was part of a writing across the curriculum team integrating writing to learn in both the history and religious studies departments. She also worked for two years in the NYU Expository Writing Center as a writing consultant. For the past ten years she has been involved in curricular reform in English, English education, and English assessment in California through her work in the California Literature Project. Patricia Schmidt currently writes, teaches, and lives in Walnut Creek, California, with her husband Neil and their critters, two dogs and two cats.